The Borzoi Reader
in Latin American History

VOLUME 1

D1533091

Consulting Editor
LEWIS HANKE
University of Massachusetts, Amherst

The
Borzoi Reader in
Latin American
History

VOLUME 1
From The Colonial Period to Independence

EDITED, WITH INTRODUCTIONS, BY
Helen Delpar
Florida State University

Alfred A. Knopf   New York

THIS IS A BORZOI BOOK
PUBLISHED BY ALFRED A. KNOPF, INC.

Copyright © 1972 by Alfred A. Knopf, Inc.

All rights reserved under International and Pan-American Copyright Conventions.
Published in the United States by Alfred A. Knopf, Inc., New York,
and simultaneously in Canada by Random House of Canada Limited, Toronto.
Distributed by Random House, Inc., New York.
ISBN: 0–394–31151–5
Library of Congress Catalog Card Number: 70–167295

Typography by James M. Wall

First Edition
9 8 7 6 5 4 3 2 1

Manufactured in the United States of America

Composed, printed and bound by Colonial Press, Clinton, Mass.

Foreword

The *Borzoi Reader in Latin American History, Volume 1 and 2* is designed to provide an introduction to Latin American civilization while conveying an appreciation of the diversity and complexity of the area. Volume 1 presents the colonial period and the growth of independence movements. Volume 2 describes nineteenth and twentieth century developments, with special sections on the Cuban and Mexican revolutions and on Peronism. Although this anthology cannot cover every aspect of Latin American history, it is the editor's hope that all the selections are both important and relevant. An attempt has been made to balance expository writings with more analytical material and to include selections by Latin American authors. A few of the articles, such as Bolívar's letter from Jamaica, will be familiar to specialists, but their intrinsic importance warrants their inclusion in a book aimed primarily at the beginning student.

Many of the readings in this collection have already appeared in the Borzoi series, and the editor gratefully acknowledges the cooperation of the editors of the earlier volumes who generously permitted use of material which they had excerpted or translated. The editor also thanks Lewis Hanke, general editor of the Borzoi series, for his assistance.

The editor of the present volume assumes all responsibility for choosing material from these books to be reprinted and for its presentation here.

Contents

ONE

THE COLONIAL PERIOD

The titles of many recent books on contemporary Latin America invariably link the words "change" and "revolution" with the area. Although Latin America is indeed undergoing a period of ferment in which traditional values and institutions are being challenged and sometimes demolished, excessive emphasis on change is likely to obscure the continuing vigor of what is usually referred to as the "colonial heritage" of the region, which in many ways seems to affect the efforts of reformers. In a stimulating discussion in 1962 on "Colonial Institutions and Contemporary Latin America," [1] the three participants, Professors Woodrow Borah, Charles Gibson, and Robert A. Potash, differed somewhat with respect to the precise meanings to be attached to the words "colonial" and "institution," but they did not dispute the cogency or relevance of the topic. Not only is it apparent to most observers that contemporary Latin America still bears the imprint of 300 years of rule by Spain and Portugal, but this proposition is usually coupled with two corollaries: first, the colonial heritage is more robust and pervasive in Latin America than in the United States; and second, it has constituted an obstacle to modernization. Indeed, this is the major premise of a recent book whose authors maintain that "in economic dependence and its syndrome of economic and social polarization we find the principal heritage of three centuries of subordination to Spain and Portugal." [2]

The nature of the colonial heritage and the extent to which it has in fact inhibited modernization are complex questions replete with semantic and conceptual difficulties. There can be little doubt, nonetheless, that colonial society was initially shaped to a large extent by the character of the "conquest culture," by the character of the indigenous cultures encountered in the New World, and by the interaction of the two. Of the formal organizations introduced to Latin America during the colonial period, perhaps the Roman Catholic Church retains the greatest vitality despite the anticlericalism and increasing secularism of the last two centuries. The occasional defiance of temporal authority by the contemporary priest may even in a sense be a distant echo of the colonial cleric's protests on behalf of the Indians. Race mixture is another Latin American phenomenon of colonial origin that has profoundly affected the area's development

---

[1] Woodrow Borah, Charles Gibson, and Robert A. Potash, "Colonial Institutions and Contemporary Latin America," *Hispanic American Historical Review*, XLIII (1963), 371–394.

[2] Stanley J. Stein and Barbara H. Stein, *The Colonial Heritage of Latin America: Essays on Economic Dependence in Perspective* (New York: Oxford University Press, 1970), p. vii.

both before and after independence. Whereas the agencies and officials of colonial government disappeared with the revolutions for independence, it can be argued that the administrative practices of the colonial period, such as centralism and institutionalized corruption, have continued to flourish to the present day in many parts of Latin America.

Although mining still remains a major industry throughout most of Latin America, the extraction of precious metals occupies a relatively smaller place in the national economies than it did during the colonial era. The emphasis on exports to which the mining booms contributed did survive independence, however, and was reinforced during the nineteenth century. Another colonial institution that has persisted during the national period is the large landed estate—both in the form of the plantation producing agricultural commodities for export and as the extensively exploited latifundium.

The readings that follow are not specifically addressed to the problem of identifying and evaluating the colonial heritage but describe and analyze many of its basic components.

The Spanish Middle Ages and the Conquest

◄━◆━►

Claudio Sánchez-Albornoz

*The conquest and colonization of America by Spain is usually inter-
preted as an extension of the medieval reconquest of the Iberian
peninsula from the Moors and consequently characterized by the
same martial and religious ethos that had marked the earlier campaign
and was in fact an outgrowth of it. In the first selection, the distinguished Spanish historian Claudio Sánchez-Albornoz develops the argument that the conquest represented the "projection of the Spanish Middle Ages in space and time" and that it had the effect of prolonging
Spain's medieval characteristics.*

*A former rector of the University of Madrid, Sánchez-Albornoz has
lived in Buenos Aires since the Spanish Civil War.*

No one disputes, nor can dispute, the fact that the discovery and settlement of America has been the great historic achievement of the
Iberian peoples. None of Hispania's other contributions to human
history can be compared to it. It is enough to repay all the debts that
Spain may owe to Europe and to counterbalance all the contributions
made by other nations to Western culture. We created the boundaries
of the Western world itself, of which the Atlantic today is the interior
sea, and we provoked the greatest shock ever experienced by the Old
World, confined for centuries to the Mediterranean by the waves of
the Atlantic. Neither the intellectual revolutions of the Renaissance
and the Reformation, creations of Italy and Germany, nor the scientific
achievements of the other nations north of the Pyrenees surpass the
great Hispanic enterprise in historic consequences. Because we incorporated America into Western life, modern scientific and technical knowledge came to rapid maturity . . . and modern capitalism could take
shape thanks to the gold that was brought from across the Atlantic:

From H. B. Johnson, Jr. (ed. and tr.), *From Reconquest to Empire* (New
York: Knopf, 1970), pp. 42–54. Copyright © 1970 by H. B. Johnson, Jr. Re-
printed by permission of Alfred A. Knopf, Inc. Deletions in text are by H. B.
Johnson. Italicized bracketed notes in the text are by Helen Delpar.

science, technical knowledge, and capitalism without whose coming together the industrial transformation of Europe would have been impossible.

.   .   .

But I think in this way, no one can accuse me of disdain for our marvelous American adventure, nor place me among those who argue about the material or spiritual damage that it may have brought to Spain. . . . But in judging the magnitude of the Spanish enterprise in America I do not always hold that all of its effects on the Spanish way of life were favorable.

Twenty-five years ago . . . I presented the theory that the Spanish conquest of America had been a projection of the Spanish Middle Ages in space and in time, and I ventured the thesis that it had prolonged the medieval character of Spain itself. For how can the conquest of America possibly be seen as anything but the most immense result of the peninsular activism created by Spain's centuries-long struggle with Islam? How can one not see in the discovery and conquest of America the last heroic age of the Western world, the last phase of the medieval epic? When Spanish activity in America is compared with that of other European peoples, does not Spanish medievalism—part crusade and part adventure—stand out as clear as day?

Unlike the Roman conquest of the West, which was planned, directed, and realized by the state, Spain's conquest of America revealed the dispersed and disordered action of the Castilian people, deprived of the effective guidance of its governing elite, almost abandoned by the Spanish monarchy, and led by a foreign dynasty into enterprises alien to its interests. And how, under such conditions, could a non-medieval nation, a nation subjected to the rigid articulations of an ancient or modern state, have been able to realize such an enterprise? How can one not see in that activity, so filled with individualism, the imprint of medieval life and society, in which the hero, the personal and isolated effort, acted with the greatest freedom and achieved the most immense results in peace and in war?

.   .   .

"At the beginning of the Modern Age," I wrote many years ago, "any European people would have had to improvise a policy of colonization if it had discovered America. Any, that is, except Spain, rich in the experience of conquest and colonization; for no other people of the West had had the opportunity to undergo a similar preparation." I continue to think the same today. The great Belgian historian, [Charles] Verlinden, has exaggerated the influence on Spanish colonization of the colonial traditions of the Italian *signorias* in the Mediterranean. . . . I cannot follow Verlinden when he affirms that Genoese merchant quarters, factories, and trading concessions prefigure those which were created by the Spanish and the Portuguese.

Some sort of filiation might be established between the colonial system of Portugal—and also of Holland, which later followed in the Portuguese wake—with that which was used in the Mediterranean during the late Middle Ages. But there were enormous differences between the medieval colonization of the Genoese Republic, which had economic aims above all, and the bellicose and evangelistic colonization of Spain.

The conquest of the great American empire, inhabited by idolatrous peoples with barbarous customs; the diffusion of Spanish faith, culture, law, and way of life throughout an immense continent; and the juridical articulation of these lands gained by the sword into the mechanism of the Castilian state have no possible parallel in the traditional methods of colonization of the Genoese *signoria*. The presence in Andalusia of a group of Genoese navigators and bankers, as well as the rare trips made by some of them to the Indies, did not exert any notable influence on the imperial colonies of Spain. The mercantile spirit, the taste for business, and the dreams of commercial gain carried little weight with them. To the possible detriment of their own imperial activity, with its seignorial and religious character, the Castilians neither learned nor tried to learn anything fundamental from the Genoese colonial system.

Verlinden recognizes that the capitulations drawn up by Columbus with Ferdinand and Isabella and the privileges which he obtained from them after his discoveries were rooted in the pure medieval Castilian tradition. And if the Genoese played a role (a role that was really less than minimal) in the first days of Caribbean exploration, the Hispanic venture soon took a direction that was entirely unconnected with medieval Italian colonization. There are, in fact, much greater differences between the Hispanic colonial techniques of the sixteenth through the eighteenth centuries . . . and European colonial enterprise of the nineteenth and twentieth centuries. The latter was the result of economic imperialism, product of the contemporary industrial revolution, which the great Belgian historian correctly distinguishes from the Hispano-Atlantic tradition. But the colonial creations of Spain in America, which were organs of power rather than economic centers, were rooted in the peninsula's medieval history.

.   .   .

"Each day it becomes increasingly clear that the whole history of medieval Castile is resumed and crystalized in an uninterrupted and gigantic enterprise of colonization," I wrote in 1930; and I continue to believe the same today. From the eighth century on, the history of Spanish Christendom is, in effect, the history of a slow but continuous restoration of Spain as an integral part of Europe; and the history of Castile, that of the constant advance of a small kingdom . . . which expanded from the mountain peaks and thickets of Asturias until it reached the blue and luminous sea to the south—the history of a people's hard-won expansion into the sunny land of Andalusia. In the wake of hard-fought battles, the Castilians spread over the plains, crept over the hills, and filed across the mountains that stood in their path—and kept on fighting and settling through space and time. Just as later in America, these eight medieval centuries[1] were a complex succession of conquests, the founding of cities, the establishment of episcopal sees and monasteries, the creation of institutions of war and of government, the mixture of cultures and peoples—in short, the transplantation of a race and a language, of a faith and a civilization.

"Although the characteristics diverged depending upon the epoch in which it occurred, each advance, from the first under the kings of Asturias to the last under the reunited crowns of Aragon and Castile, always involved a permanent colonizing activity, always carried toward the south the language born in the valleys of northern Castile, always propagated the teachings of Christ in the territory won by the sword, always installed in the new domains the peculiar ways of life that Castile's own history had been creating, always extended toward the south the municipal liberties that had arisen in the Duero valley, and always incorporated new kingdoms into the state that Castile, as the heir of classical antiquity and the Visigothic tradition, was forging bit by bit during its struggle over the centuries with Islam."

Then when the Reconquest ended and it seemed as if Castile's colonizing activity had come to an end with the attainment of the Atlantic-Mediterranean sea barrier, the naval tradition (already two centuries old) made it possible for Columbus to discover America the unknown. The bellicose energies of the impetuous Castilians were channeled into the new adventure, still unsurpassed by modern man, of the conquest of the Indies. There across the sea, Castile's medieval history was repeated and the destiny of Castile fulfilled once again. The scenery was not the same, and neither were the characteristics of her colonization, just as they had not been the same in Spain throughout the centuries. The plains, which lie to the north of the Duero river, had been populated by small freeholders, by minor nobles, and by monasteries from 850 on; great town councils brought back to life the zone between the Duero and the Tagus rivers after the conquest of Toledo (1085); the military orders accomplished the repopulation of Extremadura and La Mancha after the victory of Las Navas de Tolosa (1213); municipalities and magnates colonized lower Andalusia after the conquest of Seville (1248) . . . with each advance of the frontier new methods of colonization were applied, but the enterprise

---

[1] The author is thinking of a period extending roughly from 711 (the date of the Moorish invasion of Spain) to 1492 (the date of the reconquest of Granada). In a more limited sense, the *Reconquista* lasted from circa 850 to 1250. [H. B. J.]

was always undertaken in the same spirit of crusade and plunder, with the cross held high and one's pockets empty, with the same greed for riches and for the conversion of souls, and with the same traditions of Western liberty and civilization carried on the points of swords and lances.

Just as Spain had acted as the vanguard of the West in the face of crude, barbarous Africa during the Middle Ages, so she later was the forerunner of Europe facing a new world on American soil. Just as the ordinary peasants came down from the mountains of Asturias and Cantabria to the plains of the Duero valley greedy for liberty and riches, or the poorer nobility hungry for fortune and glory, so the penniless hidalgos and plebian adventurers embarked for America seven centuries later. Just as the monastic foundations . . . brought great depopulated areas back to life in Spain before the year 1000, so the Castilian religious missions contributed to the colonization of the American continent after 1500. And just as the colonists of the frontier in Spain near the Muslim fortresses were granted lands and liberty, so privileges and *repartimientos* (grants of Indian labor) were given to the Spanish vanguard in the new continent.

The egalitarian and integrationist policy of Castile, unique in the history of world colonization, a policy that did not treat the conquered lands as colonies but considered them simply as a prolongation of the national territory, was rooted in the oldest Castilian traditions. As they conquered diverse Muslim kingdoms, from Toledo to Granada, century after century, the kings of Asturias, León, and Castile incorporated and assimilated them on an equal footing with their own kingdoms. How can one not see in the recognition of the Indians as Castilian citizens the logical projection of the juridical doctrines of Castile in its peninsular undertakings: a Castile that had also made the conquered Moors into citizens?

We discovered, conquered, and colonized America in accordance with our medieval experience. We did not have to improvise a policy of expansion and colonization, for we continued seven centuries of peninsular history across the Atlantic. Behind the astonishing events of exploration, the titanic work of conquest, and the fruitful days of colonial settlement, a new Spain rose up between the Atlantic and the Pacific. . . . Thus we overcame the tradition of many thousands of years that had linked the development of ancient civilizations to the shores of the Mediterranean and that confined Western culture to the narrow limits of Europe. As I said at the beginning of this essay, no historic undertaking among those which contributed to the birth of the modern world had greater consequences than the American adventure. Neither the Renaissance nor the Reformation equaled its burden of decisive influences in the future of man. . . . The collaboration of Spain in creating the modern world was not inferior to any other people of the West. But, without any risk of paradox, one may also say that with the birth overseas of a new world and a new Spain, and indeed as a result of its own creation, the old Spain that had been reborn in Europe a short while before was weakened and finally destroyed. . . .

The American undertaking confirmed the providential conception of life that was already traditional among the Spanish. Aside from the incarnation and death of Christ, they regarded the discovery of the Indies as the greatest event that had occurred since the creation of the world. [Bartolomé de] Las Casas [a sixteenth-century "protector of the Indians"; see Article 2] considered Columbus as the Elect of God, designated for the accomplishment of this great task. "The conquest of the Indies began when that of the Moors was over," wrote [Francisco] López de Gómara [an historian and chaplain in the household of Cortés], "for the Spanish have always fought against infidels." They were the instrument of the Most High for the incorporation of the latter into the Mystic Body of Our Lord through the reception of the gospel from Spanish lips. The discovery and conquest were brought to a conclusion by the goodness of the Lord so that Spain, called to be the champion of the faith in Europe, could increase its power and wealth. Even men of science such as Acosta . . . whose doctrines prepared the way for the philosophy of unlimited progress, believe in the providential of the great adventure.

For the Spanish, these ideas . . . affirmed their old beliefs about the continual intervention of the Divine in the life of those below and about the continued action of Eternal God in their favor as a reward for their warlike, divine activities. And these ideas contributed to keeping alive their servile religiosity. "I serve you, therefore you owe me protection," was how these men who fought against the idolatrous Indians of America continued to think as they addressed themselves to God, in a prayer at once arrogant and presumptuous. . . .

When the frontier in Spain was closed and the clergy could no longer expand and enrich itself with lands taken from the Moors, there opened up on the other side of the Atlantic a virgin world for the diffusion and spread of the Church. In this way the Spanish church was able to replace . . . its mission with respect to the Muslims by the imperious necessity of work in America. And this activity across the sea was of great help in preserving its traditional economic power and in safeguarding its great influence within the Spanish state and society.

The expansion of the Spanish Empire in America, far from changing the equilibrium of political forces in Spain, strengthened it for several centuries more. If the medieval monarchs, by successive advances and repeated colonizations, had been able to replenish their income, which slowly diminished during the periods when the frontier was stable, so the Spanish crown accomplished similar restoration of its treasure with the riches that the galleons and fleets brought back from the Indies. If the kings of Castile, in conquering and colonizing the zones gained from the Caliphate or from the *taifa* kings [*rulers of small Muslim kingdoms*], from the Almohad empire or from Granada, had reaped a copious booty of lands and offices with which to attract and dominate both nobles and ordinary people, so the Spanish sovereigns found, in the viceroyalties, captaincies, *audiencias, corregimientos,* and *cabildos* overseas, a vast treasure of bureaucratic gifts, posts from high to low, with which to continue to attract the importunate aristocratic minorities, as well as the masses of the people, to revolve like stars around them.

The conquest and colonization of Spain contributed in a decisive way to strengthening the juridical power of the Castilian monarchy; and our action in America, in modern times, contributed no less to the omnipotence of the Spanish kingship. By the sixteenth century, the old Castilian liberties were dead. Only the legalistic spirit of Philip II's reign permitted some vitality to the ancient Cortes of Castile. But American gold also cooperated in killing and burying these liberties and in impeding their resurrection. If the Spanish monarchy had not been able to rely on the resources of America during the seventeenth and eighteenth centuries, would it have been able to remain so strong? Would it not have encountered difficulties similar to those which led to the French and English revolutions [against the crown]? If the fleets of America had not partially supplied the necessities of the treasury, would not the pressure of taxation have raised up the masses against [the monarchy]?

The reinforcement of the monarchy's political power through the American adventure contributed to make the traditional Spanish equation between power, wealth, and service a permanent one. The spreading national bureaucracy found in America a magnificent place to take root and fabulously expand. Throngs of Spaniards who had obtained royal nominations or who were in the service of Viceroys, *Adelantados,* or Captains General crossed the Atlantic, . . . thousands of *peninsulares* . . . dreamed of a post on the other side of the Atlantic. And many of them realized their dreams. [Across the Atlantic] went members of famous families (many Borgias, for example, lived in Peru), many hidalgos without means, and penniless soldiers. When the central organs of the metropolitan government for the Indies denied Cervantes' request for a post in the Indies, they unconsciously made possible the marvelous brilliance of *Don Quixote de La Mancha,* which would certainly never have been written in Guatemala. . . . How many other sharp minds, how many businessmen, how many human values were lost to the Spanish people in the security of the bureaucratic life in the Indies!

In Spanish economic life, the conquest and colonization of America also accentuated, in a manner already well-known, the fatal consequences that had already been present in the conquest and colonization of medieval Spain. The centuries of war against the Muslims and Africans, and the resulting territorial gains, drew the most daring and bravest men away from industrial and commercial activities; the discovery, the conquest, and the exploration of America was equally influential in removing many open minds and ambitious wills from economic enterprise. The hope for riches, which could be had from the conquest of infidel kingdoms, impelled the men of Castile toward the exercise of arms, in which one could easily prosper as the frontier advanced into Muslim territory; but in the same way the fantastic dream of fabulous gains in the rich provinces of America pulled thousands and thousands of Spaniards away from peaceful tasks in the peninsula to hurl them into overseas adventure. The territorial and bureaucratic booty that each new thrust of Christianity into Saracen lands put into the hands of kings and, through them, into the control of the *conquistadores,* converted many peasants, artisans, and merchants of Castile into warriors and thus separated the whole of the Castilian lower nobility from peaceful occupations. The enormous abundance of lands and offices of every sort, which the political organization of the Indies was creating, thrust a multitude of active and peaceful Spaniards, who otherwise would have pursued their economic labors in Spain, from their fields and shops into overseas exploits, toward the bureaucracy and wealth of America. . . .

And as has already been said, the attraction that America exerted on the rising industry of Castile was so great that the latter was unable to develop naturally. The rising demand for merchandise, which came to Castile from the Indies, ended by gravely damaging the development of Castilian industrial capacity. In only a few decades, the acquisitive power of the Spaniard who crossed the Atlantic was augmented fabulously and the vast native masses were converted into customers of the peninsular artisans. To fulfill such orders [from the New World], [Spain] resorted to the purchase of foreign goods. Thus was perpetuated the *ancien lien* that foreign industry had kept on our national wealth for centuries. This competition of foreign goods was facilitated and favored by the businessmen who traded in the south of the peninsula. The wave of precious metals, which arrived from America onto Spanish shores, by initiating a revolution in prices, altered the cost of living and the value of wage labor in Spain before it did so across the Pyrenees, and foreign industries could sell more cheaply than Castile the products so urgently solicited by the markets of the Indies. In the face of this series of adverse circumstances, Spanish and foreign merchants increasingly gave a greater place to non-Spanish goods in the trade with America. And this, then, is how the great American undertaking finally came, by another route, to be an obstacle to the economic development of Castile and to prolong for so long a time the great imbalance in the Castilian social structure: the weakness of our bourgeoisie and the absence of a bourgeois ethic among our citizens.

In reviving the long-standing inclination of the peninsular peoples toward warlike undertakings and in facilitating the prolongation of their old time activism, the American venture confirmed the already millennial triumph of the *homo hispanus*, given to impulse instead of calculation, and to the powers of the will over those of the mind. The ease with which the Spanish could root themselves on the land and live from the work of others reaffirmed in them the seignorial style of life proper to the nobility during the Middle Ages and extended it beyond the restricted ranks of the noble class as the sought-after archetype of existence. The possibility of obtaining sudden . . . riches kept open the doors that would permit one to rise in status and conserved the traditional fluidity of social classes in Castile. Those who experienced the novelty of reaching a high social rank became the zealous guardians of the traditions of the upper class into which they had entered and thus created the somber façade of *hidalguismo*.

The magnitude of the success achieved and the astonishing changes of fortune that came about prolonged the old strains of Spanish pride. The crudeness and the difficulty of the struggle in which life was gambled at every step and the hard, rough existence in the new settlements, perpetually at war with the land and the Indians, sharpened the edges of the already steely personality of the conquistadors and colonists. This, and the lack of close ties, which result from lasting residence from father to son in the same urban center—family connections, common traditions, common miseries and hopes—accentuated Spanish individualism and exalted their explosive egos.

An examination of the ways in which the American involvement— at once chimerical and adventurous—affected the psyche and the talent or functional contexture of the Spanish people could be extended to many other aspects of our way of life and could be deepened and detailed minutely. But what has been said is enough to prove that, as I said twenty-five years ago, the similarity between the two great stages of Spanish history—the medieval reconquest and repopulation of the peninsula and the later conquest and colonization of America—contributed to prolong, and in truth, perpetuate the whole complex of strengths and weaknesses of the peninsular way of life that had been erected on the foundations of the primitive heritage of northern Spain in the course of the age-old struggle between Spain and Islam.

The Black Legend Revisited: Assumptions and Realities

————◄◆►————

Benjamin Keen

The controversy that has always swirled around the Spanish record in America has often centered on the "Black Legend," an interpretation of the conquest which holds that the Spaniards displayed unparalleled cruelty and rapacity in their encounters with the Indian inhabitants of America. Ironically, it is a Spaniard, Bartolomé de Las Casas (1474–1566), the Dominican historian and "Protector of the Indians," who is generally considered the first writer to characterize the Black Legend. In the twentieth century many historians have questioned the validity of this interpretation and have emphasized the humanitarian aspects of Spanish colonial policy, particularly legislation such as the Laws of Burgos (1512) and the New Laws (1542), which sought to protect the Indians from mistreatment and exploitation by the colonists. In this reading, however, Benjamin Keen, Professor of History at Northern Illinois University, suggests that the Black Legend is substantially accurate and therefore not only legend, but history as well.

The term "Black Legend" has long existed in the lexicon of Latin American history. Despite its wide acceptance and use, however, it rests on premises whose validity has never been seriously questioned. This essay attempts to test these premises, to clarify the meanings attached to the phrase, and to determine its historical accuracy.

If the essence of the Black Legend is a supposed tradition of defamatory criticism of Spain and the Spaniards, then the Legend has a history much older than the term itself. [*Swedish historian*] Sverker Arnoldsson has shown that from the fourteenth century an unfavorable opinion of Spaniards prevailed among Italians as a result of the personal, economic, political, and cultural relations between the two peoples; and that the nationalist and religious struggles of the six-

From Benjamin Keen, "The Black Legend Revisited: Assumptions and Realities," *Hispanic American Historical Review*, 49 (1969), 703–706, 709–719. Reprinted by permission of the author and Duke University Press. Some footnotes deleted. Italicized bracketed notes in text are by Helen Delpar.

teenth century provoked similar attitudes toward Spain in Germany
and the Netherlands. Arnoldsson makes no systematic effort to determine how much the Spaniards deserved this unfavorable opinion, but
he concedes that the Spanish soldiery in Germany and the Netherlands
did behave with cruelty, rapacity, and licentiousness.

In 1552–1553 Bartolomé de las Casas published in Seville nine
treatises severely critical of the Spanish Conquest in America, including the famous *Very Brief Account of the Destruction of the Indies.*
Royal fear of a colonial feudalism, more dangerous to the Crown than
the shattered power of Indian kings and states, helps to explain the
remarkable tolerance which allowed publication of this exposé. But
while the Emperor Charles could allow a domestic debate on Spain's
Indian policies in the full sight and hearing of Europe, such a debate
became unthinkable under his successor, Philip II. From his accession
to the throne (1556), the dominant motive of Philip's Indian policy
was to augment the royal revenues in order to overcome the Crown's
desperate financial crisis. Simultaneously the influence of Las Casas
and his Indianist movement virtually disappeared from the Spanish
court. His immense prestige served for a time to prevent the publication of such attacks upon him as that of Captain Vargas Machuca,
who claimed that a "Huguenot translation" of the *Very Brief Account*
spread lies about Spain and her work in the Indies. But Spanish sensitivity to foreign criticism of Spain's colonial record grew as her power
in the Old and the New World declined. After 1600 the memory of
Las Casas fell under a heavy cloud.

Only one edition of Las Casas' *Very Brief Account* appeared in
Spain during the seventeenth century; appropriately enough, that edition was published in Barcelona during the Catalán revolt of 1646
against Castilian imperialism. In 1659 the Aragonese Inquisition
banned the *Very Brief Account,* and the ban was later extended to
all of Spain. A typical contemporary Spanish comment on the book
was the observation of the jurist and bibliographer Antonio de León
Pinelo that foreigners valued it not for its learning, but for its strictures
on the Conquistadores, "diminishing and destroying their exploits,
exaggerating and elaborating their cruelties with a thousand syno-
nyms: this delights foreigners." The celebrated jurist Solórzano, in
his monumental *Politica indiana* (1647), could still dissent from Las
Casas' views with expressions of respect for the learned Bishop of
Chiapas, but the historian Antonio de Solís, whose book on the conquest of Mexico was published in 1684, harshly scolded Las Casas for
his alleged services to Spain's enemies.

Eighteenth-century Spanish intellectuals continued to defend their
country's colonial record against foreign attack and to deplore the
influence of Las Casas' *Very Brief Account.* But their concessions to
foreign critics, the reasonable tone of their arguments, and their diminishing appeals to religion reflected Enlightenment influence. The

Spanish counterattack subsided further in the century that began with the liberal Cortes of Cádiz and ended with the Generation of '98 and its disillusioned self-criticism. Then it revived in the twentieth century. Facing a growing threat from the forces of liberalism and radicalism, Spanish conservatives and reactionaries developed a historical defense of the traditional order. They explained that Spain declined and lost her empire because she abandoned the spiritual values of true *Hispanidad*, values which found their fullest expression in the Spain of Charles V and Philip II, and because she embraced liberalism, rationalism, democracy, and other pagan, divisive doctrines. In the bizarre conception of some Rightist historians, the Bourbon king Charles III and Las Casas alike became instruments of a corrupting, debilitating liberalism. Meanwhile, conservative circles in Latin America, alarmed by the growth of *Indigenismo* and a variety of social revolutionary movements, identified themselves more closely with a Hispanic colonial past which they viewed through nostalgic eyes. These conditions help to explain the twentieth-century upsurge of a historical revisionism predicated on a Black Legend that falsified Spain's past and particularly her work in America.

A conservative Spanish Crown official, Julián Juderías, coined the term "Black Legend." His book, *La leyenda negra* (1914), expressed a deep sense of grievance. According to Juderías, the outside world had long viewed Spain and her past through prisms that distorted the Spanish reality. In twelve years his book went through seven editions. It was followed in both Spain and Latin America by many other apologies full of recriminations. To this tradition belong such prominent names as Carlos Pereyra, Constantino Bayle, Rómulo D. Carbia, José Vasconcelos, Salvador de Madariaga, and Ricardo Levene. Finally in 1963 the venerable Ramón Menéndez Pidal published *El Padre Las Casas, su doble personalidad,* in some respects the climactic work of this school.

Meanwhile, in the United States a more moderate revisionism, also favorable to Spain but less polemical in tone, developed among historians writing on colonial Latin America. This movement had nineteenth-century antecedents, for Yankee historians of that century regarded the Spanish Empire with kindlier eyes than is commonly supposed. There is no doubt, however, that the superb scholarship and readable style of Edward G. Bourne's *Spain in America* (1904) gave impetus to the reaction against what is now called the Black Legend by laying, in Charles Gibson's words, "a positive assessment of early Hispanic colonization before the American public." That reaction gained strength as a result of other studies. Arthur Aiton's *Antonio de Mendoza* (1927) presented an attractive portrait of a hard-working, efficient viceroy; and Irving Leonard's *Books of the Brave* (1949) demonstrated that Spanish restrictions on colonial reading were far less stringent and effective than had been supposed. The monographs of John Tate Lanning showed the high level of some Latin American thought during the Enlightenment. Lewis Hanke also contributed to the rehabilitation of Spain's colonial policies with his studies on the history of ideas, notably *The Spanish Struggle for Justice in the Conquest of America* (1949) and *Aristotle and the American Indians* (1959).

.   .   .

Let us turn to the supposed responsibility of Las Casas for the origin and diffusion of the Black Legend. First of all, how accurate were the facts and figures in his *Very Brief Account*? [*Hubert*] Herring [*author of the text* A History of Latin America], states the conventional position on these questions. Las Casas exaggerated and gave absurd statistics. His book "furnished fuel for Spain's enemies, who forthwith made capital of Spain's iniquities for their own ends. It laid a solid foundation for the 'Black Legend' which has colored the writings of the English, Dutch, Germans, and Americans ever since." From Herring's account, Las Casas emerges with the familiar aspect of a well-meaning humanitarian, admirable in his zeal, but lacking serious standards of accuracy.

It remained for Ramón Menéndez Pidal to say of Las Casas what no critic of Las Casas' own time had dared to say. Study and reflection had led Menéndez Pidal to the conclusion that Las Casas was a "paranoiac," with the fixed idea that "everything done in the Indies by Columbus and the Spaniards was diabolical and must be annulled and done all over again, whereas everything done by the Indians was good and just." Menéndez Pidal surveyed Las Casas' figures of Indian deaths and his recital of Spanish atrocities and then dismissed them with the contemptuous phrase "la enormización lascasiana."

A few comments are in order. With regard to Las Casas' figures of Indian deaths, John Fiske pointed out long ago that "the arithmetic of Las Casas is . . . no worse than that of all the Spanish historians of that age. With every one of them the nine digits seem to have gone on a glorious spree." In our own times of concern for statistical precision it is not uncommon, as Marcel Bataillon [*French scholar and student of Las Casas*] has remarked, for journals of different political views to vary by as much as 200% in their counts of the attendance at a demonstration. To be sure, Las Casas may not have been strictly accurate in his overall figures of 15 to 20 million Indian deaths in the Conquest. Nevertheless, some modern estimates of the pre-Columbian population in America (e.g., Woodrow Borah's suggestion of more than 100 millions) lend a new plausibility to Las Casas' statistics. For the rest, we have the testimony of independent witnesses, including some who cannot be charged with sympathy with Las Casas, and these confirm the very heavy mortality among Indians from causes other than epidemic disease. Bataillon, for example, cites the estimate of the conquistador and encomendero Rodrigo Lozano that the civil wars of 1544–1548 in Peru caused the death of "more than half," probably "three-fifths" of the Indians who were forced to serve the Spaniards as carriers.

We are on firmer ground when we turn to particular events related in the *Very Brief Account*. Menéndez Pidal ridicules Las Casas' stories of exhausted Indian carriers, chained by the neck, whose heads the Spaniards severed from their bodies so they might not have to stop to untie them. For Menéndez Pidal these tales are the products of the imagination of Las Casas or of his informants. But Bataillon brings together a group of witnesses who confirm this "sinister practice"; they include the chronicler Cieza de León, the royal official Pedro de la Gasca, and Gonzalo de Pizarro. Still others were the exceptionally well-informed judge Alonso de Zorita, who reported the same practice in his *Brief and Summary Relation of the Lords of New Spain*; and, for the seventeenth century, Gabriel Fernández de Villalobos, Marqués de Varinas, an eyewitness of such crimes in Venezuela. Testimony on the general reliability of the sources used for the *Very Brief Account* comes from the late Manuel Giménez Fernández, in a preliminary report on a study that he and his students were making of the sources and parallel texts of the treatise. Giménez Fernández concluded that the facts cited by Las Casas were in great part drawn from reports submitted to the Spanish monarchs and the Council of the Indies. Future archival research will undoubtedly provide further corroboration of statements made by Las Casas in the *Very Brief Account*.

Herring further makes the familiar claim that the *Very Brief Account* "laid a solid foundation for the 'Black Legend' which has colored the writings of the English, Dutch, Germans, and Americans ever since." In his luminous discussion of Las Casas, Alberto Salas acquitted him of this charge for two reasons. First, Las Casas never considered the use that Spain's enemies might make of his treatises. Second, he leveled charges of cruelty not only against Spaniards, but against Portuguese and the German conquerors in Venezuela, whom he described as "more cruel than tigers and ravenous wolves." Had he known of the crimes by English, Portuguese, and French colonizers, he would not have criticized them any more or less vigorously because they were foreigners. As Salas correctly observes, Las Casas was entirely free from nationalist sentiment.

An eighteenth-century French Dominican long ago absolved Las Casas of responsibility for Spain's ill repute with an argument that has lost none of its cogency. In his *Histoire générale de l'Amérique*, Father Touron refused to believe that the Dutch were ignorant of Spanish cruelties in the Indies before reading Las Casas' book. "The tyranny of the Conquistadors had been too widely bruited in both the Old and the New Worlds, men of good will had complained too

loudly for the past forty or thirty years, for the Dutch to be unaware
of facts so generally known throughout Europe." Obviously, too, the
Dutch had ample cause to be aware of the Spanish capacity for cruelty
without information on events in America. Sverker Arnoldsson comments in his study of Black Legend origins that the portrayal of the
Spaniards in Dutch propaganda as rapacious, cruel, and lascivious
had a "fearful basis of reality."

Certainly the *Very Brief Account* of Las Casas helped to deepen
and diffuse more widely the evil reputation that Spain already had
acquired in Europe, but to say that the book "laid a solid foundation
for the Black Legend" of Spanish cruelty in the Indies is to over-
simplify a complex process that still awaits a thorough investigation.
Consider the facts. The *Very Brief Account* was published in Seville
in 1552; the first foreign translation (Dutch) appeared in 1578, followed by French (1579), English (1583), and German (1599) versions.
Much earlier, however, the Italian traveler Girolamo Benzoni had
published his *Historia del Mondo Nuovo* (Venice, 1565), with its
moving accounts of Spanish cruelty to the Indians.

A simple style, much anecdotal detail, and a general impression
of candor and compassion contributed to the Benzoni book's great
popularity. It soon appeared in Latin (1573) and in a French (1578)
translation by the Huguenot Urbain Chauveton, his party's knowl-
edgeable specialist on American affairs, who provided the book with
elaborate annotation. Bataillon calls attention to the fact that the
famous French surgeon Ambroise Paré and the essayist Montaigne
cite Benzoni and [*Francisco López de*] Gómara [*sixteenth-century author of an account of the conquest of Mexico*]—not Las Casas—in
their denunciations of Spanish misdeeds in the Indies. Apparently it
was Montaigne's reading of Gómara, not Benzoni, that moved him to
an explosion of wrath on this subject. Gilbert Chinard contrasts the
playful tone of Montaigne's essay *On Cannibals* with the angry mood
of the essay *On Coaches*. Both dealt with the American Indians, but the
first was written in 1580, the second in 1588. What had happened in
the meantime? Montaigne had read Gómara and learned from the
lips of a Spaniard of the actions of the Conquerors in America.

Gómara was not the only imperialist chronicler, however, who
stoked Black Legend fires. The Englishman Richard Hakluyt cited
Las Casas and Benzoni in his attack on Spanish cruelty to the Indians,
but he also quoted a statement by Oviedo, "another of their own
historiographers and Captain of the Castle of Sancto Domingo."
Oviedo declared that Spaniards who had come to the Indies, "having
left their consciences and all fear of God and man behind them, have
played the parts not of man but of dragons and infidels, and having
no respect for humanitie, have been the cause that many Indians that
peradventure might have been converted and saved, are dead by

divers and sondrie deaths." Clearly the Black Legend had more than one or two "authors."

References to the Black Legend almost invariably proclaim foreign rivals' envy of Spain's American riches and their desire to take over her empire as the principal reasons for the creation and diffusion of the Legend. Hubert Herring approvingly quoted the statement of "a sagacious Spaniard," Salvador de Madariaga, that "love of tribe made it necessary for England, France, and Holland to blacken Spain; for the richest and most majestic empire the world had ever seen was for three hundred years the quarry out of which England, France, and Holland built their own empires. Spain had to be wrong so that France, Holland, and England, and later the United States could be right."

The French historian Pierre Chaunu recently restated this thesis. He lamented that it was Las Casas' unhappy fate to be exploited after his death by Spain's unscrupulous enemies. The *Very Brief Account,* wrote Chaunu, "was seized as an arm by Spain's adversaries at the height of the struggle which, in Europe, the Atlantic Ocean, America, and soon in the Indian Ocean and the Far East, opposed to the *beati possidentes* of the first Iberian wave of European expansion the second wave of robust late-comers." Foreign translations of Las Casas' treatises became weapons "in the polemical arsenal of imperialisms hostile to the Spanish Empire," "the cynical arms of psychological warfare." Thus they were turned to ends having no relation to "the noble motive that had inspired them."

Chaunu offered a statistical analysis concerning the publication history of the *Very Brief Account* and three other major tracts by Las Casas. He easily demonstrated that the great majority of editions of the four tracts appeared not in Spain but abroad. Chaunu also showed that the distribution of editions by country up to 1700 corresponded to "the hierarchy of Spain's enemies," with the greatest number of translations published in Holland, followed by France and England. Chaunu's analysis also revealed a correlation between the fortunes of the struggle between Spain and her enemies and the rise and wane of foreign interest in Las Casas' treatises.

Chaunu did not and could not prove, however, that the foreign translations of Las Casas were used exclusively or even principally for ignoble imperialist ends, as weapons "in the polemical arsenal of imperialisms hostile to the Spanish Empire." A careful examination of the circumstances surrounding specific editions of Black Legend titles suggests that nationalist aspirations and religious and other ideological conflicts with Spain of the Counter-Reformation, sometimes even an authentic humanitarianism, as well as the expansionist interests of merchant capitalist groups, all played their part in the complex process of the diffusion of the Black Legend. Such an examination quickly reveals Chaunu's error in claiming that the foreign translations of Las Casas' treatises had no relation to "the noble motive that inspired them."

The first major Black Legend work published outside Spain was Benzoni's *Historia del Mondo Nuovo* (Venice, 1565). It would require a powerful imagination to explain the appearance of this book in terms of Venetian colonial appetites for America. Furthermore, this travel account of a Milanese who passed fourteen years in the Indies is not as uncompromisingly hostile to the Spaniards as is sometimes supposed. Benzoni praised the Spanish Dominicans in the Indies for their efforts in behalf of the natives. He called the New Laws "a most holy and glorious law [sic.] truly, vouchsafed by a divine emperor." He spoke warmly of Alonso López de Cerrato, president of the *audiencia* of Guatemala. "I can testify that throughout India there never was a better judge, nor one who practiced good precepts more strictly, obeying the royal commands, always endeavouring that the Indians should not be ill-treated by any Spaniard." Benzoni even complimented Viceroy Antonio de Mendoza of New Spain for his prudence in not attempting to enforce the New Laws against the overwhelming opposition of the colonists. Curiously enough, Benzoni appears poorly informed concerning Las Casas, whose efforts to establish a colony on the coasts of Venezuela he criticized as a scheme to fish for pearls.

Las Casas found no Italian translator in the sixteenth century. This may be attributed in large part to the fact that after the treaty of Cateau Cambresis (1559) the Spaniards exercised direct or indirect control over every part of Italy except the Venetian Republic and the Duchy of Savoy. Beginning in 1616, however, a series of Las Casas' tracts in translation came off Venetian presses, including the *Very Brief Account,* his brief against Indian slavery, and the summary of his dispute with Sepúlveda.[1] In their prefaces and notes the editors or translators denounced Spanish cruelty to the Indians, drew analogies between the plight of the Indians and the condition of European peoples under Spanish rule, and endorsed Las Casas' doctrines of peaceful conversion. Ascribing this Italian use of Las Casas to colonial rivalry would be absurd. Still, this publishing activity certainly reflected the deadly enmity between Spain and Venice, an enmity which the author of a standard history of the Republic

---

[1] In 1550–1551 Las Casas and scholar Juan Ginés de Sepúlveda conducted a debate before the Council of the Indies and a panel of theologians to determine whether the Spanish conquest of America was being conducted justly. Sepúlveda argued that war might be waged on the Indians in order to compel them to accept Christianity; Las Casas, on the other hand, maintained that the Indians should be won over to Christianity by peaceful means alone. [H. D.]

accounts for by "the tolerant temper of Venice in spiritual matters, its independence of the Papacy, its friendly relations with Protestant England and the heretical Netherlands, its opposition to the Jesuits, and its indulgence to the Jews. . . ." It is difficult to comprehend why the principles of toleration, national independence, and peaceful conversion advocated by the Italian editors of Las Casas' writings are less noble than Las Casas' own ideals.

Perhaps the first French contributions to the Black Legend were Urbain Chauveton's French and Latin translations of Benzoni. One may find a hint of colonial appetite in Chauveton's assurance that the French, because of their kindlier ways, would have better success than Spaniards or Portuguese in the work of Indian conversion. But Chauveton's hostility toward Spain reflected above all the religious-political cleavage that dominated France during the sixteenth century. French published opinion of the Spanish Conquest tended to divide neatly along religious lines. If the Huguenot Chauveton denounced Spanish cruelty to the Indians, Spain found an ardent defender in the Franciscan André Thevet, royal cosmographer. Thevet poked fun at the good Sieur Chauveton for letting himself be taken in by the lies of Benzoni, who, claimed Thevet, never set foot in America. The French Franciscan turned the same suspicious eye on Las Casas' *Brief Account,* calling it a small collection of lies falsely attributed to a Spanish bishop. And Thevet poured scorn on the humanitarians, "the crack-brained men who in their counting houses and studies give themselves up to the contemplation of Platonic ideas."

Chaunu's imperialist thesis and Madariaga's "love of tribe" are even less adequate to explain the passion with which Michel de Montaigne denounced the conquest of Mexico and Peru. Montaigne did not even mention Spain by name in his essay *On Coaches.* Instead he indicted all of European civilization for its failure to approach the Indians in a spirit of "brotherly fellowship and understanding," for not respecting the rights of weaker peoples to life and liberty.

Since Chaunu assigns a special importance to the Dutch use of Las Casas, allegedly for imperialist ends, we must examine the circumstances under which the first translations of Las Casas appeared in the Netherlands. In 1578 a volume containing translations of the *Very Brief Account* and two other tracts by Las Casas was published in Holland. At that date the Dutch Revolution was fighting for life— a revolution that began, according to Pieter Geyl, by "resistance to the non-national tendencies of Philip's rule, to the Spanish troops, to the excessive centralization, and to the religious persecution." To speak of imperialist motives in connection with the first Dutch edition of Las Casas is to fly in the face of reality. The propagandist aim of the book was clearly to promote Dutch unity and fighting spirit by showing the merciless, unjust nature of an enemy who committed such great atrocities in both the Old and the New World. The same motives figured in the bitter attack on Spain's Indian policies by William of Orange in his *Apologia* (1580). The year before, a French edition of the *Very Brief Account* appeared in Antwerp, then in rebel hands. This edition seems to have been intended to gain the support of the French-speaking Walloons in the struggle for independence.

To be sure, once independence had been more or less firmly secured, Dutch merchant capitalism began to display expansionist tendencies. The first Dutch piratical expeditions to Brazil and northern South America date from the last decade of the sixteenth century; the Dutch West Indian Company was organized in 1621. A possible early instance of Dutch use of the *Very Brief Account* for the promotion of colonial designs is an Amsterdam edition (1620) whose preface refers to the liberation of the Indians from their oppressors with Dutch assistance. No doubt commercial and colonial appetites had much to do with the large number of Dutch editions of Las Casas that appeared in the course of the seventeenth century. But to assume that no other motives (religious, ideological) played a part in the appearance of these editions is to accept a very simplistic interpretation of history.

Chaunu's conviction regarding a structural link between the foreign editions of Las Casas and colonial rivalry finds no more support in the case of England. The Russian scholar Afanasiev has shown that the successive English editions of Las Casas' *Very Brief Account*: 1583, 1625, 1656, 1689, 1699, 1745, coincided either with episodes of Anglo-Spanish tension in which colonial and commercial questions dominated, or with internal political crises caused by the danger of a Stuart restoration and the "Papist" menace. In the case of the second group of editions, the colonial issue played at most a secondary role.

No name is more important in the diffusion of the Black Legend than that of Theodore de Bry. A Walloon born in Liege, De Bry left Flanders about 1570, probably to escape the "Spanish Fury," and moved to Frankfort, then ruled by the Calvinist Frederick III of the Palatinate. There De Bry established a publishing house that specialized in handsomely made, profusely illustrated travel works. He published Latin and German editions of Benzoni; and his sons brought out Latin and German editions of Las Casas' *Very Brief Account* (1598, 1599), with the famous illustrations that carried to every corner of Europe the message of Spanish cruelty. Chaunu asserts that all the Dutch, German, and Latin editions of Las Casas in the period 1594–1599 were "manifestly inspired by the United Provinces to hold (*assurer*) their clientele." In this pronouncement Chaunu was evidently taking his cue from Rómulo Carbia—with no more proof than Carbia.[2]

If this were indeed the case, we might expect the *Praefatio ad Lectorem,* which introduces the Latin edition of the *Very Brief Account,* to be unrelentingly anti-Spanish in spirit. To be sure, the brothers Jean Theodore and Jean Israel de Bry used almost the same words as Las Casas when they declared that the Spaniards in the Indies had committed such cruelties that they could more fittingly be called tigers and lions than men. But they disavowed any intent to defame the whole Spanish nation. They recognized that good and bad men were to be found in every people and region. Indeed, they affirmed that "if we enjoyed the freedom and license that the Spaniards enjoyed in America, with no superior magistrate to inspire fear and hold them in check, we would doubtless be equal to the Spaniards in savagery, cruelty, and inhumanity."

The brothers not only commended Las Casas, but complimented the Emperor Charles V, "of happy memory," for his efforts to liberate the Indians from a "harsh and intolerable slavery." Their sole aim, proclaimed these devout Calvinists, was to make men understand the terrible fruits of that root of all evil, the love of money, and to eradicate that passion from their hearts. Whoever searched his conscience seriously would find it rooted in his heart. Thus the De Bry brothers rejected the notion of a unique Spanish wickedness or cruelty.[3] Nothing in the preface to their 1598 edition of the *Very Brief Account* justifies the claim that it was designed as "a cynical arm of psychological warfare" or as a weapon "in the polemical arsenal of imperialisms hostile to the Spanish Empire."

Three tentative conclusions would seem to be justified. In the first place, the so-called Black Legend is substantially accurate, if stripped of its rhetoric and emotional coloration, and with due regard for its failure to notice less dramatic forms of Spanish exploitation of the Indians (land usurpation, peonage, and the like). Consequently it is

---

[2] According to Carbia, with the De Bry editions of Las Casas "the campaign of Dutch defamation against Spain reached its climax." *Historia de la leyenda negra hispano-americana,* 72.

[3] Theodore de Bry rejected the notion of a unique Spanish cruelty or of a special guilt attached to the Spanish nation even more forcefully in his preface to the 1594 Latin edition of Benzoni. Citing the many frauds, usuries, and abuses committed against the poor in all parts of Europe, and the cruelties committed by French, German, and Italian soldiers and by soldiers of other nationalities in their wars, he wrote: "Let us not be so hasty in condemning the Spaniards, but let us rather examine ourselves to see whether we are any better." Solórzano found the passage favorable enough to Spain to cite in his defense of the Spanish Conquest against foreign critics. Juan Solórzano y Pereyra, *Política indiana* (5 vols., Madrid, 1930), I, 127.

no legend at all, and the term lacks scientific descriptive value. Acceptance that the traditional critique of Spanish colonial practices was valid in no way implies superior practices by other imperialisms. Nor does it prelude an equal stress on Spanish colonial achievements, ranging from the devoted labors of many clergy in the fields of scholarship, education, and protection of the natives to the cultural flowering that occurred in some parts of the region during the eighteenth century.

Secondly, all major corollaries of the Black Legend concept are open to serious questioning. These include the primary responsibility of Las Casas for the rise and diffusion of the Legend, the decisive importance of colonial rivalry in its use by foreigners, and the virtual domination of historical literature by Black Legend attitudes before the time of Bourne.

Finally, the concept of a Black Legend does not illuminate the subject of Spanish-Indian relations, but rather serves to confuse and distort those relations. In particular it has served to engender a thoroughly misleading counterlegend of Spanish altruism and benevolence to the Indians. Part of this White Legend substitutes the texts of laws and pious expressions of goodwill, generally unimplemented, for the reality of Indian-Spanish relations. Another part stresses genuine cultural advances (such as the abolition of human sacrifice and cannibalism) that are largely irrelevant to the operation and effects of the Spanish colonial system. Still another part denigrates Indian lifeways with reckless generalizations that show little understanding of aboriginal culture and modern anthropological viewpoints.

.   .   .

◆§ 3 §◆

Culture and Conquest

———◆◄◆►◆———

George M. Foster

*The cultural impact of the Spanish conquest on the indigenous peoples
of the New World has long been studied by anthropologists and historians. In this selection, anthropologist George M. Foster of the University of California at Berkeley indicates that the recipient peoples
were able to exercise a degree of selectivity in adopting the tools and
techniques of the "conquest culture." He also advances the concept of
"cultural crystallization" to account for the disproportionately large
cultural influence of Andalusian and Extremaduran origins as compared
with the number of emigrants from those regions.*

I now wish to consider very briefly what happens to a conquest culture
—that of Spain, of course—in a new world. Conquest culture represents
but a small part of the totality of traits and complexes that comprise
the donor culture. Then, through a second screening process in the
geographical region of the recipient peoples, conquest culture is still
further reduced, in the process of playing its role as a builder of
colonial culture. Two distinct but related analytical approaches help
us to understand this reduction process. The first deals with the social
and psychological mechanisms whereby recipient peoples, in those
situations in which they are allowed choice, exercise discretion in accepting and rejecting elements presented to them. The second deals
with the time dimension, with the sequence in presentation of conquest
culture. It suggests a concept, which may be called "cultural crystallization," illustrating how essentially nonsocial and nonpsychological
factors may be very significant in determining what the final stabilized
forms of an acculturated society will be. These approaches, and the
conclusions they lead to, are discussed in turn.

From George M. Foster, *Culture and Conquest: America's Spanish Heritage*
(Chicago: Quadrangle Books, 1960), pp. 227–234. Copyright © 1960 by Wenner-
Gren Foundation for Anthropological Research, Incorporated. Reprinted by
permission of Quadrangle Books. This article appears as reprinted in Robert
Wauchope (ed.), *The Indian Background of Latin American History* (New
York: Knopf, 1970), pp. 189–201. Some footnotes deleted. Italicized bracketed
notes in the text are by Helen Delpar.

The operation of social and psychological mechanisms both produces and is governed by the structure of the contact situation. In relation to areas of high culture, and especially to Mexico, it is well to bear in mind that, although we tend to think only in terms of Indians acculturating to Spanish ways, there were, in fact, two recipient groups in process of change: Indian and Spanish. Every Spaniard in America represented some phase of the donor culture, and thereby helped carry conquest culture. At the same time each Spaniard was exposed not only to Indians, but also to other Spaniards, who often faced him with laws and regulations, and with less formal cultural items, many of which were very strange to him. That is, the Spaniard as well as the Indian was exposed to conquest culture. Both were faced with a similar problem of selection and adjustment. The Spaniard did not have to adjust to metal tools, domestic animals, the plow, and Christianity, but he did have to come to terms with a new sociopolitical and environmental situation and to other Spaniards and their customs as well as to the Indians.

The manner in which both Indian and Spaniard and their mestizo offspring were exposed to conquest culture was structured by the social setting, and particularly by the division of society into urban and rural components. This division, as it existed in pre-Conquest times, can be thought of in terms of the familiar folk-urban continuum with, to use Aguirre Beltrán's terminology, a "ceremonial center" pole representing the elite tradition and a "community culture" representing the peasant tradition.

In the very first years of the Conquest, acculturation must have been marked by much direct transmission from Spaniards to Indians all along this continuum, and from Spaniards to Spaniards. But as Spanish cities were founded and native cities were rebuilt, the picture changed. The native urban-elite authority structure was replaced by the Spanish equivalent so that, instead of a continuum both poles of which represented variants of a single culture, there now existed a continuum for which the authority pole was Spanish. After this modified continuum was established, and after the initial culturally mixed mestizo populations came into being, the acculturation process took the familiar pattern of flow of influence downward and outward, from the urban-elite pole to lower classes and peasants. Spanish, hispanicized, and partly hispanicized peoples all along this continuum therefore continued to be exposed to new Spanish influences as they were passed along from cities, and these peoples in turn became a point of diffusion of the items they accepted, to other populations less influenced by Spain.

The sociopsychological mechanisms whereby the peoples along this continuum screened conquest culture, accepting what they perceived to be desirable and within their reach and rejecting what they perceived to be undesirable and within their ability to refuse, can be best observed in relation to Indian culture reacting to conquest culture, since this offers the maximum contrast. Without attempting a thorough study of these mechanisms, the following observations may be made:

1. In the field of material culture and techniques, Spanish forms were welcomed when they were recognized by the Indians as useful, and when there were no indigenous counterparts or when indigenous counterparts were rudimentary. New crops, agricultural implements, and domestic animals were recognized by most Indian groups as useful. And since indigenous patterns of care of the few domestic animals known did not furnish a broad enough base on which radically to modify Spanish practices of animal husbandry, these are overwhelmingly predominant in America. Where agriculture with some other tool than the digging stick was feasible, the utility of Spanish methods, especially the plow and ox, was usually apparent; hence in much of America, Spanish agricultural techniques used in preparing the ground, sowing, and harvesting (e.g., broadcast sowing of grain and the division of fields into *melgas*) predominate. With respect to heavy transportation the Spanish solid-wheeled oxcart, the *carro chirrión,* had no native competitor in America, and it was soon widely adopted. Indigenous metalworking techniques were so limited that they offered no serious competition to European methods.

Conversely, where there were satisfactory native counterparts, Spanish influence was much less marked. This is particularly apparent with respect to food, and in the practices and beliefs associated with the life cycle. Although religious, political, and social institutions were well developed in America, and therefore might be expected to have changed less rapidly than they did, the special manner in which they were singled out for formal attention by the conquerors caused the native institutions to disintegrate at a rapid rate.

2. Again, in the field of material culture and techniques, Spanish forms set the pattern when they were recognized by the Indians as obviously superior to, or representing a significant extension of, their indigenous forms. The Moorish roof tile, the primitive Iberian potter's kiln, and the Spanish carpenter's simple tools were all widely (but by no means universally) adopted. The ubiquity of Spanish-type fishing devices certainly again reflects the fact that they were recognized by Indians as preferable to their own types. At least some Spanish costume was better than existing Indian types: outside the area of the llama, wool cloth made possible by the introduction of sheep was an enormous boon to both sexes. The fulled bayeta skirt must have brought previously unknown comfort to Indian women, and woolen blankets, blouses, and jackets must have been appreciated by all wearers in cold areas. The Spanish flat-bed loom, although by no means replacing the native back-strap loom, quickly found its place, further contributing to

more adequate clothing and a more comfortable bed. (It must be remembered that the patterns of Indian clothing in parts of Colonial America were also set by decree.) And the Old World crops of wheat, rye, barley, sugarcane, and many vegetables and fruits, as well as Spanish animals—sheep, cattle, horses, the chicken, burro, and pig—represent significant extensions of indigenous content.

3. In the field of folk culture, in a somewhat limited sense of the term, the processes at work in the acceptance or rejection of Spanish elements by Indian cultures are less clear than in the two foregoing categories. We are dealing here with areas of culture not of primary concern to State and Church and with areas of culture in which obvious superiority either does not exist or cannot be easily recognized. This is an area in which chance, and perhaps the personality of unusual individuals, both Spanish and Indian, seems to have played a very important role. With respect to such things as dietary patterns, superstitions, folk medicine, folklore, and music, Spanish traits found themselves in competition with indigenous traits, and often with no clear advantage. Here individual motivation is an important factor, but at this distance in time it is difficult to work out these motivations. We can assume that the motivations that are important in contemporary culture change—prestige and curiosity, to name two—were equally important in sixteenth-century America, but it is difficult to link these general motivations to the introduction of specific traits. To the extent that it can be done, it must be done with historical techniques.

Now let us turn to the second of the two approaches—that involving a time dimension—which help in understanding what happens to conquest culture in the recipient area. This approach concerns the question of the geographical origin in Spain of Hispanic American traits and complexes. The problem is whether we can find Spanish foci or distribution areas for prototypes of such things as agricultural tools, transportation devices, fishing techniques, clothing forms, beliefs and practices associated with the life cycle, and popular religious observances. If we find such distribution areas, what implications do they hold for understanding the sequence of presentation of conquest culture to America? And what do they have to do with the concept of "cultural crystallization"?

Although peninsular distribution areas for Hispanic American prototypes have not been worked out in detail, certain broad patterns, which will shortly be pointed out, do exist. That is, Spanish culture in America does not represent an equal and balanced selection from all parts of the country; some areas of Spain are much more heavily represented than others. Why is this? A common explanation is based on the theory of what may be called "proportional representation." Since we know that cultures meet through their carriers, each individual—each emigrant of a donor culture—is a potential device for transmitting something of his local culture to the new region. Therefore, it might be expected that each geographical area of such a country as Spain would be represented culturally in America in proportion to its share of the total numbers of emigrants who left the peninsula. The apparent predominance of Andalusian and Extremaduran traits in America is therefore often "explained" by saying that "a majority of conquistadors and settlers came from these areas."

If we utilize the data presented to determine whether in fact the cultures of Andalusia and Extremadura are most heavily represented in America, we come to the conclusion that this popular belief is essentially correct. Minor modifications are needed: eastern Andalusia appears less important, and much of New Castile and the southerly parts of Old Castile and León must be included in the area of greatest influence. Here are samples of the data that lead one to this conclusion:

Agriculture

In America the Andalusian and Extremaduran plow is found to the apparent exclusion of all other peninsular forms. The highly useful Castilian threshing sledge (tribulum) is unknown, while the absence of the modern Andalusian threshing cart (the ancient plostellum) can be explained on the basis of its nineteenth-century reintroduction into southern Spain, so that it was not available in earlier centuries for export to America. For drawing plows and carts the north-Spanish neck yoke is uncommon or absent in America, its place taken by the central-southern Spanish horn yoke.

Fishing

American net types and terminology, especially the various parts of the jábega-chinchorro seine, suggest the Andalusian coast rather than Galicia or Catalonia. I have no explanation, however, for the puzzling fact that the term "chinchorro" appears to be used in all Spanish America to the complete exclusion of the more common Spanish term "jábega," and the near exclusion of the term "boliche." Perhaps American net forms are drawn from a very limited area of Andalusia where the term "chinchorro" predominated. In view of the great variation in terminology applied to similar nets along Spanish coasts, this is certainly a possibility.

Arts and Crafts

Spanish American folk pottery techniques of peninsular origin appear to draw most heavily on Spanish forms found from Granada west, and then north to León, while American manufacture of finer ware, such as Talavera, is due to Sevillian and Toledan influence. With respect to the textile arts, the south-Spanish horizontal spinning wheel rather than the north-Spanish upright model is found in America. Spanish American folk costume suggests south Spain rather than north Spain; for example, the garments of peasant women from Old Castile north are surprisingly different from those of women in rural America. Some specific items, like the *tapada* of colonial Peru, quite obviously come from Andalusia. Salamancan jewelry, especially such things as articulated silver fish, appears to be ancestral to many Peruvian and Mexican forms.

Social Patterns

To the extent that a peninsular type of *compadrazgo* is ancestral to Hispanic American variants, it is Andalusian. Negatively, the absence in America of the widespread Old Castilian-Leonese institution of bachelors' societies, and of most of the popular wedding customs and forms of horseplay of north-central and northwest Spain, is significant.

Funerary Practices

On the basis of available data the customs of Extremadura, Huelva, and parts of New Castile are particularly suggestive of America, although the *baile del angelito*[1] points to the southeast. At the time of the Conquest, however, this custom may well have been much more widespread. Negatively, the north-Spanish funeral orgy appears not to have characterized America, nor have paid mourners been noted in the New World. Likewise, north-Spanish inheritance patterns seem to have had little influence in America, whereas south-Spanish forms have been important.

Popular Religious Practices

A number of widespread central and northern Spanish activities are little known or lacking entirely in America. Among these are the pig of St. Anthony, the Candlemas torte, the festivities of Santa Agueda and the married women's *cofradía* [*sisterhood*], and *la maya* [*a May queen or any girl who takes part in festivities connected with the month*]. The "burial of the sardine" [*to mark the end of Carnival*], general in central and northern Spain in earlier years, was absent in Andalusia, and very rare in America.

---

[1] The baile del angelito, or dance of the little angel, was a dance performed in southern Spain at the wake of a young child. Since a child who died was believed to go directly to heaven, his death might be considered an occasion for rejoicing. [H. D.]

Speech

Although linguistic acculturation is an enormously complicated subject, which cannot be touched upon here, in a general way it seems that southern and western Spanish variants of Castilian were more important in America than central and northern forms.

This list deals primarily with cultural elements brought to America through informal channels. It is clear that the formally transmitted categories of culture, in which Church and State policy were predominant, are Castilian rather than Andalusian-Extremaduran. This is to be expected, for the obvious reason that Castile was the kingdom of the ruling house and of the administrators and churchmen most concerned with government.

If we therefore ignore these formally transmitted categories of culture, it looks as if we have a good case for the hypothesis of "proportional representation" as it is popularly expressed: a preponderance of southern and western influences, because of a preponderance of emigrants from these areas. But we know now that the old belief in the importance of settlers from Andalusia and Extremadura is not borne out by demographic data. Sufficiently large numbers of emigrants came from nearly all parts of the country, so that we might logically expect less Andalusian-Extremaduran influence and more from Old Castile, Asturias, Navarre, Aragón, León, and Galicia. What explanation can be advanced to explain the seeming anomaly of a disproportionately large total of cultural influences stemming from Andalusia-Extremadura as compared with the numbers of emigrants from these regions?

The answer appears to lie in the *sequence* of formation and presentation of conquest culture. It is probable that at any given time undirected conquest culture (i.e., that not controlled by Church and State) was made up of elements which reflected at least a rough correlation between subcultural areas and numbers of emigrants from these areas. This means that conquest culture was not formed overnight, to remain essentially static over a long period of time. Rather, it was fluid, changing over the years as the composition of its carriers changed. At any specific time it was given shape by the culture type of the most numerous groups of emigrants, at least as far as informally transmitted elements are concerned.

In its earliest manifestation, then, it must have represented the local culture of the first waves of conquistadors and settlers. And these people, we know, did come in significant numbers from Andalusia and Extremadura. While it is true that, if we consider the entire sixteenth century or even the first fifty years of widespread emigration, nearly all parts of Spain were represented in significant quantity, it is also true that during the first two or three decades the provinces of western Andalusia, Extremadura, New Castile, southern León, and southern Old Castile were particularly well represented. This is by no mean a homogeneous culture area, but there are basic similarities which stem from the fact that its northern part had recolonized its southern part several centuries earlier.

Therefore, during the very first years of conquest and settlement in America, in its unplanned aspects conquest culture represented southwest and west-central Spain rather than the north. This initial phase was relatively short, although I hesitate to set a time span. It was a highly fluid, formative period in America in which the basic answers to new conditions of life had to be found, and a rapid adaptation to changed conditions on the part of both Indians and Spaniards was imperative. This was the period of the blocking out of colonial cultures. Quick decisions, individual and collective, conscious and unconscious, had to be made on innumerable points. And the information on which settlers had to draw, in making these decisions, was the knowledge that characterized their particular variants of Spanish culture.

The basic outlines of the new colonial cultures took shape at a rapid rate. Once they became comparatively well integrated and offered preliminary answers to the most pressing problems of settlers, their forms became more rigid: they may be said to have crystallized. After crystallization, and during a period of reasonably satisfactory adjustments to social and natural environments, the new Spanish American colonial cultures appear to have become more resistant to continuing Spanish influence. These stabilizing cultures were then less receptive to change and less prone to accept new elements from the parent culture which had been left behind or rejected in the initial movement.

When, then, increasing numbers of emigrants from more northerly areas reached the New World, they encountered a going concern to which they had to adapt themselves. The culture they brought with them, which would have been perfectly adequate in working out solutions to new problems in America, was now less important, simply because it came later in the time sequence.

The duration of the initial period of fluid cultural conditions and hospitality to Spanish forms is difficult to determine. It varied from place to place, depending on the date of effective conquest. On the mainland this initial period began and ended first in central Mexico, whereas in South America it came some years later. Writing about Yucatan, [*France V.*] Scholes says that the basic pattern of Hispano-Indian society

was clearly marked out by the end of the sixteenth century or about sixty years after the Conquest. By that time a new ruling caste of foreign origin, extremely jealous of its privileges, had obtained firm control over the destinies of the Maya race; . . . and a considerable amount of fusion of culture, especially in the realm of religion, had taken place. *During the remainder of the colonial period these basic problems of provincial society remained essentially the same.* [Italics mine, G. M. F.] [2]

There is evidence for the validity of the concept of cultural crystallization from other sources. [*Melville J.*] Herskovits, faced with the problem of reconciling the fact that slaves were drawn from a wide African area but that major Negro influences in America apparently represent a relatively restricted area on the west coast, has come to similar conclusions. He believes the answer to his problem lies in the fact that "the slaves who came late to the New World had to accommodate themselves to patterns of Negro behavior established earlier on the basis of the customs of the tribes" that preceded them,[3] just as Spaniards who came to America after the earliest phases of conquest had to adjust to prevailing circumstances.

Pursuing this line of reasoning further, he suggests that in colonial United States the early Senegalese arrivals

were overshadowed by the traditions of the more numerous Guinea coast Negroes; while as for late-comers such as the Congo Negroes, the slaves they found were numerous enough, and well enough established, to have translated their modes of behavior . . . into community patterns.[4]

I believe that similar processes explain the apparent predominance of southern and western Spanish forms in America. In the very early years of the conquest of America, Andalusian and Extremaduran emigrants were numerically superior to those from all other areas, even though well before the end of the sixteenth century this pattern had shifted drastically. Moreover, to the extent that items of material culture were carried to America—plows and nets, for example—they would certainly be objects locally manufactured near the seaports which traded with the Indies. Poor internal transportation in Spain would preclude the hauling of Castilian plows and Navarense yokes to Sevilla, when perfectly adequate local models were available.

The early decades in America were decades of decision, a time when new adjustments and colonial cultures were roughed out and the basic outlines set. To the extent that Church and State did not take charge, the customs and ways of the earliest immigrants had the best chance of surviving, of finding niches in the new societies. Equally satisfactory competing forms, which came with more northerly immigrants only

[2] France V. Scholes, "The Beginnings of Hispano-Indian Society in Yucatan," *Scientific Monthly*, 44 (1937), 531.

[3] Melville J. Herskovits, *The Myth of the Negro Past* (New York: Harper, 1941), p. 52.

[4] *Loc. cit.*

a few years later, would find the functions they fulfilled already taken care of, and their carriers, like the later African slaves in the United States, had to adjust to the forms already set. After the first several decades a comparative hardening of colonial cultures occurred which, for a significant period of time, made these cultures less receptive to new items and less tolerant in their appraisal of later Spanish cultural influence.

If the concept of cultural crystallization is valid, it is clear that the common anthropological emphasis on social and psychological phenomena to explain acceptance or rejection of new elements by a subordinate people can never fully explain what takes place in an acculturation situation. The time sequence of formation and presentation of conquest culture plays an equally important role in determining the final selection of imported traits by native and colonial cultures. The sociopsychological reasons for acceptance and rejection can never be fully understood until they are placed in the perspective of time sequence and until it is recognized that new hybrid and drastically altered native cultures must make rapid decisions and then abide by most of these decisions, if they are to endure.

Indian Policy in Brazil

————◄◆►►————

Mathias C. Kiemen

Although royal legislation attempted to protect the Indians, its enforcement in America was at best fitful, and colonists tended to regard the natives primarily as a source of tribute and labor. The most vigorous defenders of the Indians, especially in the early years of colonization, were the clergy, particularly the members of the religious orders. In Brazil, the most important order was the Society of Jesus, whose first representatives arrived in the colony in 1549. Conflict over Indian labor between seventeenth-century settlers and the great Luso-Brazilian[1] Jesuit, Antônio Vieira, is described here by the Reverend Mathias C. Kiemen, o.f.m., former editor of The Americas, *a journal published by the Academy of American Franciscan History.*

The Jesuit effort on behalf of the Indians of Maranhão and Pará was intensified during the years 1652–1662 largely through activities of Father Antônio Vieira.

Antônio Vieira, whom many consider the most celebrated sacred orator in the Portuguese language, was born in Lisbon on February 6, 1608, of parents of moderate means. The family moved to Bahia when he was six years old. He attended the Jesuit College in Bahia, and in 1623 entered the Jesuit Order. In 1614 he returned to Portugal where he soon gained the confidence of King John IV. From 1652, when he was sent to Maranhão with royal authority to organize the Indian missions, until the day of his death in Bahia in 1697, he was intimately connected with the legislation passed in favor of the Indians.

On February 23, 1652, by decree of the king, Maranhão and Pará became separate captaincies, independent of each other. Each was now

From Mathias C. Kiemen, *The Indian Policy of Portugal in the Amazon Region, 1614–1693* (Washington, D.C.: Catholic University of America, 1954), pp. 79–117. Reprinted by permission of the Catholic University of America. This article appears as reprinted in Fredrick B. Pike (ed.), *The Conflict Between Church and State in Latin America* (New York: Knopf, 1964), pp. 90–97. Italicized bracketed notes in text are by Helen Delpar.

[1] "Luso" refers to Portugal (from Portugal's Roman name: *Lusitania*).

to have a *capitão-mor* who would exercise the highest civil authority. In accordance with the new law, Ignacio de Rego Barreto on March 3, 1652, was appointed for Pará, and Baltasar de Sousa Pereira on April 16, 1652, for Maranhão. Pereira arrived in São Luiz [the capital of Maranhão] in November or December of 1652, provided with a *regimento* which obliged him, among other things, to free the Indians who had been enslaved up to that time. Unfortunately for Vieira, Pereira published this part of his *regimento* only fifteen days after Vieira's arrival, and this led many of the people who were in favor of the *status quo* to blame the Jesuit for Pereira's action. A riot eventually broke out, during which people shouted, "Away with the Jesuits," but nothing more was accomplished. On March 2, 1653, the following Sunday, Vieira told the faithful from the pulpit that those who held slaves unjustly were on the road to eternal damnation.

On May 20 Fr. Antônio Vieira wrote a long letter to the Portuguese monarch. He spoke of the miserable lot of the Indians, both free and slave, especially of those who lived with the Portuguese. The free Indians worked for the governors and captains, especially in the growing and curing of tobacco, and they treated them as though they were actually slaves. Many of them died under their heavy yoke. Under the circumstances, the governors and captains, Vieira believed, should be forbidden to grow tobacco or any other product, or from using or distributing Indians in any way, except for public projects, such as the building of fortifications. Nor should they be permitted to place the *aldeias* [Indian communities] in the hands of laymen. On the contrary, no white man should be allowed in the *aldeias* except the missionary who lived there.

While Vieira was thus trying to influence the Crown, the settlers of the two captaincies were alert to the threat to the *status quo*. They therefore sent delegates (*procuradores*) to plead their case and obtain legislation favorable to their interests. The case, as presented by Vieira and the procurators, was resolved in Lisbon by the law of October 17, 1653, an attempt at a compromise solution.

Under given circumstances, the king allowed Indians to be captured as slaves. *Entradas* [entries into unpacified Indian territory] were permitted, with the choice of leader up to the captain or governor, in conference with the members of the town council, and the prelates of religious orders and the vicar general. Religious must accompany these expeditions, and the decision as to the legality of enslavement was up to this accompanying religious. The last part of the law absolutely forbade to the governor or captain-major the use of Indians in any way at all, except for public causes, such as building fortifications.

Such was the law of October 17, 1653. It was not entirely pleasing to Vieira, and he left for Lisbon in 1654, hoping to be able to improve it.

[Prior to leaving for Portugal] Vieira told the king quite specifically what should be done for the missions and the Indians in his letter of April 16, 1654. He outlined his ideas in nineteen paragraphs. [In the last of these Vieira insisted that the king] should place the missions in the hands of a single Order. Not every Order, in his opinion, would do. The work should be entrusted to an Order known for the virtue, disinterestedness, zeal and learning of its members. Moreover, the Indians should be independent of the authority of the governor.

Vieira left São Luiz in June, 1654, and arrived in Lisbon after a perilous voyage in November of the same year. There was much for him to do. The two procurators of the Town Councils of Belém [the capital of Pará] and São Luiz were already active at Court, protecting the interests of the colonists. The new governor of Maranhão-Pará [the two captaincies were now joined together under the rule of one governor] André de Vidal Negreiros, appointed on August 11, 1654, was ready to depart for his post. The king, however, anxious to settle this Indian question once [and] for all, called a full-dress junta of the most prominent theologians in the country to decide the thorny question of Indian enslavement. The king first of all sent out, on March 15, 1655, copies of the older laws on the subject to a group of theologians, asking them for their opinions on the matter.

After giving the theologians time to form their opinions the king ordered the junta to meet, probably in early April. The meeting was presided over by the Archbishop of Braga, Dom Pedro de Alemcastre. Coincidental with this meeting, a similar meeting was held to discuss practical details. It was attended by the new governor, Fr. Vieira himself, and the two procurators.

The result of the deliberations of these two juntas was the law of April 9, 1655, which regulated Indian enslavement. The body of the law began with a prohibition against capturing Indians except in the cases to be enumerated. The first is in a just offensive war against the Indians, which is defined as a war fought with the written authority of the king, after he had asked the opinion of all the civil and religious officials in the state. This effectively took away the power to wage offensive war from the governor. The second case in which the Indians could be captured as slaves would be one in which they impeded the preaching of the Holy Gospel, for they were obliged to allow it to be preached to them, even though they could not be forced with arms to accept it and believe it. The third case would be if the Indians were ransomed while being *presos a corda para serem comidos* [prisoners who were to be eaten by their Indian captors]. The fourth case in which Indians could be legally enslaved would be if they were purchased from other Indians, whose legitimate slaves they were, having been taken in a just war of the Indians among themselves.

[In] the next section of the law the king forbade all governors to work tobacco, or to use or distribute the Indians in any way at all, nor could the governor place lay captains in the *aldeias,* since these villages were to be ruled by their pastors and the Indian chiefs.

It can easily be seen that the law of April 9 was concerned with only one facet of the Indian problem. It was supplemented in many practical details by the *regimento* given to André Vidal de Negreiros on April 14, 1655. The Indians were to serve six months of each year, divided into terms of two months at a time, after which they must spend two months at home. The payment for the two-month service must be made before the Indians left for the work. The *regimento* decreed concerning *entradas* that on the years when these were undertaken, the Indians of service would serve proportionately less time in working for the colonists. *Entradas* were to be made only for the purpose of the propagation of the Faith. The Prelate of the Missions would give the order for the *entrada,* and the governor was commanded to furnish him with the soldiers necessary and a suitable leader, who, however, should have nothing to do with the religious side of the expedition, only caring for the military preparations. The Jesuit prelate shall decide the time and place of the *entradas.*

These two documents of 1655, together with the inevitable appointment of Fr. Vieira as Superior of the Missions, were to be the foundations upon which the Jesuits attempted to build control of the Indians. Vieira left Lisbon on April 16. When he arrived in São Luiz, Negreiros was already there. Largely because of the governor's interest, the law and the *regimento* were immediately put into practice. The choice of governor had been a wise one. Negreiros knew the country well, being a Brazilian by birth. He was, moreover, openly in favor of missionary activities. The discontent of the colonists at the arrival of Negreiros and Vieira with such a strong law was general. It was hard for the settlers to realize that the Indians, the great source of wealth in the colony, were now completely entrusted to the Jesuits. Yet they had no alternative. The presence and prestige of Negreiros were sufficient to ensure the carrying out of the royal will in both Maranhão and Pará.

The colonists, however, were not all resigned to the new situation. Open trouble began in 1656. In Belém and São Luiz the residents suffered in silence, because of the closeness of the seat of government. But in Gurupá, many leagues from Belém, the settlers decided to take matters into their own hands. With the support of the soldiers of the fort, the colonists put the two local Jesuits in a canoe, took them to a spot near Belém and warned them not to return. The colonists did not know the temper of Governor Negreiros. Accompanied by thirty soldiers and sixty Indians, he immediately restored the Jesuits to their former position. Two of the guilty were sent in chains to Lisbon to be judged there. The other lesser culprits were exiled to Brazil. Clearly the new governor was not to be trifled with. For the time being, at any rate, Vieira could congratulate himself on the victory.

But *requerimentos* continued to be sent to Lisbon against the law. The complaints of the colonists, however, would be useless as long as Father Vieira kept his influence at Court and could count on the protection of the royal family.

Early in 1661 the troubles of the Jesuits with the colonists and government officials reached a critical stage. Repeated complaints of the people to the Jesuits in Maranhão and Pará in 1659 and 1660 had had no effect. On January 12, 1660, the Town Council of Belém had written to the officials of São Luiz, suggesting a united front of complaints against the Jesuits' temporal power. But São Luiz turned down this proposal. One last series of appeals was made in 1661 by the Town Council of Belém to Fr. Vieira. On January 15, the town council in a long reclamation, declared the utter helplessness of the colony without more Indian workers. The town council then resolved to send a procurator to see the governor in São Luiz to tell him about conditions, and also to send a supplication to the Court. The complaint to the Court was sent off on April 9. So far all the agitation had been in Belém. The scene now shifted to São Luiz, where some private letters of Fr. Vieira to the bishop who had been confessor of the king were made public in early 1661. These letters were full of complaints against the lawlessness of the people concerning the protective legislation for the Indians. On May 17 the procurator or commissary sent by the Town Council of Belém left that city on his way to São Luiz. His arrival in São Luiz and the story he told, together with the publication of the recent letters, was enough to cause a riot in São Luiz, which ended in the imprisonment within the college of all Jesuits. That the revolt succeeded was due in part to the indecisiveness of the governor, Pedro de Melo [Negreiros had returned to Portugal after serving only eighteen months as governor], when the fatal moment of the revolt arrived. It must be said, however, that his military guards deserted him at the crucial moment. In a letter to Fr. Vieira which the governor sent off on May 23, he asked Vieira what he could have done with five or six faithful soldiers against five or six hundred rioters.

Vieira was sailing from Belém in Pará and stopped midway at the captaincy of Cumá, where the letter of the governor reached him. He immediately returned to Belém, where, he trusted, the news had not yet arrived, and where he could possibly still save the situation. He arrived in Belém on June 21 and immediately addressed himself to the town council, urging them to repudiate the actions of São Luiz. On July 7 the emissary that had been sent by Belém to the governor some time before returned to Belém and made his report. The governor had granted part of their request: that the Jesuits be removed from their temporal control over the Indians. When news of the happenings in Maranhão spread through the city, the excitement grew. On July 17 a tumult arose among the people, who demanded the immediate election of a *juiz do povo* [*people's tribune*] to settle the Indian question. The town council elected Diogo Pinto, one of their number, to this position, and the tumult died down. The new judge immediately imprisoned Vieira and his companions and sent them to São Luiz. From there the fathers were sent to Lisbon on the first available ship. By the following year, 1662, all the fathers, even those in the faraway missions, had been rounded up and put into custody. The revolt was complete.

In Lisbon, Vieira immediately set about repairing the situation, and was having marked success, when, unexpectedly, on June 21, 1662, a palace revolution unseated the queen regent, Luisa. Her son, Alfonso VI, became king in fact as well as name. Unfortunately for his cause, Fr. Vieira had backed the losing faction which had supported Prince Pedro against his brother the king. Alfonso now turned on Vieira. The Jesuit was banished from Court, and, in fact, was in the toils of the Inquisition from 1663 to 1667. He returned to royal favor in 1668, when Pedro became regent, but he never regained his former preeminence. In 1669 he went to Rome, and there he stayed until 1679. After that he went to Bahia, where he spent his declining years until his death in 1697.

❧ 5 ❧

A Despotic Utopia in Paraguay

Robert Southey

*The Jesuits were relative latecomers to Spanish America, arriving in
New Spain in 1572, but they quickly became active as missionaries and
educators and engaged in a variety of profitable economic enterprises.
The most celebrated as well as controversial missions of the Society of
Jesus were those established in the seventeenth century in the Rio de
la Plata area, which formed the Jesuit province of Paraguay. Here
the Jesuits exercised complete civil and military authority over their
charges. Royal suspicion of the actual or potential disloyalty of the
Jesuits of Paraguay undoubtedly contributed to the suppression of the
order in Spain and the Indies in 1767, especially since Indians under
the fathers' charge had forcibly resisted execution of the Treaty of
Madrid (1750), which provided for the transfer of mission territory
to Portugal and the removal of the Indians residing there. These events
probably had an even greater impact on the Portuguese government,
which anticipated Spain by expelling the Jesuits in 1759.*

*Although the English poet and man of letters Robert Southey (1774–
1843) never visited America, his three-volume* History of Brazil *(1810–
1819) is still considered a classic. In this excerpt, Southey depicts the
missions of Paraguay as a despotic utopia in which every aspect of the
Indians' life was regulated by the Jesuit fathers.*

Here [in Paraguay] were innumerable tribes, addicted to the vices,
prone to the superstitions, and subject to the accumulated miseries of
the savage life; suffering wrongs from the Spaniards, and seeking
vengeance in return; neither acknowledging King nor God; worshipping the Devil in this world, and condemned to him everlastingly in
the next. These people the Jesuits undertook to reclaim with no other
weapons than those of the Gospel, provided they might pursue their
own plans, without the interference of any other power; and provided

---

From Robert Southey, *History of Brazil* (London, 1817), Vol. 2, pp. 332–364
passim. This article appears as reprinted in Magnus Mörner (ed.), *The Expulsion of the Jesuits from Latin America* (New York: Knopf, 1965), pp. 55–62.
Deletions in the text are by Magnus Mörner.

the Spaniards, over whose conduct they could have no control, were interdicted from coming among them. The Spanish Government, whose real concern for the salvation of the Indians within its extensive empire, however erroneous in its direction, should be remembered as well as the enormities of its first conquest, granted these conditions; and the Jesuits were thus enabled to form establishments according to their own ideas of a perfect commonwealth, and to mould the human mind, till they made a community of men after their own heart. Equally impressed with horror for the state of savage man, and for the vices by which civilized society was every where infected, they endeavoured to reclaim the Indians from the one, and preserve them from the other by bringing them to that middle state wherein they might enjoy the greatest share of personal comforts, and be subject to the fewest spiritual dangers. For this purpose, as if they understood the words of Christ in their literal meaning, they sought to keep their converts always like little children in a state of pupillage. Their object was not to advance them in civilization, but to tame them to the utmost possible docility. Hereby they involved themselves in perpetual contradictions, of which their enemies did not fail to take advantage: for on one hand they argued with irresistible truth against the slave-traders, that the Indians ought to be regarded as human, rational, and immortal beings; and on the other they justified themselves for treating them as though they were incapable of self-conduct, by endeavouring to establish, that though they were human beings, having discourse of reason, and souls to be saved or lost, they were nevertheless of an inferior species. They did not venture thus broadly to assert a proposition which might well have been deemed heretical, but their conduct and their arguments unavoidably led to this conclusion.

Acting upon these views, they formed a Utopia of their own. The first object was to remove from their people all temptations which are not inherent in human nature; and by establishing as nearly as possible a community of goods, they excluded a large portion of the crimes and miseries which embitter the life of civilized man. For this they had the authority of sages and legislators: and if they could have found as fair a ground-work for the mythology of Popery in the scriptures as for this part of their institutions, the Bible would not have been a prohibited book wherever the influence of the Jesuits extended. There was no difficulty in beginning upon this system in a wide and thinly-peopled country; men accustomed to the boundless liberty of the savage life would more readily perceive its obvious advantages, than they could be made to comprehend the more complicated relations of property, and the benefits of that inequality in society, of which the evils are apparent as well as numerous. The master of every family had a portion of land allotted him sufficient for its use, wherein he cultivated maize, mandubi, a species of potatoe, cotton, and whatever else he pleased; of this land, which was called *Abamba,* or the private possession, he was tenant as long as he was able to cultivate it; when he became too old for the labour, or in case of death, it was assigned to another occupier. Oxen for ploughing it were lent from the common stock. Two larger portions, called *Tupamba,* or God's possession, were cultivated for the community, one part being laid out in grain and pulse, another in cotton; here the inhabitants all contributed their share of work at stated times, and the produce was deposited in the common storehouse, for the food and clothing of the infirm and sick, widows, orphans, and children of both sexes. From these stores whatever was needed for the church, or for the public use, was purchased, and the Indians were supplied with seed, if, as it often happened, they had not been provident enough to lay it up for themselves: but they were required to return from their private harvest the same measure which they received. The public tribute also was discharged from this stock: this did not commence till the year 1649, when Philip IV, honouring them at the same time with the title of his most faithful vassals, and confirming their exemption from all other services, required an annual poll-tax of one *peso* of eight *reales* from all the males between the ages of twenty-two and fifty; that of all other Indian subjects was five *pesos.* There was an additional charge of an hundred *pesos* as a commutation for the tenths; but these payments produced little to the treasury; for as the kings of Spain allowed a salary of six hundred *pesos* to the two missionaries, and provided wine for the sacrament and oil for the lamps, which burnt day and night before the high altar, (both articles of exceeding cost, the latter coming from Europe, and the former either from thence or from Chili) the balance upon an annual settlement of accounts was very trifling on either side. . . .

As in the Jesuits' system nothing was the result of fortuitous circumstances, but all had been preconceived and ordered, the towns were all built upon the same plan. The houses were placed on three sides of a large square. At first they were mere hovels: the frame-work was of stakes firmly set in the ground, and canes between them, well secured either with withs or thongs; these were then plastered with a mixture of mud, straw, and cow-dung. Shingles of a tree called the Caranday were found the best roofing; and a strong compost, which was water proof, was made of clay and bullock's blood. As the Reductions became more settled they improved in building; the houses were more solidly constructed, and covered with tiles. Still, by persons accustomed to the decencies of life, they would be deemed miserable habitations, . . . a single room of about twenty-four feet square being all, and the door serving at once to admit the light and let out the smoke. The houses were protected from sun and rain by wide porticos, which formed a covered walk. They were built in rows of six or seven each; these were at regular distances, two on each of three sides of the square; and as many parallel rows were placed behind them as the population of the place required.

The largest of the Guaraní Reductions contained eight thousand inhabitants, the smallest twelve hundred and fifty, . . . the average was about three thousand. On the fourth side of the square was the church, having on the right the Jesuit's house, and the public work-shops, each inclosed in a quadrangle, and on the left a walled burial-ground; behind this range was a large garden; and on the left of the burial-ground, but separated from it, was the Widows'-house, built in a quadrangle. The enemies of the Jesuits, as well as their friends, agree in representing their churches as the largest and most splendid in that part of the world. . . . They had usually three naves, but some had five; and there were numerous windows, which were absolutely nec-essary; for though the church was always adorned with flowers, and sprinkled upon festivals with orange-flower and rosewater, neither these perfumes nor the incense could prevail over the odour of an unclean congregation. . . .

An Indian of the Reductions never knew, during his whole progress from the cradle to the grave, what it was to take thought for the mor-row: all his duties were comprized in obedience. The strictest disci-pline soon becomes tolerable when it is certain and immutable; . . . that of the Jesuits extended to every thing, but it was neither capricious nor oppressive. The children were considered as belonging to the com-munity; they lived with their parents, that the course of natural affec-tion might not be interrpted; but their education was a public duty. Early in the morning the bell summoned them to church, where having prayed and been examined in the catechism, they heard mass; their breakfast was then given them at the Rector's from the public stores; after which they were led by an elder, who acted both as overseer and censor, to their daily occupations. From the earliest age the sexes were separated; they did not even enter the church by the same door, nor did woman or girl ever set foot within the Jesuit's house. The business of the young girls was to gather the cotton, and drive away birds from the field. The boys were employed in weeding, keeping the roads in order, and other tasks suited to their strength. They went to work with the music of flutes, and in procession, bearing a little image of St. Isidro the husbandman, the patron saint of Madrid . . . this idol was placed in a conspicuous situation while the boys were at work, and borne back with the same ceremony when the morning's task was over. In the afternoon they were again summoned to church, where they went through the rosary; they had then their dinner in the same manner as their breakfast, after which they returned home to assist their mothers, or amuse themselves during the remainder of the day. . . .

Equal care was taken to employ and to amuse the people; and for the latter purpose, a religion which consisted so much of externals afforded excellent means. It was soon discovered that the Indians possessed a remarkable aptitude for music. This talent was cultivated for the church-service, and brought to great perfection by the skill and assiduity of F. Juan Vaz: in his youth he is said to have been one of Charles the Fifth's musicians; but having given up all his property, and entered the Company, he applied the stores of his youthful art to this purpose, and died in the Reduction of Loretto, from the fatigues which in extreme old age he underwent in attending upon the neophytes during a pestilence. . . .

The system upon which the Reductions were founded and administered was confessedly suggested by that which Nobrega and Anchieta had pursued in Brazil; the persons who matured it, and gave it its perfect form in Paraguay, were Lorenzana, Montoya, and Diaz Taño. Never was there a more absolute despotism; but never has there existed any other society in which the welfare of the subjects, temporal and eternal, has been the sole object of the government: the governors, indeed, erred grossly in their standard of both; but, erroneous as they were, the sanctity of the end proposed, and the heroism and perseverance with which it was pursued, deserve the highest admiration. . . .

But if the Jesuits were placed in circumstances where even their superstition tended to purify and exalt the character, calling into action the benevolent as well as the heroic virtues, it was far otherwise with the Indians; they were kept by system in a state of moral inferiority. Whatever could make them good servants, and render them happy in servitude, was carefully taught them, but nothing beyond this, . . . nothing which could tend to political and intellectual emancipation. The enemies of the Company were thus provided with fair cause of accusation: why, they said, was no attempt made to elevate the Indians into free agents? why, if they were civilized, were they not rendered capable of enjoying the privileges of civilized men? If the system were to lead to nothing better, then had the Jesuits been labouring for no other end than to form an empire for themselves? This argument was distinct from all those which originated in the enmity of political or religious parties, and undoubtedly had its full weight in latter times. In vain did the Jesuits reply that these Indians were only fullgrown children, and that they knew not whether their obtuseness of intellect were a defect inherent in the race, or the consequence of savage life. Such an answer was no longer relevant when generations had grown up under their tuition: they dared not insist upon the first alternative, which would have been admitting all that the *Encomenderos* and slave-dealers desired; but if there were no original and radical inferiority in the race, then was the fault in that system upon which the Reductions were established. Why, it was asked, will not the Jesuits recruit themselves from these Indians who are born and bred among them, when it is so difficult to procure missionaries from Europe, so expensive to transport them, and impossible to obtain them in sufficient numbers? Why does not the Company, which in other countries had acted with right Christian indifference toward casts and colours, admit Guaranies into its bosom? The answer was, that their superiors had determined otherwise, . . . that things were well as they were; the object was accomplished; the Indians were brought to a state of Christian obedience, Christian virtue, and Christian happiness; their *summum bonum* was obtained; their welfare here and hereafter was secured. To those who look forward for that improvement of mankind, and that diminution of evil in the world, which human wisdom and divine religion both authorize us to expect, the reply will appear miserably insufficient: but the circumstances of the surrounding society into which it was proposed that these Indians should be incorporated, must be considered, and when the reader shall have that picture before him he will hold the Jesuits justified.

6

A Corn Riot in Mexico City, 1692

Hubert Howe Bancroft

The mission system of the Jesuits and of the other religious orders was based in part upon their conviction, shared by the Spanish crown, that the spiritual and physical welfare of the Indians would be safeguarded best by their segregation from the white, mestizo, and African segments of the population. In practice, the segregationist policy of Church and state broke down, and although many communities retained an exclusively Indian character, the population of the larger cities typically contained representatives of all the ethnic groups in the colonies. The association of Spaniards and Indians, the miscegenation that resulted, and the social and economic distinctions that divided the various groups in colonial society created strains that occasionally erupted into violence. One such episode—the corn riots of 1692 in Mexico City, the immediate cause of which was a severe shortage of grain—is described in this selection. The author, Hubert Howe Bancroft (1832–1918), was a businessman-turned-historian whose collection of books became the nucleus of the Bancroft Library of the University of California.

With the loss of the wheat crop [*as a result of bad weather, floods, and pests*] the consumption of corn increased, its price being further advanced by the partial failure of the crop, due to excessive moisture and cold. The situation was indeed critical. Maize was the food staple of the natives, and since the loss of the wheat crop the tortilla had taken the place of wheat bread, not only among all the lower and laboring classes of the capital, but also to some extent among the wealthy. Such was now the increasing scarcity that by the beginning of September [*1691*] the price of wheat had more than doubled. The bakers in consequence refused any longer to make bread, for at the price at which they were compelled to sell it they found the business unprofitable,

---

From Hubert Howe Bancroft, *The Works of Hubert Howe Bancroft* (San Francisco: A. L. Bancroft & Company, Publishers, 1883), Vol. 11, pp. 229–247 *passim*. Some footnotes deleted. Italicized bracketed notes in text are by Helen Delpar.

and a disturbance was averted only by the prompt measures taken by the viceroy to insure a sufficient supply.

Murmurs began to be heard on all sides, and notwithstanding the strenuous efforts of the viceroy [*the Conde de Galve*] to provide a supply of grain the suspicious and unreasoning populace would not credit the reported failure of the crops until a special commissioner was sent into the valley to verify the report. From the beginning Galve adopted every measure that experience and prudence could suggest to prevent or at least mitigate the suffering and dangers of a prolonged famine. Officials were sent among the farmers of the valley and interior districts to purchase all the surplus grain, and with orders to seize it if necessary. The sale of grain and flour in the city by private individuals was forbidden, all that could be found being collected by the government for distribution at the public granary. . . .

The public granary was now placed in charge of the municipal authorities, and grain could be purchased only there. In November of 1691, the daily allowance for each individual was one *quartilla*,[1] and the daily consumption from one thousand to thirteen hundred *fanegas*.[2] In the surrounding country the suffering was still greater than in the city, as the governor having seized most of their grain, many of the inhabitants were compelled to beg food in the capital.

Meanwhile the viceroy did not relax his efforts to maintain the supply. In April 1692, a meeting of the principal civil and ecclesiastical authorities was called for this purpose, and commissioners were kept constantly busy in the neighboring districts as well as in those more remote, collecting and forwarding corn. In May an abundant crop of wheat was harvested from the irrigated lands in the valley, and under the belief that the prevailing high price would induce the farmers to bring their grain to the capital, permission for its free sale was given. Many, however, sold it elsewhere, and this, together with the partial failure in the remoter districts, owing to a snow storm early in April—a rare occurrence in the valley of Mexico—caused the stock in the capital to run low toward the end of May. Vigorous measures were now required, and fresh commissioners were despatched with orders to confiscate all grain wherever found. The daily allowance of corn in the city was also reduced, although a suffcient quantity of grain was obtained by the commissioners to insure a moderate supply until the next harvest.

By this time the price of grain had increased so enormously that a load of wheat which usually sold for three or five pesos could not now be purchased for less than twenty-four pesos.

---

[1] Equal to about two quarts. [H. H. B.]

[2] A fanega is about equivalent to a bushel and a half. [H. H. B.]

The suppressed murmurs of the populace previously heard against the government, now gave place to complaints in which the viceroy was openly accused of speculating in grain; and not withstanding the publicity of all his measures and the character of the persons commissioned for the collection and distribution of supplies, this unjust charge gained a ready credence among the natives and lower classes. This grave accusation and the hostile attitude toward the government to which it gave rise were encouraged by the imprudent language of a Franciscan friar, during a sermon preached in the cathedral at the beginning of Easter. Notwithstanding the presence of the viceroy, *oidores,* and the officials of the various tribunals, he alluded in such terms to the existing scarcity as to confirm the suspicions of his audience, who loudly applauded him.

The populace, urged by the pangs of hunger and by their fancied grievances, were now in a mood which boded ill for the peace and safety of the capital. Yet, although previous outbreaks had shown their turbulent nature, no precaution whatever appears to have been taken to guard against a disturbance. Affairs were ripe for an outbreak. The city was divided into nine wards, six of which were inhabited wholly by natives having their own governors. The total population was over one hundred and forty thousand, of whom the Spaniards and mixed races formed but a small proportion. A large part of the lower classes were idle and dissolute, and among them were many criminals. The name *saramullos* was then applied to them and later they were called *léperos.*

The usual resorts of this class were the shops where pulque was sold, and the *baratillo,*[3] where the natives also congregated, and where all plotted against and denounced the government at will, free from the interference of the officers of justice.

The natives at this period, especially the men, were restless, indolent, and vicious, and so addicted to the use of pulque [*a beverage made from the fermented juice of the maguey plant*], the consumption of which had never been so great, that all contemporary writers concur in affirming that they were daily under its influence. They were the chief complainers against the government, and were constantly encouraged by the saramullos, who eagerly desired an outbreak because of the opportunity thus afforded them for plunder.

To oppose these dangerous elements there was in the capital but a single company of infantry, of less than one hundred men, who did

---

[3] A shop or collection of shops in the main plaza where cheap and second-class wares were sold, and where stolen articles were also disposed of. It was frequented by vagabonds and criminals, and several attempts had already been made by the authorities to abolish it.

duty as palace guard, and even these were indifferently armed and equipped. There was no artillery, no store of small arms and ammunition, and no organized militia.

.   .   .

Such was the condition of the capital in the beginning of June 1692. Though the scarcity of grain still continued, the careful distribution of the supply daily received at the public granary sufficed to keep starvation from the city. The natives, however, daily grew bolder and more insolent, and awaited but a pretext to revolt, encouraged, as they were, by the inaction of the authorities which they construed into fear.

The desired opportunity soon arrived. On Friday June 7th the corn at the public granary gave out at six o'clock in the evening, whereupon several native women who remained to be served, gave vent to their disappointment in shrill outcries and insulting epithets. On the following day they were still more disorderly, shouting, fighting, pushing, and crowding each other, so as to make it impossible for the officers to proceed with the distribution. Taking advantage of this confusion, several attempted to help themselves to corn, whereupon one of the officials, finding peaceful measures ineffectual, seized a whip, and by laying it on right and left succeeded in driving them back. In a few minutes, however, they surged forward again, headed by one more daring than the rest. The official again made use of his whip, and seizing a cane rained a shower of blows on the head and shoulders of the leader and her companions. Exasperated by this treatment, some of them seized their leader, and raising her on their shoulders rushed out of the granary, whence, followed by nearly two hundred of their companions, they hastened across the plaza to the palace of the archbishop and demanded to see him. The attendants refused, but listened to their complaints, consoled them as best they could, and dismissed them. Not content with this reception, the crowd, still carrying the injured woman, proceeded to the viceregal palace, filling its lower corridors and clamoring for an interview with the viceroy. On being told that he was absent, they tried to force their way into the viceregal apartments, but were pushed back by the guards. Thereupon they returned to the archiepiscopal palace, not a single man having joined them thus far, and were met by the primate. To him they repeated their complaints, adding that the injured woman had just died. Through an interpreter he sought to pacify them, and despatched a messenger to the granary officials, requesting that the Indians should in future be treated with more consideration. After another fruitless attempt to obtain an interview with the viceroy, the tumult ended for the day.

On the return of the viceroy in the evening he gave orders that in future an oidor should be present during the distribution of corn, for to a lack of system in this matter the outbreak was attributed. Instructions were also issued to the captain of the palace guard to take every precaution to prevent any repetition of the disturbance. Pikes were to be made ready, ammunition to be distributed to the troops, and all fire-arms to be kept loaded. No uproar occurred during the night, nor does an attempt appear to have been made by the authorities to ascertain the state of affairs in the native wards or among the saramullos. On the following day, the 8th of June, the native women appeared as usual at the public granary, and with the exception of pushing and crowding in their attempt to gain the foremost place, the presence of the oidor prevented a repetition of the previous disorder. During the early hours quiet reigned throughout the city, and the authorities, fearing no danger, neglected to take further precautions.

The viceroy, however, was ill at ease. Leaving his breakfast untouched, he repaired to the convent of Santo Domingo to hear mass, and his appearance was greeted with a murmur of disapproval by the assembled worshippers, who regarded him as the cause of their present sufferings. About four o'clock in the afternoon he attended service at the Augustine convent, and thence proceeded, as was his custom, to the convent of San Francisco. The usual procession ended, he entered the convent to converse with the friars, when suddenly the sound of tumult, accompanied by the report of fire-arms, was heard. The viceroy started up to go to the palace, but in this he was prevented by his few attendants, and by the friars, who, gathering about him, represented the danger of such an attempt, the streets being already filled with excited natives, who with loud cries were hurrying from all quarters toward the plaza.

But five hundred fanegas of corn were received at the public granary on this day, and by five o'clock in the afternoon the supply was exhausted, while there were still many to be served. This caused a great commotion among the native women, during which one of them fell to the ground, whether intentionally is not known, and was trampled upon and injured by her companions.

The rôle of the previous day is again performed, but with more fatal results. The injured woman is placed on the back of an Indian, who runs with her to the baratillo, and thence, having been joined by a number of the saramullas, to the palace of the archbishop, the crowd following with wild cries and shouts of rage. A demand to see the archbishop is again made, and is again denied by the attendants, whereupon they are assailed with the vilest language. Growing impatient at the non-appearance of the archbishop the constantly increasing mob proceeds across the plaza to the viceregal palace, the women taking up a position at the corners of the streets. Then they begin to abuse the viceroy in set terms, and to throw stones at the balcony of the viceregal apartments, which are soon destroyed. After some delay a dozen or more of the guard appear, and joined by an equal number of volunteers charge the rioters, now mustering about two hundred. The latter fly for refuge to the stalls and the cathedral cemetery, but being reënforced rally and drive back their assailants. A few of the guard ascend to the roof and fire blank cartridges. This of course only emboldens the rioters, who answer with shouts of derision and volleys of stones.

As the first party return from their charge, driven back by overwhelming numbers, a squad of soldiers come forward, and are joined by the count of Santiago and a few other gentlemen; but the rioters are now assembled in such force that the troops are compelled again to retire. It is then resolved to close the palace doors, which is done with such haste that two or three of the guard are shut out, and are seized and torn in pieces. A shout of triumph arises from the crowd, now numbering ten thousand. "Death to the viceroy and corregidor," they cry, "death to those who have all the corn and are killing us with hunger!" It is half past six; and though thirty minutes have scarcely elapsed since the beginning of hostilities, the plaza is filled with the populace. Eager for plunder they join in the cries against the government, shouting, "Death to the viceroy and all who defend him!" while the echo from hundreds swells the uproar, "Death to the Spaniards and gachupines who are eating our corn!"

At this juncture the archbishop approaches on foot with uplifted cross, and surrounded by his attendants. Little regard is shown him, however, for his coachman, who was sent on before, is knocked from his seat by a stone, and missiles begin to fall so thickly that the primate and his companions are glad to make good their escape. The guards in the palace make no further attempt to disperse the rioters. After some thirty shots from the roof, firing ceases; for not only are many of the soldiers disabled, but their ammunition is exhausted.

The rioters continue to storm the palace, but finding that little harm is done they resolve to burn it down, no longer fearing those within. The booths in the plaza afford an abundance of combustible material, and dry rushes and reeds are soon heaped against the wooden doors and set ablaze. The city hall is also fired; and while some are thus engaged, others seize the coach of the corregidor, whose residence forms a portion of that building, set fire to it, and with the mules attached drive it in triumph around the plaza, finally killing the wildly affrighted animals. The corregidor and his wife are fortunately absent; else their lives were lost. The opportunity for plunder sought for by the saramullos has arrived. With the exception of the burning of the gallows, also situated in the plaza, none of the lower classes appear to have taken part with the natives in the work of destruction, but there is little doubt that they were the chief instigators in the matter. Almost simultaneously with the burning of the palace the adjacent stalls are set on fire.

And now follows a scene which no pen can fully describe. It is between seven and eight o'clock, and the spacious plaza is made as light as day by the conflagration. Filling the plaza and adjoining streets, the maddened populace may be seen surging to and fro in dense masses like an angry sea, and above the roar of the flames rise hoarse shouts of exultation as the work of destruction goes on. Few Spaniards are visible. From the palace corridors, with despairing form and features, the archbishop and his attendants gaze in silence, while on the outskirts of the plaza groups of citizens watch in speechless terror the progress of the conflagration. Suddenly the cry is raised, "To the stalls!" "To the stalls!" and the human sea surges in that direction. The places where hardware was sold are first attacked, and knives, machetes, and iron bars secured, the last named for defense as well as for breaking open doors. And now let chaos come; innocent and guilty, friend and foe, are one; robbery and rape, fire and blood; the people have become raving maniacs! As fast as the houses are broken open and robbed the torch is applied. Gradually the infuriated yells sink to a low murderous hum of voices, interrupted only by the crash of falling buildings. Rapidly the flames spread, and by the lurid light may be seen the dusky forms of the rioters flitting in and out and among the buildings, or disappearing in the darkness laden with plunder.

A singular phase of riot and robbery now presents itself. Among the rabble are many owners of stalls who dare not openly protect their property, yet are unable to witness its loss with indifference. Merchants yesterday they are robbers now, and may as well rob themselves as be robbed by their comrades. So they join in the attack on their own stalls, being sometimes the first to enter, and if possible to seize and carry to a place of safety some of their own effects. Others, affecting an air of resignation, encourage the pillage of their stalls, and then stealthily follow the plunderer and relieve him of his load by a sudden blow or deadly thrust. Many of the rioters are run through at the entrance to the streets by the groups of exasperated Spaniards, as they are tauntingly defied by the passing rabble, and not a few perish in the flames.

While the many are thus engaged, a few hasten to the palace of the marqués del Valle, to fire it. The flames have reached the balconies, when the treasurer of the cathedral, Manuel de Escalante y Mendoza, arrives accompanied by a few ecclesiastics, and bearing the uncovered host. All other means proving unavailing, this pious proceeding is adopted, in the hope of saving the city. Exhortations accompany the act of elevating; and finally a number of the more religious rascals temporarily extinguish the flames in the palace of the marqués. Here, however, their forbearance ceases, for they at once hurry away to join their companions in the work of plunder elsewhere. To add to the solemn terror of the occasion all the bells begin to ring, but it is the call to prayers, and not to arms. Following the example of the cathedral treasurer, the religious orders next appear marching in procession, with uplifted crosses and solemn chants. Their efforts, however, avail but little; they are greeted with a shower of stones, and dispersed; and although singly or in groups they continue their exhortations in different parts of the plaza, the rioters disregard them, or reply with jeers.

These exciting events have occupied but a short time, for it is yet hardly nine, and the plaza, which for the last three hours has been thronged with the canaille of the capital, is fast becoming deserted. The rioters have for the most part retired with their plunder, and among the few that remain the religious still continue their fruitless exhortations. Despite the efforts of the guard and those of the few citizens who have ventured to show themselves, the fire in the viceregal palace and city hall still burns, and the stalls and booths are one mass of flames.

At this juncture the count of Santiago with a number of armed citizens, collected by order of the viceroy, appear in the plaza and open fire on the crowd, but are induced to stop by the religious, who declare that many innocent persons will thus be slain. As there is nothing further to be feared from the people remaining in the plaza, the citizens direct their efforts to subduing the flames. With the aid of the prisoners from the palace jail, who have barely escaped with their own lives, and of the inmates of the viceregal palace who are forgotten by the mob while intent on plundering the stalls, everything of value in the viceregal apartments is saved, and the females of the household are conveyed in safety through the plaza to the palace of the archbishop. . . .

The riot was now virtually at an end, and additional assistance arriving, the further progress of the fire was checked, although it continued to burn fiercely until the following Tuesday. . . .

Armed citizens patrolled the streets in the Spanish quarters during the remainder of the night, but no further disturbance occurred. The sun rose upon a mass of smouldering ruins in the plaza, while the bodies of the dead lay scattered here and there among the various articles of plunder dropped by the rioters in their hasty flight. . . . The loss of property caused by this outbreak was estimated at three million pesos. The number of lives lost did not exceed fifty, and was possibly not so great; nor is there any evidence to show that excepting the two or three victims among the palace guard, a single Spaniard was seriously injured.

.   .   .

There was still much apprehension lest the Indians should return, and this was increased by the discovery that the native ward of Santiago Tlaltelulco was deserted. The most active measures were therefore taken to prevent another uprising, and for the arrest and punishment of the rioters, and the recovery of the stolen property.

.   .   .

Although the saramullos took part in the pillage of the stalls, if not in setting fire to the viceroy's palace, they for the most part escaped punishment, the principal victims being natives. The first execution took place on the 11th of June. Three Indians, taken in the act of setting fire to the palace, were shot in the plaza under the gallows, erected in place of the one destroyed; and in the afternoon their hands were cut off, and some nailed to the gallows, and others to the door-posts of the palace. Between this date and the twenty-first of the following August thirty-six Indians of both sexes and a few mestizos were publicly whipped, and eleven natives and one mestizo were hanged. A Spaniard who took part in the riot, and died of his wounds in hospital, was exposed on the gibbet. The last one put to death was a lame Indian, who was believed to have been the captain of the rioters.

7

Mestizaje in New Granada

Jaime Jaramillo Uribe

Throughout the colonial period mixed-bloods experienced social and legal discrimination in the Spanish colonies. However, the extent of miscegenation and the emergence of many different racial types led to the blurring of racial lines, particularly in the eighteenth century, to the great dismay of the whites and especially the Creoles (American-born offspring of Spaniards), who fought tenaciously for the preservation of their privileges. In this selection, Colombian historian Jaime Jaramillo Uribe discusses miscegenation in New Granada (modern Colombia) and the conflicts that it produced in the eighteenth century.

A member of the faculty of the National University of Colombia, Professor Jaramillo was a founder of the Anuario Colombiano de Historia Social y de la Cultura *and has written numerous works, including* El pensamiento colombiano en el siglo XIX *(Bogotá: Editorial Temis, 1963).*

Character of Granadine Society in the Eighteenth Century

If we accept the classification of societies into two great categories—open and closed—each formed in accordance with the degree of social mobility it presents, how should we classify Granadine society at the end of the eighteenth century? Was New Granada's colonial society, as it was structured in the decades before independence, an open, mobile society and, in this sense, democratic? Or was it a closed society? In this case, as in so many other fields of social history, the student of Spanish American history encounters great difficulties, given the character of the social development of this part of the continent. Even if the two types of society are considered only as ideal types in the sense given by Max Weber to social categories—that is, as formations that never occur in a pure state, but with a greater or lesser degree of ap-

From Jaime Jaramillo Uribe, "Mestizaje y diferenciación social en el Nuevo Reino de Granada en la segunda mitad del siglo XVIII," *Anuario Colombiano de Historia Social y de la Cultura*, 2 (1965), 21–48. Reprinted by permission of the author. Translated by Helen Delpar. Some footnotes deleted.

proximation to the ideal type, some approaching it more than others, as the caste society of India approached the closed society and North American society of the seventeenth and eighteenth centuries approached the open type—even so, the historian of Spanish American colonial society, above all in a case like that of New Granada, would hesitate to describe it as an open or closed society, for in reality it was neither one nor the other. Or perhaps it was both, with openness and mobility being dominant at times and rigid stratification and social immobility at others.

In considering New Granada from this point of view, at least two situations are clear. The sixteenth and seventeenth centuries were the formative period of the new society which emerged from the contact between the Indian society and the Spanish society that arrived with the conquerors and colonists. On the other hand, the last years of the seventeenth century and above all the eighteenth century constitute a period marked by separation and then consolidation of perfectly differentiated strata. . . . Only then could people speak . . . of belonging to "good society" or of being members of the "society" of Santa Fe [colonial name of Bogotá] or Popayán or Cartagena, in contrast to those who did not belong because they were part of the strata considered plebeian or "infamous,". as the language of the period put it. This does not mean that relationships between the rulers and the ruled, between the privileged and the dispossessed, or, as one would say in Marxist terminology, between the exploiters and the exploited did not exist from the very beginning of the Conquest. We know that the Spanish *encomenderos* and proprietors of lands, mines, textile factories, haciendas, and public offices, along with the Indians, made up the two earliest categories and forms of social differentiation, and that during the sixteenth century itself there began to develop within the Spanish group superior categories, which embraced those considered "well-deserving of the Indies" (*beneméritos de Indias*), the conquerors and their sons, and categories corresponding to the mass of immigrants of varied and generally low social levels who came to seek fame and fortune, not to mention the incipient process of *mestizaje* [miscegenation, especially between Indians and whites] with all its groups and subgroups nor the relationship between masters and slaves. But in this first period neither the demographic density nor the complexity of relationships was sufficient to produce a highly differentiated society in which there could appear forms of group consciousness, discrimination, and conflicts of interest capable of generating the tensions and strife characteristic of an elaborately stratified society. The process of mestizaje, which was the dynamic and differentiating factor *par excellence,* had to advance during the seventeenth century before a highly stratified society could appear. The emergence of such a society also required the development of wealth and patrimonial distinctions and of a conspicuous division of labor among miners, farmers, landowners, artisans, and bureaucrats, as well as a division between residents of urban and of rural areas.

These conditions are found in a mature state only in the eighteenth century, and especially in the second half of that century. By the end of the sixteenth century the relationship between Spaniards and Indians had served merely as a basis for the establishment of two poles which, because they were so dissimilar and so far apart, did not produce the socioracial tensions that occurred in the eighteenth century when the "castes" [1] were numerous and, at the same time that distinctions were sharply drawn, [their] proximity [to the whites] was such that self-awareness was all the more irritating, discrimination more intolerable, and conflicts more violent. The case of eighteenth-century Granadine society confirms what seems to be a constant rule of social development, namely, that conflicts between groups which, though different, are contiguous are more intense than conflicts between highly dissimilar extremes. For this reason the friction and the struggles between mestizos and whites and between creoles and Spaniards at the end of the colonial period were much more violent than those that occurred between creoles and Indians and even between masters and slaves. For the same reason the tensions between mestizos and whites and between creoles and *chapetones* constituted the wellspring of conflict in society, and it was their clashes that eventually created the social climate of the revolution for independence.

The Process of Mestizaje

We have said that the dynamic factor *par excellence* of the new society was mestizaje, imposed upon the Spaniards more by historical circumstances than by a conscious desire for racial fusion or by the absence of a sense of superiority. Indeed, without the process of mestizaje, which was especially rapid and thorough in New Granada, Colombian society would have had a much more rigid structure and would have been constituted in a much less national and organic form. There would have been fewer possibilities of forming a nation, and to the elements that today differentiate the various social groups, such as economic resources and cultural level, would be added, to a greater degree than at present, others much more rigid and difficult to conquer, such as racial and cultural heterogeneity, as has occurred in Spanish American countries where the process of mestizaje was in-

---

[1] In the Spanish colonies, the term "caste" was used to designate mestizos, mulattoes, and Negroes. It did not mean a rigid and hereditary social system such as that associated with India. [H. D.]

complete or was much less intense and rapid than in Colombia. Historical experience shows that wealth and scientific and technical skills are conquered with much greater speed by groups occupying low social strata when . . . racial differences representing a heritage of domination . . . do not persist in the society. . . .

For the reasons noted, the intensity of the process of mestizaje, in which cultural and racial factors are indissolubly linked, can serve as a yardstick for determining the extent to which Spanish American societies are open or closed, and the correlation of the elements that tend to close or stratify them and those that foster openness and dynamism can be the thread by which the social history of Spanish America is interpreted. Such a correlation, with the specific character it presents in each of the Spanish American republics, will give us one of the keys to its national character and to its distinctive features. It will also reveal those elements it shares with the other countries. On the basis of these methodological concepts, let us examine the situation in New Granada toward the end of the eighteenth century.

Since the process of mestizaje constituted the dynamic element in colonial society, it is useful to keep in mind an outline of the Granadine population with respect to socioracial relations. First, it should be remembered that in the present territory of Colombia the process of mestizaje occurred with a certain celerity, though there were, of course, regional variations. The process was made easier by the relatively low demographic and cultural density of its pre-Hispanic population or, if you will, by the speed with which it was dominated or destroyed. Characteristic of the social history of New Granada is the fact that by the end of the eighteenth century the Indian languages had practically disappeared from the central region of the territory, including that of the most compact of the native groups, the Chibchas. By this time the surviving Indian population can be considered to have spoken Spanish and to have practiced Catholicism, ignoring for the moment the degree of authenticity and the depth of the religious observances of the Indians; to use the eighteenth-century expression, it was a *"ladino"* ["Latinized"] population. After the middle of the seventeenth century royal inspectors did not need interpreters—or "tongues," in the jargon of the colonial administration—at least in the most densely populated regions of New Granada, and when Madrid ordered the elimination of the teaching of the Muisca language in Santa Fe in 1783, the measure could not be put into effect because such instruction, being unnecessary, had disappeared several years earlier.

From the point of view of mestizaje, a very eloquent picture is presented by Francisco Silvestre, efficient functionary of the crown and perceptive observer of colonial society in New Granada; it is probably based on the most complete census of the period, that of 1778. In the

558 cities, towns, villages, hamlets, and parishes that comprised the jurisdiction of New Granada, excluding other dependencies of the viceroyalty, there were 277,068 whites, 368,093 *"libres"* (a term that designated mestizos in the language of the period), 136,753 Indians, and 44,636 slaves in a total population of 826,550 inhabitants. The white and mestizo groups, therefore, represented nearly 80 percent of the population, the Indians 15 percent, and the Negro slaves 5 percent. The greater part of the Indian population was concentrated in three places, Sante Fe, Tunja, and Cauca, above all in the first two, which correspond to the departments of Cundinamarca and Boyacá in modern Colombia. The percentage of Indians was still high, but for the problem that concerns us, we should keep in mind that it was a ladino Indian population, that is, one that spoke Spanish and was highly acculturated. . . .

Hidalguía[2] and Nobility

But if mestizaje represented the dynamic process that tended to eliminate socioracial differences because it afforded a possibility of upward mobility and of improved status, the legal and de facto prerogatives and privileges, both social and economic, with which certain groups were surrounded ended by creating in the eighteenth century a stratified, compartmentalized society of a closed tendency, divided into well-differentiated socioracial groups, or "castes." There is a large measure of truth in the assertion that the Spaniard had fewer racial prejudices than the Anglo-Saxon and that his Catholic conception of the human personality, in addition to his tradition of contact and mixture with Africans and Moors, facilitated the process of miscegenation with Indians and blacks and made his conduct toward the dominated peoples more equalitarian and less hostile. This attitude of greater sympathy and humanitarianism is evident in the laws for protection of the Indians and in numerous practices of Spanish colonial administration. But the objective historian who does not wish to idealize the past should not forget that, over and above these extenuating factors, the Spaniard who came to America was fully aware of his character as a conqueror and of his superiority vis-à-vis the Indian and that those who came to the new continent in search of fame or fortune demanded advantages and privileges from the beginning.

That such privileges existed and remained in force until the end of the eighteenth century is shown by the testimony of Francisco Silvestre. With a clear vision of what the modern state should be, in the final

---

[2] The quality of pertaining to the lower nobility of Spain, whose members were called *hidalgos*. [H. D.]

recommendations of his *Descripción del Nuevo Reino de Santa Fe,* he makes direct reference to these privileges and requests that they be eliminated in the name of justice and for the benefit of the crown. Silvestre, as a former governor of the province of Antioquia and a high official of the viceroyalty, had realized that the latent danger to Spanish domination of the colonies lay in the Creole group, which was excessively sure of itself and which showed "great enthusiasm for nobility and haughty pride and attachment to florid and pompous titles," as he said of the creoles of Antioquia. On the subject of dignities, privileges, and exemptions, these are his exact words: "It is similarly necessary to suppress all legal privileges (*fueros*), which serve only to multiply lawsuits and tribunals and to complicate the administration of justice to the general detriment of the vassals and of Royal Jurisdiction, which . . . is the only one by which a State should be governed since there is only one body of law, and it should apply to all, though modified in certain cases and circumstances."

In addition, the crown was sparing in granting privileges because it did not wish to create in America strong groups or classes that might in any way lessen the jurisdiction of the state, as the Spanish grandees had done during the feudal era, the monarchy being able to limit their privileges only after a long struggle. For political reasons it always refused to make *encomiendas* perpetual or to create a nobility with a juridically protected body of privileges. . . .

Even hidalguías were conceded with a certain parsimony. Those who hoped to obtain them or have them recognized had to apply to the chanceries of Valladolid and Granada in order to prove their descent from Spanish *hidalgos,* making considerable expenditures and often waiting years for a decision. Colonial authorities were parsimonious in granting this title because they undoubtedly did not want the Indies to become filled with hidalgos as Spain was in the eighteenth century. Although purity of blood [3] (*limpieza de sangre*) and even what the Granadines called "nobility" could be proved before the Royal Audiencia, even by means of witnesses, the recognition of hidalguía as a rule had to come from the metropolis. . . .

In this atmosphere of distinctions and desires for nobility and privilege, both those who aspired to enjoy their real or apparent advantages and the Spanish authorities who did not want to grant them in excess developed an intricate casuistry. On the one hand, there were hidalgos, on the other those who were called "nobles," as well as those who were Spaniards or descendants of Spaniards, and finally those who were simply white or "pure." . . . However, everything seems to indicate that, apart from the right of hidalgos to use coats of arms and to enjoy

---

[3] Purity of blood signified ancestry free of Jewish and Moorish blood and therefore free of the taint of heresy. [H. D.]

certain immunities, such as exemption from imprisonment for debt, all these types and subtypes tended to become confused; what was decisive was to prove whiteness or purity of blood, which meant that a person was classified as a Spaniard or at least a descendant of Spaniards, or, negatively, that he was not a mestizo or a mulatto. Once purity of blood had been proved, an individual was not subject to the discriminatory restrictions that weighed upon the so-called castes.

Evaluation of the Mestizo

With the purpose of protecting the Indians, the Spanish authorities began to enact discriminatory measures against mestizos in the second half of the sixteenth century. They were forbidden to live in Indian villages, to trade with the Indians, or to employ them as servants or bearers. To fill certain public offices, such as those of municipal councilor (*regidor*) or magistrate (*alcalde*), they had to prove purity of blood or that they were persons of importance.

Colonial officials did not have a good opinion of the mestizo. He was generally described in official documents as unsettled, unstable, and abusive, especially with respect to the Indians. . . .

From the beginning of the seventeenth century, when the mestizo population had attained certain development, conflicts with this group multiplied, and the terms mestizo, mulatto, and *zambo* were converted into pejorative designations which constituted such a grave slur on the honor of those who considered themselves creoles or whites descended of Spaniards that they were accepted in law as capable of damaging the reputation of an individual and therefore of serving as a basis for charges of defamation. . . .

Conflicts with mestizos, who were branded as unstable troublemakers and people of irregular life and bad habits, occurred unceasingly. At the beginning of the seventeenth century, in 1623, the governor of the province of Pamplona addressed himself to the archbishop of the New Kingdom [of Granada], don Fernando Arias Ugarte, requesting that celebration of only one saint's feast day be permitted each year, for the Indians celebrated several such holidays, and they were a motive for "the occurrence of great drunkenness and excesses of all kinds, especially on the part of the mestizos of both sexes, who live from fiesta to fiesta." . . . The archbishop issued a decree forbidding the celebration of more than one fiesta a year, under the penalty of one hundred lashes and exile from the province for four years for women and the same penalty and four years' service as galley slaves in Cartagena for the men. . . . Twenty years later, in the same province of Pamplona, there took place a noisy suit against a group of eighteen mestizos on the occasion of an inspection (1642) to the Real de Minas de Vetas by the visitor of the Royal Audiencia, don Diego Carrasquilla. The mestizos were accused of abusing the Indians, of leading them into vice, and of causing disturbances. The visitor, after hearing the declarations of the Indians, encomenderos, alcaldes, and priests of the Real de Minas, decided to expel the mestizos and require them to live four leagues from the place. . . .

In the eighteenth century—when the white group had increased considerably, the process of mestizaje was far advanced, and society was structured into very well-defined socioracial groups—the terms mestizo and mulatto became even more defamatory and offensive. The white, Spanish group became more conscious of its advantages and privileges and, seeing them threatened by the increasing number of mestizos, defended them with greater zeal and intransigence. Life in Granadine society was now soured by judicial and extrajudicial disputes motivated by honor and matters related to ancestry. This was the century . . . of proofs of purity of blood. This expression pullulates in private and official documents as the motive for petitions for exemptions and favors and, most significantly, as a weapon of social rivalry among those who had enemies or were involved in criminal or civil lawsuits. In certain regions where small municipal aristocracies of real or alleged purity of blood were formed as in Santander and Antioquia, judicial records bear witness to these contests, true fairs of vanity and pride which poisoned the atmosphere of society and often had a bloody ending. Those who defended their hidalguía and nobility did so, moreover, not only to defend their honor—the refuge of the soul, as one litigant said, recalling the phrase of Calderón—but also with the conviction that they were thereby defending justice and the social order.

In the year 1725 in the city of Socorro, Diego de Vargas conducted a long and costly criminal suit against José Delgadillo, a carpenter, because the latter "had made fun of his parchments and had spread rumors regarding his honor and ancestry, saying that he and his family were zambos, mulattoes, and Inquisition penitents (*ensambenitados*)." . . . And Pedro Galindo, a captain of militia in the town of Purificación, came personally to Bogotá in 1766 to settle a long dispute with [a certain] Narciso Trujillo because the latter "without fear of Our Lord God or conscience, and influenced by others, treated me as a mulatto." . . . In 1802 in the . . . city of San Juan de Girón, where quarrels of this type were numerous, Juan Ordóñez and José Román accused each other of offenses against honor because the first had treated the second as a zambo and the latter had insisted on proving the "infamous ancestry" of Ordóñez.

But in spite of the legal and social disabilities that weighed upon the mestizo, there were not a few cases in which mestizos still considered Indians asked to be declared mestizos so that they could be freed from the obligation of paying tribute and from their condition as Indians, for it was evident that, regardless of the mestizo's position of inferiority vis-à-vis the white and the discrimination that he faced, mestizaje opened a possibility of change that was not available to the Indian. Above all, it opened the possibility of being considered "white," which was feasible, for the mixture of races had reached such a point that it was already difficult to determine with certainty, at least on the basis of external facts, who was white and who was mestizo. Many mestizos publicly declared themselves white and pure of blood though they admitted having an Indian ancestor. . . .

Marriage and Education

The distinctions we have been examining played a very important role in two aspects of social life: marriage and education. With respect to marriage, everything indicates that the Spanish authorities leaned in the eighteenth century toward a markedly segregationist policy designed to preserve the homogeneity of the white group or, as the official documents put it, "to maintain the integrity of the good families of the kingdom," threatened by the rise of mestizaje. In addition to the traditional legislation governing the family, which obliged those under twenty-five who wished to marry to obtain the consent of their parents or in their absence that of their closest relatives, dispositions like the Real Pragmática of April 1778 on marriage between persons of unequal lineage reinforced parental authority by establishing the racial inequality of the prospective partners as a motive for objecting to a marriage. It is true that in this, as in many other aspects of colonial legislation, there was a divorce between the written law and social reality and that the principles of tribunals and functionaries were generally uncertain and variable. Thus in cases of "matrimonial dissent" (*disenso matrimonial*), which were very frequent in the eighteenth century, the authorities attenuated the rigor of the laws by giving them a tolerant interpretation, by accepting without difficulty the proof of purity of blood of the accused party, or, most frequently, by failing to give a decision in the case. But here, as in other aspects of social life, the laxity of the authorities in enforcing the laws did not prevent the tensions and family conflicts created by the segregationist legislation.

Opposition [to a marriage] often occurred with mestizo families, a fourth or eighth part of mestizaje more or less being sufficient to produce litigation. Although he was unable to prove his alleged ancestry, Francisco de Aguirre of the city of Antioquia interposed a suit of disenso matrimonial to prevent the marriage of his daughter to Luis Sarrazola, whom he labeled a mulatto. The case reached the Royal

Audiencia, which authorized the wedding on the grounds that there was equality since Aguirre could not adequately prove his purity of blood. The reply of Sarrazola to his proud prospective father-in-law is a model of the history of mestizaje, all the more typical because it reveals an intricate network of family relationships between those accused of impurity and the relatives of the one who alleged nobility, perhaps because of an additional fraction of whiteness. As was frequently the case in such suits, the way to defend oneself from an accusation of being a mulatto, mestizo, or plebeian was to prove that it was the other fellow who was the mulatto, mestizo, or plebeian. In reply to the accusation of Francisco de Aguirre, Luis Sarrazola's lawyer said:

> They [the Aguirres] have never objected to their relatives' marrying mulattoes. Manuel de Aguirre, brother of the said Francisco de Aguirre, while their father, don Manuel de Aguirre, was still alive, married a *mulata* called Estefanía Sarrazola, who was a sister of Tomas Sarrazola, father of my father. José Maria de Aguirre, nephew of the said Francisco de Aguirre, is married to another mulata, called Olaria Erron. Segunda Pérez, his second cousin, married Narciso Martínez, natural son of María Rosa Mendoza, who was a slave of doña Rosa de Hibarbuen; Nicolasa Torres, also a second cousin, married the Negro Pedro Ibarra, son of the Negroes Fermín and Joaquina, who were slaves of the priest don Ignacio Ibarra. . . .[4]

Access to establishments of higher education—universities, secondary schools, and seminaries—was limited by strongly discriminatory provisions. In order to study and obtain degrees for the only existing professions, jurisprudence and the ecclesiastical career, it was necessary to prove purity of blood. Here there were also exceptions, but they were obtained only after long and vexing suits and always as a special, exceptional favor on the part of the authorities. To enter the Thomist University, legitimate birth and purity of blood were required, for . . . the secretary would later have to certify that the prospective graduate was *vir purus ab omni macula sanguinis atque legitimus et natalibus descendens* (a man of legitimate birth and free from any stain of blood). The same was required in the Colegio Mayor de Nuestra Señora del Rosario. . . .

The conflict between law and reality, between nobiliary concepts of privilege and the impulse toward equality represented by mestizaje, was also evident in this area. The Spanish authorities were subject to two pressures. On the one hand, they had to contend with the demands of the creoles, who were sometimes more orthodox than the Spaniards

---

[4] Archivo Histórico Nacional de Colombia, Bogotá, "Genealogías," v. VI, ff. 47 r. and v.

themselves in the defense of prerogatives which in the metropolis corresponded to the nobility and the horde of hidalgos, but which in America were sought by the creole families of Spanish origin. On the other hand, they were faced with the political necessity of offering opportunities for social mobility to the growing mestizo group while preventing the ambitious and arrogant creoles from becoming overly strong. The poverty of men trained for certain positions in administration and teaching sharpened the conflict.

All the foregoing can be seen very clearly in what must have been a resounding case in Cartagena in 1801. After the priest Vicente Ambrosio resigned the chair of philosophy in the Seminary of San Carlos, the rector ordered the beginning of competition to fill the position, and the doctors Pedro Carracedo, Bernardo Garay, Juan José Sotomayor, and José de los Santos presented themselves. The academic degrees of all were in order, but Garay, Sotomayor, and de los Santos denied the right of Carracedo to take part in the contest, claiming that he had not presented the proof of purity of blood required by the statutes of the seminary. Carracedo could not meet this requirement because he was a mulatto of humble origin, but he held a bachelor's degree from San Bartolomé and a doctorate from the Thomist University and could produce statements from eminent personages in Bogotá, such as . . . the Archbishop Caicedo y Florez and don Pablo Plata, rector of the Seminary of San Bartolomé, attesting to his intelligence, application, and capacity for letters. The archbishop of Cartagena declared that the petition of Carracedo's adversaries was impertinent and maintained his right to participate in the competition.

The suit was apparently a long one, and the documents do not indicate its final outcome, but the briefs presented by both sides reveal the currents of opinion that were aired in such cases. Carracedo gave an account of his merits and insisted that the traditional rules were modified by the royal will when the crown wished to reward certain subjects who, even though they could not prove purity of blood, had distinguished themselves by their talents and services to the state. "Your august predecessors," he said, referring to the King, "wisely disposed that positions of honor ought to be given to individuals because they were deemed good and not because they were the sons of magistrates or officials."

The most impassioned of Carracedo's opponents, the priest Sotomayor, said for his part:

> . . . The constitution of [our] colegio absolutely requires descent from Spanish parents free of any evil race. This requirement is not really met by the parents of our opponent, the procurator Matías Carracedo and Manuela Iraola, whose low origin is not clearly indicated by the

word "humility" which he uses in his statement, it being necessary to add . . . that they are considered mulattoes, especially the mother, the illegitimate daughter of a Negress who is still alive. . . .[5]

And rejecting the ideas that degrees alone were sufficient for granting academic appointments because they were frequently authorized by the charity of the monarch without regard to the indispensable requirement of purity of blood, he said:

> . . . Academic degrees, which by themselves ennoble those who receive them, exempting them from the condition of plebeians, are not conferred and should not be conferred on persons of this class. From the presence of the clause *purus ab omnia macula sanguinis* in the text of the degrees, it can be inferred that *pardos* [free persons of African ancestry] are to be rigorously excluded from aspiring to these distinctions unless the sovereign, moved by charity, wishes to exempt them. . . .

Noble and Ignoble Occupations

The same differentiating effect was realized by the division of offices and occupations into noble and plebian ones, the former being reserved for those who were pure of blood and the latter for mestizos, Indians, and Negroes. Government employment, even of the most modest sort, such as the position of notary, as well as the legal profession and ecclesiastical offices, was considered a noble activity. On the other hand, anything that implied manual labor, such as the crafts and even the occupations of schoolteacher and surgeon, were deemed suitable for mestizos, pardos, and other persons of mixed blood. All litigants in suits to prove purity of blood or nobility or in cases of disenso matrimonial alleged, as a means of showing their social distinction, that they had never engaged in ignoble occupations and, on the contrary, that they had held [public office]. . . .

Forms of Address: The Case of the *Don*

In the use and evolution of certain forms of social address like the "don," we can also follow the differentiating process in New Granada's colonial society and the progression of the forces that, on the one hand, tended to stratify it and, on the other, gave it an open and mobile character. The "don," although it was used very exclusively in the eighteenth century by a minority that demanded it as a sign of white-

---

[5] Archivo Histórico Nacional de Colombia, Bogotá, "Colegios," v. I, f. 286.

ness and nobility, nevertheless underwent a process of deterioration that indicated the progress of leveling forces and the weakening of lineage as the basic component of social status.

The "don" as a form of social address had from its medieval origins a nobiliary character and continued to be used in America in the same sense. But the Spanish tendency toward self-ennoblement of the lower classes, visible in Spanish history from the time of the Reconquest, popularized its use in the peninsula until . . . in the age of Cervantes, even as it served as an attribute of the new class of lawyers (*letrados*) and as a title of honor and reverence granted only to the nobility, it was demanded by the petty hidalgos and used by the lower classes and even by public prostitutes, who called themselves *doñas*. . . .

If this occurred in Spain, in America both facets of the process were intensified. In the presence of the dominated Indian population, the "don" strengthened its differentiating character and gave expression to the craving for honor and nobility that possessed the Spaniards who came to America. It was thus the first noble title conceded to or appropriated by the conquerors. . . . Every Spaniard who came to America, no matter how low his status, wished to be addressed as "don." . . .

But it was in the eighteenth century when the use of the "don" was most strongly desired and defended by Creoles and Spaniards and when the largest number of conflicts over its use and usurpation took place. Lawsuits over usurpation or withdrawal of the title were innumerable, especially in the regions of dense white and mestizo populations, such as Santander (particularly in the south), Antioquia, and some coastal cities like Mompós, Tolú, and Cartagena.

The prestige of the "don" as a differentiating social element is reflected in the anger that was produced in the small provincial aristocracies by the denial of the title or its inappropriate application. . . . As in the case of offenses against honor through application of racial pejoratives that cast doubt on purity of blood, bitter and expensive lawsuits occurred which frequently reached the Royal Audiencia. A good example of these is a long suit in 1808 between José Miguel de Olarte Salazar of Puente Real (Santander) and the priest of the same town, Fr. Pedro Pardo. According to the plaintiff, the latter had deprived Olarte of the title, which "he had always enjoyed" and the suppression of which, Olarte said, "directly affected his honor." . . . Being addressed as "don" was also a sign of being considered white and pure of blood. A witness in the suit for offenses against honor brought by Miguel Vanquezel against Miguel Cano asserted that he considered the latter to be white because he had heard others addressing him as "don." Vanquezel replied to this that the "don" had become so common in those days "that even Negroes use it in addressing each other. . . ."

The *donomanía* of which [José] Cadalso [eighteenth-century Spanish poet and satirist] spoke, referring to eighteenth-century Spain, also spread throughout the colonies in the same century. Don Joaquín Vallejo, a resident of Girón, wrote to the viceroy on September 27, 1802:

> . . . Let the application of the "don" to those who have no right to it be expelled like a moth which gnaws at the public felicity. . . . It should be attained only by those who deserve it because of their status, special service to the State and Fatherland, employment, or declared nobility. This would put an end to those many fanatics who . . . consider it an indignity to engage in decent and honorable activities and occupations which they think will make them lose the imaginary luster that sustains them and wish only to live in idleness, . . . thereby causing grave damage to society and the interests of the Fatherland.[6]

With the advent of the republic, the devaluation of the "don" took an even more accelerated course. The republican constitutions prohibited the use of titles of nobility or titles that simply evoked pretensions toward nobility with the democratic idea of replacing them all with the title of citizen. "Speaking of forms of address," [Colombian philologist] Rufino Cuervo wrote in his *Apuntaciones críticas al lenguaje bogotano,* "we recall that in Colombia, as in other parts of America, the 'don' was eliminated from the written language, being considered dangerous to democracy." And [Colombian publicist and businessman] Miguel Samper observed with melancholy in the second half of the nineteenth century: "The title is no longer linked among us to the ancestral home of the lofty Castilian noble. Any muleteer who through hard work and thrift acquires a team of mules and a pasture automatically obtains the title of 'don.' "

---

[6] *Anuario Colombiano de Historia Social y de la Cultura,* I (1963), No. 2, 538.

✎§ 8 ೩≈

The Evolution of the Great Estate

———◄●►———

James Lockhart

Settlers in the colonies consistently endeavored to avail themselves of whatever labor the Indians might be willing or able to supply. One of the earliest and most important of the labor systems imposed on the indigenous population by Spain was the encomienda, *introduced in Hispaniola early in the sixteenth century. The* encomienda *was a grant of the tribute (and initially of the labor as well) of a designated group of Indians to a Spaniard who was obliged to provide for their Christianization and to render military service to the crown if the need arose. It is generally conceded that an encomienda did not include a grant of land, yet historians have puzzled over the possible relationship between the encomienda, which declined after the sixteenth century, and the large landed estate, which has been a prominent feature of Spanish American life to the present day. In this selection, Professor James Lockhart of the University of Texas explores the processes by which the encomienda may have evolved into the hacienda. Professor Lockhart is also the author of a fine study of Spanish Peru.[1]*

What the Spanish colonial period added to pre-Columbian America can be described briefly as the contents of two complementary master institutions, the Spanish city and the great estate. Historians have now begun to penetrate deeply into these subjects, and soon it will be possible to deal with Spanish American colonial history from its vital center rather than from its surface or periphery. While the colonial city is the less well explored of the two themes, its study can proceed on a firm footing, since the continuity of location, function, and even formal organization must be evident to all. Understanding the great estate has proved more difficult, for the estate had a greater diversity

---

From James Lockhart, "Encomienda and Hacienda: The Evolution of the Great Estate in the Spanish Indies," *Hispanic American Historical Review,* 49 (1969), 411, 419–429. Reprinted by permission of the author and Duke University Press. Some footnotes deleted. Italicized bracketed notes in text are by Helen Delpar.

[1] James Lockhart, *Spanish Peru, 1532–1560: A Colonial Society* (Madison: University of Wisconsin Press, 1968).

of forms and changed more than the city, both in law and in sub-
stance. The most serious problem, not always recognized as such, has
been the apparent lack of connection between the encomienda of the
Conquest period and the hacienda of the mature colony.

． ． ．

Legal history yields few links between these two institutions, which
dominated the Spanish American countryside, while any actual line
of descent cannot yet be traced in detail. Accordingly, the only means
available to establish the connection is a phenomenological comparison
of the two. This in itself could never prove—nor is it meant to prove
—that the hacienda arose out of the encomienda, but it can show
that the change was far less than a transformation. The comparison,
to be just and fruitful, must range broadly over associated practices
and structures which, one could maintain, were not a part of the
institutions proper. This procedure is necessary because the true com-
parability exists at the level of de facto practice, social organization,
and broader functions. Neither encomienda nor hacienda ever found
adequate legal expression of its full impact on society.

First of all, we may compare the two institutions as to proprietor-
ship.[1] It will be immediately apparent that the encomendero and the
later hacendado were cut from the same cloth; they were patriarchs
of a special kind who ruled both the countryside and the city. Following both custom and law, the encomendero lived and maintained a
house in the city to whose jurisdiction his encomienda belonged. Similarly the hacendado, while not a full-time urban resident in most
cases, kept a large town house and held citizenship in the nearest city.
The urban role played by both types expressed itself in the domination
of the municipal council. In the Conquest period, the councils of most
cities consisted exclusively of encomenderos. The later hacendados
never achieved such a complete monopoly of urban office, since miners
in some places and merchants in others were also council members,
but nevertheless the dominance of the hacendado over municipal
councils was the norm.

Each institution in its time was a family possession, the main re-
source of a numerous clan. Each gave rise to many entails; but, with
or without legal devices of perpetuation, each had a strong tendency

---

[1] The treatment that follows is so generalized that specific footnoting seems
inappropriate. . . . The whole comparison applies primarily to regions of
sedentary Indian settlement. It holds above all for the former centers of Indian
civilization, Peru and Mexico, and with slightly diminished force for adjacent
regions such as Colombia, Chile, or Guatemala. In fringe areas like Paraguay
or Venezuela, the encomienda assumed a great variety of forms, though it appears to the author that these various arrangements were in each case as close
an approach to the classic estate form as conditions permitted, with some re-
sidual influence of the tradition of *rescate,* a mixture of trade and booty.

to remain in the family. As the effective heads of society, both encomenderos and hacendados felt themselves to be an aristocracy whatever their origins and negotiated for honors and titles from the king,
particularly coats of arms and membership in Spain's military orders.

The balance between country and city shifted considerably from
encomendero to hacendado. The encomendero stayed ordinarily in his
city residence, as luxurious as he could afford to make it, and went to
his encomienda as rarely as once a year on a trip which combined a
pleasant country excursion and a tour of inspection at tribute-collect-
ing time. He did not have a house for himself on the encomienda,
though he would often build or preempt structures there to house
his subordinates and to store products. In contrast, the typical hacienda had an impressive country house as one of its outstanding
features. Yet though some hacienda houses were like palaces, at least
as many were fortress-warehouses, massive and utilitarian compared to
the hacendado's town house with its carved balconies and fountains.

The hacendado and his family could be counted on to live in town
as much as possible. On occasion, for example in the depressed seventeenth century, an hacendado might not be able to afford the heavy
expenses of ostentatious town living, and would sit out many months
of involuntary exile in the country. But when times were good, he
would live mainly in the city and travel out to the hacienda for one
good long vacation and inspection tour, much like the encomendero.
Both types were rural-urban, with their economic base in the country
and their social ties in the city. Only the balance between the two
poles changed, corresponding to the slow and uneven movement of
Spaniards and Spanish life out into the countryside through the course
of the colonial period.

What one might call the staff of the two institutions was nearly
identical. Both encomendero and hacendado had large collections of
relatives, friends, and guests who partly lived on the bounty of the
patron, partly worked for him. More specifically, both encomendero
and hacendado had in their hire a steward called a majordomo, who
took over nearly all the practical management of the estate. The man
in this post would be well educated and would enjoy reasonably high
standing in the Spanish world; yet he remained socially subordinate
to the employer. Like his master the steward was urban-oriented; he
was at home in the city markets, where he borrowed money, bought
supplies, and sold the estate's produce.

On the encomienda, or at least on large encomiendas, there were
beneath the majordomo a number of combined tribute-collectors, labor
foremen, and stock-watchers, often called estancieros.[2] Though their

---

[2] "Estanciero" clearly derives from *estancia*. On the face of it, this would
seem to constitute a linguistic proof of the intertwining of tribute collection,

function was of considerable importance, their status was the lowest possible within the Spanish sphere. Typically they originated in the humblest strata of Spanish peninsular society or came out of marginal groups such as sailors, foreigners, or Negroes. The later hacienda had exactly the same kind of low-level supervisory personnel, sometimes still called estancieros—which significantly was the first word for cowboys on cattle haciendas. They still came from the same social strata, belonging to the Spanish world, but at the very fringes of it. By this time, mestizos were commonly found in such work, along with Negroes, mulattoes, and poor Spaniards, but their relationship to Spanish society as a whole was precisely that of the earlier estancieros. These people lived more in the country than in the city, though often against their preference. In any case, they spoke Spanish, rode horses, used Spanish weapons, implements, and techniques, and thus constituted a Spanish-urban extension into the countryside, taking their norms from the cities.

At the lowest level, raw labor in both cases was done by Indians or near-Indians, divided into two distinct worker types, as will be seen shortly. We must also take into account the ecclesiastical personnel of the great estate. Each encomienda was supposed to have its *doctrinero* to minister to the Indians, and this person would also serve as the encomendero's private chaplain. The priest present on the larger haciendas duplicated these functions.

In one aspect it would be natural to expect a thorough transformation—in the evolution from public to private, from a semigovernmental office to an agricultural enterprise. Here too, however, a great deal of continuity can be observed. On the governmental side, en-

---

labor use, and land exploitation in the encomienda, since "estancia" was the most commonly used word all over the Indies in the Conquest period for private holdings whether devoted to livestock or crops. If the encomienda's tribute collectors were named after their agricultural functions, that would be a very strong indication that such functions were seen as an important regular feature of the encomienda in practice. The present writer believes that such an interpretation is essentially justified, but there are two factors tending to obscure it. First, "estancia" had another meaning, particularly well established for Mexico by Gibson (*The Aztecs under Spanish Rule*, Stanford: Stanford University Press, 1964, pp. 33 and 475, n. 13). In this sense it designated an area where a small group of Indians lived remote from the main group. Estancieros would often be found in such places, so that this sense of "estancia" could have influenced, or conceivably have been the real origin of their name. Both meanings of "estancia" go back to the Antillean period, and examples can be found in the Laws of Burgos. . . . Second, "estanciero" was not the only word applied to the lowest employees of encomenderos. They could be called simply majordomos like the head stewards, and in Mexico they often went by the name of *calpisque*, after the Aztec tribute collectors. A third alternative name, *capataz*, had the strongest agricultural connotations of all, but was quite rare.

comenderos had the nominal paternalistic duties of protecting and instructing their Indians. Although their post was not supposed to entail true jurisdiction, it is clear that they did in fact rule over these Indians during the early period, openly calling themselves their *señores* or lords. Hacendados, as mere property owners, lacked any legal justification whatever for such a role; yet they too achieved it in practice. As recognition of their power, the authorities would often give them positions such as captain of the militia or alcalde mayor, and they would exercise formal jurisdiction as well. Both encomenderos and hacendados envisioned themselves as lords with retainers and vassals.

Even on the economic side, in the evolution toward a private agricultural enterprise, there was no lack of common elements in encomienda and hacienda practice. On the encomienda traditional, unsupervised Indian production ordinarily had primacy, but the encomendero would regularly go on to take possession of land, often on or near his encomienda. (Usually, but by no means always, he received a formal land grant from the town council or the governor.) On these holdings, most commonly called estancias,[3] he would raise crops and livestock for his own establishment and for sale in town markets or mining camps.

Of great importance in the agricultural labor force of the estancias were Indians falling outside the legal framework of the encomienda. Almost everywhere certain Indians soon came to be attached personally to individual Spaniards, who might or might not be encomenderos; in the circum-Caribbean region these Indians were called naborías, and in Peru yanaconas. Indians of this type, plus some Negro and Indian slaves, formed a permanent skeleton crew for the estancias, under the supervision of the estancieros. They were aided by a much more numerous force of encomienda Indians performing "tribute labor," particularly at times of maximum work load.[4] In the case of Peru we know that the yanaconas of the Conquest period had the use of plots which they cultivated for their own sustenance. From a very early time there were also non-encomenderos with much the same kind of estancias, though their position was rather precarious, and their possibilities were limited at first because of uncertain access to seasonal labor by encomienda Indians.

All of the above characteristics persisted into the hacienda period.

---

[3] In Peru and adjacent areas, often *chácaras*.

[4] For the sake of clarity, the above presentation makes a clean distinction between estancia activity and unsupervised tribute producing. Actually a common practice was for the encomienda Indians to grow tribute products on certain land set aside for the purpose, under as much or as little supervision as the majordomo saw fit to apply. There was no basic difference between this and an estancia.

We should not forget that our term "hacienda" is a scholarly convention; seventeenth-century Spanish Americans used "estancia" at least as often to designate a large landed property, retaining the earlier meaning of this word. Ownership of land by Spaniards expanded greatly as the hacienda began to emerge, but the Indian villages still held much land. Even more important, the hacienda did not exploit all its vast holdings intensively; instead, certain restricted areas were cultivated under the direction of majordomos. To do this work the hacienda possessed a more substantial crew of permanent workers than the estancias of the Conquest period. (The workers' names at this time were "gañán" in Mexico and still "yanacona" in Peru.) But they were still aided by a large seasonal influx of laborers from the independent Indian villages, impelled now by direct economic considerations rather than by encomienda obligation. Sometimes the villagers floated in and out according to their own and the hacienda's temporary needs, but in some places, as in Yucatán, they had a regularized obligation very reminiscent of earlier labor arrangements.

Both resident labor and nonresident labor, under both encomienda and hacienda, were still very close to pre-Columbian systems of periodic obligatory work. All types of workers performed something less than full-time duties, and obligations were usually reckoned by the household rather than by the individual. Also rooted in the pre-Columbian period were the so-called personal services which were so prominent a feature of the early encomienda. Most of these were inherited by the hacienda. This is especially clear for Peru, where in the twentieth century hacienda workers still delivered produce to town and provided rotating servants in the town house of the hacendado, as they once did for the encomendero.[5]

The renowned self-sufficiency of the hacienda was also anticipated in the Conquest period. Using their rights to Indian labor and produce as a base, encomenderos created networks of enterprises in almost all branches of economic activity that were locally profitable, though livestock and agriculture always occupied a prominent place. They did their best to make coherent economic units of these varied holdings, each part supplementing and balancing the others. The

---

[5] Beyond the bare statement that the main elements of the Spanish American estate were brought from Spain, the present article hardly touches on the question of antecedents, because both the Spanish estate and possible Indian forerunners are very incompletely studied. It is clear, here as in other facets of Spanish American life, that Spanish influence was concentrated in the upper and middle levels, Indian influence at the lowest, and that the Indian element was recessive. Often it is hard, when analyzing any one trait, to make a clear decision on whether it is Spanish, Indian, or a coincidence of both. This is true even for something as distinctively Indian as the special services of the Incas, some of which were very close to practices on European estates.

whole estate was under unified management, since the majordomos were responsible both for official encomienda activities and for enterprises of a more private nature, as were the estancieros at a lower level.

The tendency to build complete, diversified estates, then, was already observable at a time when the Spanish sector of the economy was generally booming under the influence of newly opened mines and the demand of the nascent Spanish towns for all kinds of supplies. This fact throws a new light on the self-sufficiency so characteristic of the later hacienda, which has often been explained very largely as a response to depressed conditions. Much the same type of structure appeared earlier in response to social and economic forces of quite a different kind. The vision of society which the Spaniards brought with them to America included a clear picture of the attributes of a great estate and its lord. Aside from his mansion and numerous servants, guests, and vassals, he must have land, cattle, and horses, and various agricultural enterprises from wheat farms to vegetable gardens. From the early Conquest period, this ideal constituted a fixed pattern of ambitions for successful Spaniards. First the encomenderos and then the hacendados exerted themselves to carry it out to the last detail, even where local conditions rendered it economically irrational.

But by and large the great estate scheme was economically rational as well as socially desirable. Everything the estates produced was wanted in the cities; taken together these products helped create a Spanish as opposed to an Indian economy. The desire to assemble a complete set of varied holdings was not inconsistent with a thoroughly commercial orientation. Self-sufficiency is very hard to distinguish from the diversification or integration of a commercial enterprise, and the complete refusal to specialize, which may strike us today as amateurish, characterized not only the lords of estates, but colonial merchants as well. In an age of commercial rather than industrial capitalism, there was little thought of expansion and usually little justification for it. The constant effort of the most acute commercial minds was to monopolize, drive out competition, and sell at high prices to the severely limited market. The hacienda would carry the tendencies toward self-sufficiency and monopoly to their logical conclusion, without ever giving up a strong element of market orientation.

In fact, though inspired in part by social ambition, the hacendados' desire for lands which they would not exploit fully made very good economic sense. Monopolizing the land discouraged the rise of competitors in the immediate neighborhood. If the hacendado actually developed production on the whole vast expanse, however, he would have flooded the city market, as sometimes happened in any case. It seems probable that the size of urban markets and the amount of silver available were the real factors limiting hacienda production at any given time. The most market-oriented establishments in the Spanish Indies, the sugar plantations, still did not typically become specialized, but raised much of their own maize, wheat, and cattle. A drive toward self-sufficiency, diversification, or completeness—for the three cannot be separated—was a constant in Spanish colonial estates from the early sixteenth century onward.

All in all, the replacement of the encomienda by the hacienda involved only a shift in emphasis, whatever the factual details of institutional development. A semigovernmental domain, serving as the basis of a private economic unit, gave way to a private estate with many characteristics of a government. There was also a significant movement into the countryside, but both institutions stretched from the city into the country, and indeed their main function was to connect the two worlds. The estate ruled the countryside in the city's name; it brought country products to the city and the elements of Spanish culture and society to the country. After the city itself, the estate was the most powerful instrument of Hispanization in Spanish American culture. During the early period, when Indian structures were relatively intact and Spanish cities relatively small, the estate could emphasize government and tribute collection over active supervision. As Indian structures deteriorated and the cities grew, supervision increased; the city came into the country.

The perspective here suggested makes it possible to treat the evolution of the great estate as one single line of development underneath the changing forms on the institutional surface. To judge from certain portions of their works, scholars like [Silvio] Zavala, [José] Miranda, and [Charles] Gibson have long had a good subjective understanding of this deep continuity, but they have never chosen to give it methodical expression. The standard works still tend to speak in terms of three successive systems: encomienda, repartimiento, and hacienda. The internal history of each system is worked out separate from the others; each new stage is seen as requiring a much greater transformation than was in fact the case.

But looking beneath the level of formal institutions and administrative policy, the evolution could be expressed in simplest terms as follows. At all times there were private Spanish holdings in the countryside with workers attached to them, and these holdings always drew temporary labor from the Indian villages. From the Conquest period until the present century, the constant trend was for the Spanish properties and their permanent crews to grow, while the Indian villages and their lands and production shrank. It now begins to appear that Spanish agricultural enterprises, generally speaking, never achieved complete reliance on a resident working force during the colonial period. (Scholars familiar with conditions in the late nineteenth and twentieth centuries may have projected into the colonial period the solid, sedentary force of debt peons thought to characterize more recent times.) The villagers came to work on the estancias and later haciendas, first through encomienda obligations, then through the mechanism of the repartimiento, and finally through individual arrangements, but they were always the same people doing the same things. In the Conquest period the greatest landowners were the encomenderos, whose estancias formed an integral if informal part of their estates. Yet from the very beginning there were other Spaniards with similar holdings, both small and large. Encomendero families or their legal successors seem often to have retained, consolidated, and even expanded their properties, which may have had a special aura of permanence and nobility. But the lands of the non-encomenderos increased even more, until the countryside contained several times the number of great estates present in the Conquest period. This development paralleled the great expansion of the Spanish or (broadly speaking) urban sector. The organization and social composition of those who owned and managed the estate hardly changed from the age of the encomienda to the hacienda of the eighteenth century.

Giving importance to these basic social and economic continuities does not require one to believe that the encomienda as an institution involved landholding, or that it evolved directly into the hacienda. As far as agriculture and landownership are concerned, the technical antecedent of the hacienda was the estancia rather than the encomienda. One may retain a narrowly legal definition of the encomienda as the right to enjoy labor and tribute and of the hacienda as pure landownership (though the latter interpretation is more rarely made). At the same time, it is quite possible to appreciate that the Spaniards tried to use each legal framework in turn as the basis of the same kind of great estate. Ideally this would have combined jurisdiction over vassals with vast possessions of land and stock. In the encomienda only the governmental aspect was formally expressed, and the rest was left to the spontaneous action of socioeconomic ambitions and opportunities. The hacienda was just the opposite, giving legal status only to landownership and leaving the jurisdictional aspects to de facto patterns. This basic, essentially unitary social institution, the great estate, was quite fixed as to ideal attributes and social organization, and it maintained constant its function as intermediary between the growing Spanish towns and the receding Indian villages. It evolved along two simple lines—constant rise in the legal ownership of land and change in the balance of the labor force, as permanent workers increased and temporary workers decreased.

Let us view the great estate, therefore, as a basic social pattern with certain permanent attributes and a few recognized principles of evolution. By so doing, we can hope to understand the increasingly complex picture that is emerging as research proceeds to areas other than Mexico. Each region in the Spanish Indies seems to have produced a different form of the encomienda and a different timetable for its downfall. The same is true for the repartimiento or mita. Some areas suffered great population loss, while others did not; still others had little or no population to start with. Some estates arose from holdings associated with encomiendas, others from lands accumulated by administrative and judicial officials, others from humble wheat farms. From region to region the hacienda veered toward pastoralism, cereal production, sugar growing, and other activities. But we can cope with all these variations if we understand them as retarding, hastening, or modifying an institution that was ultimately embedded in Spanish social practice and had its own coherence, its own dynamics of development.

One may conclude that the rise of the hacienda was essentially a development rather than a struggle. The evolution of the great estate responded to such realities as the size of cities and Spanish populations, the degree of acculturation among the Indians, and the nature of Spanish society in early modern times. The royal policy of discouraging an independent aristocracy and the humanitarian campaigns to protect the Indians deserve intensive study in themselves, but the struggles over these matters cannot be said to have greatly affected the evolution of the great estate. Wherever it might appear that the Crown or the Church became a prime mover in its development, one will find on close examination that deeper forces were at work. Crown policy has been credited with the destruction of the encomienda, but natural developments in the colonies had doomed the institution. On the one hand, the fortunes arising from commerce and mining were not directly dependent upon the encomienda; on the other hand, the sheer growth of Spanish society produced newly powerful families who began to carve out estates of their own, undermining the inflexible encomienda system.

Historians have commonly observed the general tendency of the Conquest period to set basic patterns for later times. The hacienda, taking shape in the late sixteenth and seventeenth centuries, has appeared to be a major exception. But the interpretation of the great estate set forth here reintegrates the hacienda into the general picture. From the broader perspective one may argue that the Conquest period created the function and the basic social and economic modes of organization, while following years brought mainly growth or shrinkage —in other words, quantitative change. Such a view implies that perhaps scholars investigating the history of the hacienda should begin at the beginning. One of the few complaints that one might bring against the magnificent work of [François] Chevalier [see Article 28] is that, faced with a vast body of material on the hacienda, he accepted a conventional view of the Conquest period and the encomienda, without submitting them to the same kind of analysis which he applied to his more immediate subject.

In general, those who engage in future research on forms of the great estate should take into account the institution's multiple dimensions and not limit themselves to "hacienda studies," or to the study of "land and labor systems," or most especially to "rural history." In all known embodiments the Spanish American great estate was closely related to the city, indeed almost inseparable from it. Spanish American colonial history has three principal elements: the city, the great estate, and the Indian village. Of these only the village was truly and thoroughly rural. The function of the great estate was to mediate between city and country, to carry back and forth supplies, people, and ideas that were vital to the growth of Spanish American civilization.

⚜ 9 ⚜

Big House and Slave Quarters

Gilberto Freyre

The native population was less numerous in Brazil than in the principal centers of Spanish settlement, and the relatively primitive culture of the Brazilian Indians made them less adaptable to the demands of the Portuguese settlers. As a result, the labor of Negro slaves became an increasingly important factor in the colonial economy, especially on the sugar plantations of the coastal zone of the northeast. Sugar proved to be Brazil's most valuable product during the colonial period, although exports declined after the mid-seventeenth century because of the competition of Dutch, French, and English producers in the West Indies.

The patriarchal society that developed on the sugar plantations of colonial Brazil received its classic delineation in Gilberto Freyre's Casa-Grande e Senzala ("Big House and Slave Quarters"). An excerpt from the English translation, called The Masters and the Slaves, *appears here. Although the soundness of Freyre's documentation and many of his generalizations have been questioned, the publication of his book in 1933 is considered a landmark in the development of Brazilian nationalism because of his positive evaluation not only of the effects of miscegenation but also of the African contribution to Brazilian culture. Freyre was born in 1900 in Recife (Pernambuco).*

In Brazil the relations between the white and colored races from the first half of the sixteenth century were conditioned on the one hand by the system of economic production—monoculture and latifundia— and on the other hand by the scarcity of white women among the conquerors. Sugar-raising not only stifled the democratic industries represented by the trade in brazilwood and hides; it sterilized the land for the forces of diversified farming and herding for a broad expanse around the plantations. It called for an enormous number of slaves.

From Gilberto Freyre, *The Masters and the Slaves: A Study in the Development of Brazilian Civilization,* translated by Samuel Putnam (New York: Knopf, 1956), pp. xxviii-xliv. Copyright 1946, © 1956 by Alfred A. Knopf, Inc. Reprinted by permission of the publisher. Italicized bracketed notes in the text are by Helen Delpar.

Cattle-raising, meanwhile, with the possibilities it afforded for a democratic way of life, was relegated to the backlands. In the agrarian zone, along with a monoculture that absorbed other forms of production, there developed a semi-feudal society, with a minority of whites and light-skinned mulattoes dominating, patriarchally and polygamously, from their Big Houses of stone and mortar, not only the slaves that were bred so prolifically in the *senzalas,* but the sharecroppers as well, the tenants or retainers, those who dwelt in the huts of mud and straw, vassals of the Big House in the strictest meaning of the world.[1]

Conquerors, in the military and technical sense, of the indigenous populations, the absolute rulers of the Negroes imported from Africa for the hard labor of the *bagaceira,*[2] the Europeans and their descendants meanwhile had to compromise with the Indians and the Africans in the matter of genetic and social relations. The scarcity of white women created zones of fraternization between conquerors and conquered, between masters and slaves. While these relations between white men and colored women did not cease to be those of "superiors" with "inferiors," and in the majority of cases those of disillusioned and sadistic gentlemen with passive slave girls, they were mitigated by the need that was felt by many colonists of founding a family under such circumstances and upon such a basis as this. A widely practiced miscegenation here tended to modify the enormous social distance that otherwise would have been preserved between Big House and tropical forest, between Big House and slave hut. What a latifundiary monoculture based upon slavery accomplished in the way of creating an aristocracy, by dividing Brazilian society into two extremes, of gentry and slaves, with a thin and insignificant remnant of free men sandwiched in between, was in good part offset by the social effects of miscegenation. The Indian woman and the *"mina,"* [3] or Negro woman,

---

[1] On the relation between building materials and the formation of aristocratic societies, see George Plekhanov: *Introduction à l'histoire sociale de la Russie* (translation) (Paris, 1926).

[2] The *bagaceira* was the place where the bagasse, or refuse of the sugarcane after the juice had been pressed from it ("cane trash"), was stored. The word in Brazil comes to mean the general life and atmosphere of the sugar plantation. A famous modern novel by José Américo de Almeida is entitled *A Bagaceira* (Rio de Janeiro, 1928); this work is looked upon as the beginning of the school of social fiction of the 1930's and the present day. [Tr.]

[3] Name given to highly respected Negro women of Bahia who became "friends," concubines, and "housewives" *(donas de casa)* of their white masters. The name is derived from Forte de el Mina on the west coast of Africa, one of the places from which the Portuguese imported their slaves. The *"minas"* were light-skinned, with features that resembled those of a white person, and were looked upon as "excellent companions." They were probably the first Negro women to be legally married to Europeans. See Donald Pierson: *Negroes in Brazil,* pp. 145–6. [Tr.]

in the beginning, and later the mulatto, the *cabrocha*,[4] the quadroon, and the octoroon, becoming domestics, concubines, and even the lawful wives of their white masters, exerted a powerful influence for social democracy in Brazil. A considerable portion of the big landed estates was divided among the mestizo sons, legitimate or illegitimate, pro-created by these white fathers, and this tended to break up the feudal allotments and latifundia that were small kingdoms in themselves.

Bound up with a latifundiary monoculture were deep-rooted evils that for generations impaired the robustness and efficiency of the Brazilian population, whose unstable health, uncertain capacity for work, apathy, and disturbances of growth are so frequently attributed to miscegenation. Among other things, there was the poor supply of fresh food, subjecting the major part of the population to a deficient diet, marked by the overuse of dried fish and manihot flour (and later of jerked beef), or to an incomplete and dangerous one of foodstuffs imported under the worst conditions of transport, such as those that preceded the steamboat and the employment in recent years of re-frigerator compartments on ships. The importance of the factor of hyponutrition, stressed by Armitage,[5] McCollum and Simmonds,[6] and of late by Escudero,[7] a chronic hunger that comes not so much from a diet reduced in quantity as from its defective quality, throws a new light on those problems vaguely referred to as due to racial "deca-dence" or "inferiority" and, thank God, offers greater possibilities of a solution. Prominent among the effects of hyponutrition are: a decrease in stature, weight, and chest measurement; deformities of the bony structure; decalcification of the teeth; thyroid insufficiency, pituitary and gonadial, leading to premature old age, a generally impoverished fertility, apathy, and, not infrequently, infecundity. It is precisely these characteristics of sterility and an inferior physique that are commonly associated with the execrated blood-stream of the so called "inferior races." Nor should we forget other influences that developed along with the patriarchal and slave-holding system of colonization: syphilis, for example, which is responsible for so many of those "sickly mulat-toes" of whom [*Brazilian ecologist E.*] Roquette Pinto speaks and to whom [*German social scientist*] Ruediger Bilden attributes a great importance in his study of the formation of Brazilian society.

---

[4] A dark-skinned mestizo type. [Tr.]

[5] F. P. Armitage: *Diet and Race* (London and New York, 1922).

[6] E. V. McCollum and Nina Simmonds: *The Newer Knowledge of Nutrition: the Use of Foods for the Preservation of Vitality and Health* (New York, 1929).

[7] Pedro Escudero: *"Influencia de la alimentación sobre la raza,"* La Prensa (Buenos Aires), March 27, 1933. The articles of the Argentine professor are interesting, even though they add little that is original to the studies of North American and European physiologists: Armitage, McCollum, Simmonds, Lusk, Benedict, McCay, Nitti.

The formative patriarchal phase of that society, in its virtues as well as in its shortcomings, is to be explained less in terms of "race" and "religion" than in those of economics, cultural experience, and family organization; for the family here was the colonizing unit. This was an economy and a social organization that at times ran counter not only to Catholic sexual morality but to the Semite tendencies of the Portuguese adventurer toward trade and barter as well.

. . .

Admitting the tendency of the physical environment, and especially of the biochemical content, to re-create in its own image those individuals who come to it from various places, we still must not forget the action exerted in a contrary direction by the technical resources of the colonizers: their effect in imposing upon the environment strange cultural forms and accessories such as would permit the preservation of an exotic *race* or *culture*.

The patriarchal system of colonization set up by the Portuguese in Brazil and represented by the Big House was one of plastic compromise between the two tendencies. At the same time that it gave expression to the imperialist imposition of an advanced race upon a backward one, an imposition of European forms (already modified by colonizing experience in Asia and Africa) upon a tropical milieu, it meant a coming to terms with the new conditions of life and environment. The plantation Big House that the colonizer began erecting in Brazil in the sixteenth century—thick walls of mud or of stone and lime, covered with straw or with tile, with a veranda in front and on the sides and with sloping roofs to give the maximum of protection against the strong sun and tropical rains—was by no means a reproduction of Portuguese houses, but a new expression, corresponding to the new physical environment and to a surprising, unlooked-for phase of Portuguese imperialism: its agrarian and sedentary activity in the tropics, its rural, slave-holding patriarchalism. From that moment the Portuguese, while still longing nostalgically for his native realm, a sentiment to which Capistrano de Abreu [*Brazilian historian and authority on Indian dialects*] has given the name of "transoceanism"—from that moment he was a Luso-Brazilian, the founder of a new economic and social order, the creator of a new type of habitation. One has but to compare the plan of a Brazilian Big House of the sixteenth century with that of a Lusitanian manor house (*solar*) of the fifteenth century in order to be able to perceive the enormous difference between the Portuguese of Portugal and the Portuguese of Brazil. After something like a century of patriarchal life and agrarian activity in the tropics, the Brazilians are practically another race, expressing themselves in another type of dwelling. As Spengler observes —and for him the type of habitation has a historical-social value superior to that of race—the energy of the blood-stream that leaves identical traces down the centuries must necessarily be increased by the "mysterious cosmic force that binds together in a single rhythm those who dwell in close proximity to one another." [8] This force in the formation of Brazilian life was exerted from above downward, emanating from the Big Houses that were the center of patriarchal and religious cohesion, the points of support for the organized society of the nation.

The Big House completed by the slave shed represents an entire economic, social, and political system: a system of production (a latifundiary monoculture); a system of labor (slavery); a system of transport (the ox-cart, the *banguê*,[9] the hammock, the horse); a system of religion (a family Catholicism, with the chaplain subordinated to the paterfamilias, with a cult of the dead, etc.); a system of sexual and family life (polygamous patriarchalism); a system of bodily and household hygiene (the "tiger," [10] the banana stalk, the river bath, the tub bath, the sitting-bath, the foot bath); and a system of politics (*compadrismo*).[11] The Big House was thus at one and the same time a fortress, a bank, a cemetery, a hospital, a school, and a house of charity giving shelter to the aged, the widow, and the orphan. The Big House of the Noruega plantation in Pernambuco, with its many rooms, drawing-rooms, and corridors, its two convent kitchens, its dispensary, its chapel, and its annexes, impresses me as being the sincere and complete expression of the absorptive patriarchalism of colonial times. An expression of the gentle and subdued patriarchalism of the eighteenth century, without the air of a fortress that characterized the first Big Houses of the sixteenth century. "On the plantations it was like being on a field of battle," writes Theodoro Sampaio,[12] with reference to the first century of colonization. "The rich were in the habit of protecting their dwellings and manor houses by a double and powerful row of stakes, in the manner of the natives, and these stockades

---

[8] Oswald Spengler, *The Decline of the West* (translation). (New York, 1926, 1928), vol. II. The significance of the dwelling-place had already been stressed by G. Schmoller, in the classic pages that he has written on the subject.

[9] In northeastern Brazil the *banguê* was a variety of litter with leather top and curtains. [Tr.]

[10] The *"tigre"* was a vessel for the depositing and carrying away of fecal matter. [Tr.]

[11] *"Compadrismo"* was a system of oligarchic nepotism and patronage; the author refers to it later in this chapter. From *compadre:* literally, a godfather or sponsor, a friend, etc. [Tr.]

[12] Theodoro Sampaio: *"S. Paulo de Piratininga no fim do século XVI"* ("S. Paulo de Piratininga at the End of the Sixteenth century"), *Revista do Instituto Histórico de São Paulo,* Vol. II.

were manned by domestics, retainers, and Indian slaves and served also as a refuge for the neighbors when they were unexpectedly attacked by savages."

.   .   .

The truth of the matter is that around the plantation-owners was created the most stable type of civilization to be found in Hispanic America, a type that is illustrated by the squat, horizontal architecture of the Big Houses: enormous kitchens; vast dining-rooms; numerous rooms for the sons and guests; a chapel; annexes for the accommodation of married sons; small chambers in the center for the all but monastic seclusion of unmarried daughters; a gynæceum; an entryway; a slave hut. The style of these Big Houses—style in the Spenglerian sense—might be a borrowed one, but its architecture was honest and authentic. Brazilian as a jungle plant. It had a soul. It was a sincere expression of the needs, interests, and the broad rhythm of a patriarchal life rendered possible by the income from sugar and the efficient labor of Negro slaves.

This honesty, this expansiveness without luxurious display, was sensed by various foreign travelers, from [*William*] Dampier [*seventeenth-century British buccaneer*] to Maria Graham, who visited colonial Brazil. Maria Graham was enchanted with the residences in the vicinity of Recife and with the plantation houses in the province of Rio de Janeiro. The only bad impression that she got was due to the excessive number of bird and parrot cages hung up everywhere. But these parrot cages merely served to confer upon family life a bit of what today would be called local color. As for the parrots themselves, they were so well trained, Mrs. Graham adds, that they rarely screamed at the same time.[13] So far as that goes, d'Assier notes a still more significant instance: that of monkeys receiving the benediction from Negro lads, just as the lads received it from the aged blacks, who in turn were blessed by their white masters.[14] The hierarchy of the Big Houses was extended even to parrots and monkeys.

The Big House, although associated particularly with the sugar plantation and the patriarchal life of the northeast, is not to be looked upon as exclusively the result of sugar-raising, but rather as the effect of a slave-holding and latifundiary monoculture in general. In the south it was created by coffee, in the north by sugar; and it is as Brazilian in the one case as in the other. In traveling through the old coffee-plantation zone of the Rio Grande and São Paulo region, one sees the ruins of former mansions with the land round about bleeding

---

[13] Maria Graham: *Journal of a Voyage to Brazil and Residence There during the Years 1821, 1822, 1823* (London, 1824), p. 127. [Mrs. Graham traveled to Brazil in the company of her husband, a captain in the British navy. H. D.]

[14] Adolphe d'Assier: *Le Brésil contemporain—Races—Mœurs—Institutions—Paysages* (Paris, 1867), p. 89.

still from the wounds of the ax and the processes of latifundiary labor, and one realizes that they are the expression of the same economic impulse that in Pernambuco created the Big Houses of Megaipe, of Anjos, of Noruega, of Monjope, of Gaipió, of Morenos, laying waste a considerable part of the region known as *"mata,"* or jungle forest. It is true that certain variations are to be noted, some of them due to a difference in climate, others to psychological contrasts, and to the fact that, in São Paulo at least, a latifundiary monoculture was a regime imposed at the end of the eighteenth century upon a system of small ownership.[15] In passing we should not overlook the fact that "while the inhabitants of the north sought out for their habitations elevated sites, on the mountain slopes, the Paulistas commonly preferred the lowlands, the depressions of the earth, as the place to erect their dwellings. . . ." [16] These latter houses were "always built on a steeply inclined slope as a protection against the south wind, in such a manner that on the lower side the house had a ground floor that gave it the appearance of a two-story edifice." The southern mansions have more of a closed-in, aloof air than do the houses of the north; but the "terrace from which the planter with his gaze could take in the entire organism of rural life" is the same as in the north, a terrace that is pleasing, hospitable, and patriarchal in character. Coming down the river from Santos to Rio in a small steamer that puts in at all the ports along the way, one has a glimpse at the water's edge—in Ubatuba, São Sebastião, Angra dos Reis—of town houses that recall the patriarchal dwellings of Rio Formoso. And at times, as in the north, one

---

[15] Alfredo Ellis, Jr., in *Raça de Gigantes* (*Race of Giants*), basing his statements upon the old *Inventories* and *Allotments* of colonial days, asserts that down to the end of the eighteenth century a small-property regime was the dominant one in São Paulo, the dwelling-houses being no more than stucco-walled structures, originally covered with sapé. "They ordinarily had three rooms with a garden and were very badly furnished. . . ." They were, however, very large, with enormous dining-rooms, and already had a "house for Negroes," or *senzala*. In the seventeenth-century house of Francisco Mariano da Cunha the same writer found sixteen rooms of huge dimensions and a dining-room 13 meters by 5.4 [about 43 feet by 18]. Oliveira Vianna, in his *Populações Meridionais do Brasil* (*Southern Populations of Brazil*), stresses the contrast between the São Paulo plantations prior to the century (the nineteenth) in which coffee was introduced—"diminutive estates measured in cubits, the majority of them being a league in circumference"—and "the estates of Minas and the Rio Grande region, which are latifundia of 10,000 alquiers or more." But the real latifundia were those of Pernambuco and Bahia, of the type of the Garcia d'Avila plantation.

(The alquier [alqueire] is a land measure varying in extent from 24.2 to 48.4 square meters. [Tr.])

[16] João Vampré: *"Fatos e festas na tradição"* ("Facts and Festivals as Handed Down by Tradition"), in the *Revista do Instituto Histórico de São Paulo,* Vol. XIII.

encounters churches with a porch in front—gently inviting and typically Brazilian.

The social history of the Big House is the intimate history of practically every Brazilian: the history of his domestic and conjugal life under a slave-holding and polygamous patriarchal regime; the history of his life as a child; the history of his Christianity, reduced to the form of a family religion and influenced by the superstitions of the slave hut. The study of the intimate history of a people has in it something of Proustian introspection—the Goncourts had a name for it: *"ce roman vrai."* The architect Lúcio Costa has given us his impression in the presence of the old mansions of Sabará, São João d'El-Rei, Ouro Preto, and Mariana, the old Big Houses of Minas: "How one meets oneself here. . . . And one remembers things one never knew but which were there inside one all the while; I do not know how to put it—it would take a Proust to explain it." [17]

It is in the Big Houses that, down to this day, the Brazilian character has found its best expression, the expression of our social continuity. In the study of their intimate history, all that political and military history has to offer in the way of striking events holds little meaning in comparison with a mode of life that is almost routine; but it is in that routine that the character of a people is most readily to be discerned. In studying the domestic life of our ancestors we feel that we are completing ourselves: it is another method of searching for the *"temps perdu,"* another means of finding ourselves in others, in those who lived before us and whose life anticipates our own. The past awakens many strings and has a bearing on the life of each and every one of us; and the study of this past is more than mere research and a rummaging in the archives: it is an adventure in sensitivity.

---

[17] Lúcio Costa: *"O Aleijadinho e a Arquitetura Tradicional"* ("Aleijadinho and Traditional Architecture"), *O Jornal,* Rio de Janeiro, special Minas Geraes edition.

❧ 10 ❧

Silver Mining in Potosí

------◄◆►------

Antonio Vázquez de Espinosa

Although settlers in the Spanish colonies and in Brazil always evinced interest in the acquisition of land and its exploitation through agriculture or stock raising, their primary concern in the early years of colonization was the discovery of precious metals. In this quest the Spaniards were initially more successful than the Portuguese, for in the middle of the sixteenth century vast deposits of silver were found in several places in the Viceroyalty of New Spain and in Potosí in the Viceroyalty of Peru. The products of these regions helped to finance the expensive foreign policy of the early Hapsburg rulers of Spain and also contributed to the rise of prices in that country. Mining operations in Potosí are described here by Antonio Vázquez de Espinosa (d. 1630), a Spanish friar who spent many years as a missionary in America. The excerpt is from Vázquez de Espinosa's Compendium and Description of the West Indies, *published in full for the first time in 1942 by the Smithsonian Institution.*

The famous Potosí range, so celebrated all over the world for the great wealth which God has created unique in its bowels and veins, lies in the Province of the Charcas, 18 leagues from the city of Chuquisaca, which was later called La Plata, on account of the great richness of this range. It is in the midst of the Cordillera, and since that is high-altitude country, that region is usually colder than Germany, so much so that it was uninhabitable for the native tribes. It is scant 20° S.; on account of the cold, not a fly, mosquito, or [any] other unpleasant creature can live there; there was no living thing on that waste but guanacos, vicuñas, ostriches, and vizcachas, which are characteristic of that cold country.

The Cordillera, at the point where the Potosí range stands, is bare and treeless, with occasional plains, which in that country they call pampas; but there are a few ranges in the region, 5 leagues to the E. of the old Porco mines. The outline of this rich hill is like that of a

From Antonio Vázquez de Espinosa, *Description of the Indies (c. 1620)*, translated by Charles Upson Clark (Washington, D.C.: Smithsonian Institution Press, 1968), pp. 621–627. Reprinted by permission of the publisher.

89

pile of wheat or a sugar loaf, handsome and well proportioned, standing up and lording it over the others, as if their prince. It is almost deep red in color, and is over half a league high, the ascent covering more than a league, with a steep grade but all negotiable on horseback over the roads and paths which climb up it; at the top, it forms a round summit; its circumference along the base of the slope is over a league around. At present it is all hollowed out and shored up, on account of the great amount of ore they have taken out from the veins in its bowels and center, and the long tunnels they have bored from the sides to get the ore out with less labor, though it remains considerable, for there are veins they have followed and keep following, for over 300 stades[1] inward; it was to facilitate these operations that they have made those tunnels on many sides of the hill. It is joined to another lower ridge which they call Guayna Potosí, meaning Young Potosí.

This marvelously rich range was discovered at the beginning of the year 1545, 14 years after the discovery of that Kingdom by Marqués Don Francisco Pizarro and his comrades. The first to discover it was an Indian of Chumbivilca Province, which is at one side of Cuzco, by the name of Hualpa, who was at the Porco mines. He spoke of it to another native, from the Province of Jauja, which is up above Lima; this man was a servant or Yanacona of a Porco miner named Villarroel. He told his master about it, and he went over to verify the richness of the range; when assured of it, he registered his claim on April 21, 1545, staking it on the vein which they have named Centeno; staking (estacandose) is the same as taking possession of the extension in varas permitted by the law to those who make the find, so that they can work it as their own, registering it before His Majesty's officials for the proper payment of the 20 percent impost; then they discovered the vein called Estaño (tin), very rich in ore, and late in August, the Mendieta vein. The first vein, discovered by the Chumbivilca Indian, was 300 feet long and 13 broad; it had a great outcrop above ground the height of a lance, half silver, and in parts all virgin silver with flukes projecting out from the hill level.

These four chief veins were on the E. side of the hill, running N. and S. into its depths toward the slopes. They had other branches springing from them, like those springing from the trunk of a tree. On each of these principal veins there were different mines divided up between many proprietors or miners; by law, the largest mine cannot run over 80 varas,[2] and the smallest, 4. The rich vein had 78 mines on it; the Centeno, 24, and the others rather more. These ore veins in

---

[1] A stade (*estado*) is a Spanish measure of length equal to slightly over six feet. [H. D.]

[2] A *vara* is a measure of length equal to about a yard. [H. D.]

general run between two cliffs which stand like sentries over them, and are called Caja (strongbox). They do not always run even, but in some places rich and others poor; they break open the cliffs or cajas to get it out, although they are the hardest of flint in some cases. They call the rich ore tacana; it is almost amber colored; it comes also red, ashy, and other colors.

These ores were treated by smelting for 26 years, because the Spaniards in that Kingdom knew no other method; they used it from the discovery of the richness of that range in 1545 until the year 1571, when, in the days of [*Spanish viceroy*] Don Francisco de Toledo, they began treating the ore with mercury, the benefits of which had been discovered in the Huancavelica mines. . . .

The way they smelted these ores was in little ovens which the Indians set up on the tops and slopes of the sierras and mountains; they fed them with wood or charcoal and when lighted they glowed under the draft of the wind the Indians call guayra, and so they called these ovens guayras; every night over 6,000 flamed on those ridges and mountains under the fresh wind blowing through them; it was a pleasant sight to see so many lights at night; it looked as if there were bonfires all over the hills, and gay celebrations, and so it surely was for the Spaniards, with the Indians getting out the silver for them. They even had rogations, Masses, and other pious acts for God to send them wind for their guayras, just as sailors do when there is a calm at sea for a wind to help them on their course. In this smelting they used the rich ore and dumped in soroche, which is plumbeous, so that it would melt and liquefy better. Thus the slag separated off under the flame, the lead melted, and the silver swam or ran on top of it, until the heat consumed it and the silver was left, which kept on refining and purifying itself until it became liquid and pure; they used tin also in the process. Smelting could not get all the silver except at too great effort and cost; so they did not smelt low-grade ore, the residue and the discard (desmontes) for the reason given, it being too difficult and the cost more than the profit, until the quicksilver process arrived; that gets it all (varrelo), and so all grades of ore, rich and poor, and whatever discard and residue there was, were treated, and are treated, with it, better and more easily; and yet at the present day there are many guayras on the Potosí range and its neighborhood, operated by poor miners and Indians. . . .

According to His Majesty's warrant, the mine owners on this massive range have a right to the mita of 13,300 Indians in the working and exploitation of the mines, both those which have been discovered, those now discovered, and those which shall be discovered. It is the duty of the Corregidor of Potosí to have them rounded up and to see that they come in from all the provinces between Cuzco over the whole of El Collao and as far as the frontiers of Tarija and Tomina; this

Potosí Corregidor has power and authority over all the Corregidors in those provinces mentioned; for if they do not fill the Indian mita allotment assigned each one of them in accordance with the capacity of their provinces as indicated to them, he can send them, and does, salaried inspectors to report upon it, and when the remissness is great or remarkable, he can suspend them, notifying the Viceroy of the fact.

These Indians are sent out every year under a captain whom they choose in each village or tribe, for him to take them and oversee them for the year each has to serve; every year they have a new election, for as some go out, others come in. This works out very badly, with great losses and gaps in the quotas of Indians, the villages being depopulated; and this gives rise to great extortions and abuses on the part of the inspectors toward the poor Indians, ruining them and thus depriving the caciques and chief Indians of their property and carrying them off in chains because they do not fill out the mita assignment, which they cannot do, for the reasons given and for others which I do not bring forward.

These 13,300 are divided up every 4 months into 3 mitas, each consisting of 4,433 Indians, to work in the mines on the range and in the 120 smelters in the Potosí and Tarapaya areas; it is a good league between the two. These mita Indians earn each day, or there is paid each one for his labor, 4 reals. Besides these there are others not under obligation, who are mingados or hire themselves out voluntarily: these each get from 12 to 16 reals, and some up to 24, according to their reputation of wielding the pick and knowing how to get the ore out. These mingados will be over 4,000 in number. They and the mita Indians go up every Monday morning to the locality of Guayna Potosí which is at the foot of the range; the Corregidor arrives with all the provincial captains or chiefs who have charge of the Indians assigned them, and he there checks off and reports to each mine and smelter owner the number of Indians assigned him for his mine or smelter; that keeps him busy till 1 p.m., by which time the Indians are already turned over to these mine and smelter owners.

After each has eaten his ration, they climb up the hill, each to his mine, and go in, staying there from that hour until Saturday evening without coming out of the mine; their wives bring them food, but they stay constantly underground, excavating and carrying out the ore from which they get the silver. They all have tallow candles, lighted day and night; that is the light they work with, for as they are underground, they have need of it all the time. The mere cost of these candles used in the mines on this range will amount every year to more than 300,000 pesos, even though tallow is cheap in that country, being abundant; but this is a very great expense, and it is almost incredible how much is spent for candles in the operation of breaking down and getting out the ore.

These Indians have different functions in the handling of the silver ore; some break it up with bar or pick, and dig down in, following the vein in the mine; others bring it up; others up above keep separating the good and the poor in piles; others are occupied in taking it down from the range to the mills on herds of llamas; every day they bring up more than 8,000 of these native beasts of burden for this task. These teamsters who carry the metal do not belong to the mita, but are mingados—hired. . . .

The mills to grind the ore are run by water, like water mills (aceñas) or gristmills; for that purpose they have around the range or at some distance from it 16 reservoirs; the most remote, called Tavaconuño, is 3 leagues off. In these they collect the water which falls in the rainy season; the mills are all built and arranged in order, and when the grinding is to start, they let the water into a channel passing from one to another, for as soon as it issues from one, it goes into another; the whole Potosí range is like that. Most of the mills have two heads (of water?), with great heavy stone hammers which pound the ore, the ones rising and the others falling, just as in a fulling mill, until the ore, hard as flint though some of it is, has been reduced to meal; then they sift it through sieves set up for that purpose; in 24 hours they will sift over 30 quintals.

They set great store on the water in these reservoirs; as soon as one is empty, they start on another, for although they are all divided up and apportioned, they are arranged in such a way that each distributes its water to the first mill, and from that on in order. This Potosí range is the larger; most years, when the water gets low, they have processions and prayers for rain to fill the reservoirs; and according as the year is wet or dry, they run the mills a longer or shorter time, to grind the ore. The Tarapaya range is the shorter; the mills there grind with the water of a stream on which they are built.

After grinding and sifting the ore they dump it into containers for the furnaces and saturate it with brine, using for every 50 quintals[3] of ore, 5 of salt, more or less, according to the quality of the ore, for it to eat and consume it, or part of it, and scour it. Then they put the mercury in, so that by this arrangement it may better embrace and combine with the silver, and shorten the process, and bring about a union of the mercury with the silver, having thrown salt in with it; they knead it twice a day with their feet, just as they do clay in the making of tile or brick, and they remix with mercury twice a day; then they put the containers on furnaces and start the fires underneath in small ovens, so that the heat may cause the mercury to amalgamate more quickly with the silver.

Although the ore all comes from one range, the mines and the ore

---

[3] A *quintal* is equivalent to one hundred pounds. [H. D.]

are usually of different grade, and so different materials are necessary for their treatment; for some they put in salt and lime, and iron or copper ground up in water, for which processing they have some small mills; in others, they put lead and tin; other ore—the negrillo (stephanite)—is first roasted in ovens for its grinding in the mills. Thus in some cases they use all these materials, in some, many, and in some, fewer, according to the need and to the grade of the ore; if low, the quicksilver is hampered in its union and amalgamation with the silver. With all this preparation and solicitude, in one case it may come to 20, in others more or less; with the fire or heat they apply, and these materials mentioned, the quicksilver absorbs the silver within 8 days.

At the moment which seems right to them, according to the ore and the treatment given it, the mercury having already absorbed the silver, they dump this ore into large tubs with water running into them. These have a device with paddles or wheels in continual motion inside the tubs, so that the ore dust is carried off by the running water, and the combined mercury and silver, being heavier, goes to the bottom and settles there in the tubs. The rest of the ore, which was not well washed in these tubs or other puddling operations, they finish refining, until the silver and mercury alone are left, without any dust. This lump, which is soft as dough, is put in a linen cloth and squeezed hard until they press out and separate all the mercury they can from the silver. Then they put the lumps of silver which have had the mercury squeezed out, into clay forms or pots shaped like sugar loaves, with an aperture at the end of the narrowest point, and set them in ovens specially made for the purpose; when they start the fire, the mercury goes out through the hole as vapor or smoke, but nothing is lost, thanks to the preparation made.

After the fire has severed the mercury from his friend the silver, the cone (piña) of pure silver comes out the size and shape of a loaf of very white sugar, for silver looks very white and spongy. Each cone is usually of 40 silver marks, slightly more or less; that is the ordinary product from one container; but if the grade and richness of the ore permit, they may get two cones, as happened at the beginning when the rich range was first exploited; the same is true of certain new mines; but ordinarily it is only one. They make up a bar by melting two together. The silver refined by the mercury process is so fine and white that it is always above the 2,380 grade; and to make it fit for use by the silversmiths, they reduce the grade to the 11 dineros and 4 grains which is the legal sterling standard, by addition of copper or other alloy. . . .

The silver which is extracted and collected from the ore dust, is much finer than that which they get first from the ore; it is the most delicate part that runs off with the mud and ore dust in the first washings and rewashings of the ore in the tubs. Of this dust, which contains much silver that has passed through and escaped the mercury process, they treat every year more than 300,000 quintals, roasting it in more than 200 furnaces maintained for this purpose on the Potosí and Tarapaya ranges. Thus they recover a large amount of silver, which will amount each year to over 300,000 pesos; this is the finest and highest-grade silver of all that is handled. Together with it they recover more than 2,000 quintals of mercury carried off with it in the ore dust; this amount, plus over 6,000 more brought from the Huancavelica mines, is used up every year at Potosí alone in the reduction of the ore and the silver.

After this silver has been run into bars, the Assayer takes a bit from each and weighs it by itself to see what grade it is. He puts each bit of silver into a receptacle made of ashes from ground burnt bones, cast in a mold, each with its label; these are like the little molds used by the silversmiths in casting silver or gold. These jars or molds are used for the assay sample and when they take it for the assay, His Majesty collects his royal 20 percent.

. . .

So huge is the wealth which has been taken out of this range since the year 1545, when it was discovered, up to the present year of 1628, which makes 83 years that they have been working and reducing its ores, that merely from the registered mines, as appears from an examination of most of the accounts in the royal records, 326,000,000 assay pesos have been taken out. At the beginning when the ore was richer and easier to get out, for then there were no mita Indians and no mercury process, in the 40 years between 1545 and 1585, they took out 111,000,000 of assay silver. From the year 1585 up to 1628, 43 years, although the mines are harder to work, for they are deeper down, with the assistance of 13,300 Indians whom His Majesty has granted to the mine owners on that range, and of other hired Indians, who come there freely and voluntarily to work at day's wages, and with the great advantage of the mercury process, in which none of the ore or the silver is wasted, and with the better knowledge of the technique which the miners now have, they have taken out 215,000,000 assay pesos. That, plus the 111 extracted in the 40 years previous to 1585, makes 326,000,000 assay pesos, not counting the great amount of silver secretly taken from these mines to be registered in others paying only 10 percent tithes, the silver in the 20 percent impost, the currency circulating in those Kingdoms, the silver plate and vessels of private individuals, that in the churches in the form of chalices, crosses, lamps, and other vessels for decoration and use in divine service, and that that has been taken secretly to Spain, paying no 20 percent or registry fee, and to other countries outside Spain, and to the Philippines and China, which is beyond all reckoning; but I should venture to imagine and even assert that what has been taken from the Potosí range must be as much again as what paid the 20 percent royal impost.

Over and above that, such great treasure and riches have come from the Indies in gold and silver from all the other mines in New Spain and Peru, Honduras, the New Kingdom of Granada, Chile, New Galicia, New Vizcaya, and other quarters since the discovery of the Indies, that they exceed 1,800 millions.

Minas Gerais in the Gold Mining Era

---◆◀◆▶◆---

José João Teixeira Coelho

Gold was discovered in Brazil in 1693–1695, when several strikes were made in the region that became known as Minas Gerais. Like Potosí, the mining centers of Minas Gerais became turbulent, lawless boom towns, as José João Teixeira Coelho, who spent eleven years in the region, indicated in an "Instruction for the Government of the Captaincy of Minas Gerais" (1780). The gold strikes in Minas Gerais and subsequent discoveries of gold in Matto Grosso and Goiaz and of diamonds in Minas Gerais not only enriched prospectors and increased royal revenue but also stimulated the economic development of the mining regions. The mining era also had the less beneficial effect of further attaching the colony to an economy based on a cyclical pattern of boom and bust.

The Poverty of the Miners

Without means and burdened with debt, the miners cannot undertake costly projects; in the majority of cases, because of their poverty, they are content to be simple prospectors. They know that in some places on their lands rich lodes and veins of gold lie hidden. However, because its excavation requires investments beyond their abilities, they show no enthusiasm to carry out projects for which they do not have the capital. They know that the banks and bed of the stream of Carmo contain much gold, but as this cannot be obtained without great expenditure, which one miner, and even many, cannot afford, the gold remains untouched.

At other places, because there is no one able to control the waterfalls, drain the deep water, or dig away hills, there exists the same inability to get at the natural resources. The presence of hostile Indians along other rivers likewise prevents gold mining. Lately along the

Rio das Velhas many projects have been abandoned because the miners did not have enough equipment to encourage them to carry on, and they frequently failed to complete their work during the dry season so that when the rains fell the swollen streams washed away equipment and the deposits being searched for gold.

If some miners own the necessary number of slaves for mining along the river banks, they divert part of that number for other tasks because they show no talent as prospectors. They are able to get a small quantity of gold with which to pay the necessary expenses, but they become discouraged because the return is so small and do not fully pursue their vocation.

Other miners, having just enough Negroes for the mining of gold, use some of them to work in the fields which lessens the production of gold, and so they extract less gold than they might if all the Negroes were at work looking for gold.

Lack of Negroes, Monopoly of Them, and Taxes on Them

There is a severe shortage of slaves in the captaincy of Minas Gerais because there is no systematic method of obtaining them along the African coast and because in Rio de Janeiro there is a monopoly over the slave trade.

In 1779, when I was in Rio de Janeiro, two shiploads of Negroes arrived in the port, and immediately a group of merchants bought the entire cargo.

These merchants, as they own all the Negroes, are arbiters of their price, and the miners who are poor and find the Negroes expensive do not buy as many as they need. For that reason they never are able to run their mining operation at full capacity.

There is no doubt that a miner with fifty slaves and a yearly production of 1,000 oitavas[1] would be able to double his production with one hundred slaves and the same thing would happen proportionally with the other miners. A more systematic exportation of slaves from Africa and an abolition of the monopoly in order to reduce the price of slaves are matters which deserve particular attention.

There is no doubt that slaves are cheaper than they were in former times. Even so, they are expensive because the mining industry no longer enjoys the same prosperity it did in the past. The easy gold has been removed, and now it is necessary to work harder in more difficult places to excavate less gold.

---

[1] An *oitava* equals 3.586 grams. [E. B. B.]

The taxes on slaves are excessive because in addition to what they charge in Africa, it is still necessary to pay the following: in Rio de Janeiro each Negro on landing, 4$500 réis;[2] for documents and transactions, 500; on crossing the Parahyba and Parahybuna rivers, 160; and to the soldiers that guard them, 40; for each one shipped beyond the Parahybuna, 640; as some of the slaves are detained because of sickness and do not proceed with their group, it is necessary to pay an additional 640; and to register their entrance into the province is another 3$000 réis.

In addition to these charges, in Rio de Janeiro it is necessary to pay to the secretary of the police 40 réis for each Negro. There have been differences in this practice over the last decades. At first it was required to pay 40 réis for each passport which might include one person or many if they were a family group. Later the Viceroy Conde da Cunha suspended those payments. During the succeeding administration once again a charge of 40 réis a passport was made, but four or five years later it became necessary to pay 40 réis per person no matter whether they were alone or a part of a family. The practice of paying for each Negro is current today.

For more than twenty years a subsidy of 4$800 was paid for every Negro, but that subsidy has ended.

All these taxes on Negroes, as well as the other reasons given, raise the price of slaves and make it difficult for the miners to buy as many as they need. None of the miners has a sufficient number. This is a constant and known fact to which I can attest because I have visited the principal mining regions of Villa Rica, Sabará, and Rio das Mortes.

It is calculated that each year about four thousand Negroes enter Minas Gerais. Subtracting from that number the slaves needed for household and field services there remains but a handful to work in mining, and by these calculations alone it is possible to see that the mines are underworked.

Poor Mining Methods

Governor Antônio de Albuquerque Coelho de Carvalho in a letter written to His Majesty on August 7, 1711, spoke of the necessity of establishing regulations for gold mining and of using the knowledge of science to increase production. His recommendations have not been implemented and the miners go about their work according to their

---

[2] The basic monetary unit is the *real* (plural réis). 1,000 réis is expressed as 1$000 and is called a *milreis*. The value of the milreis has varied considerably over the years. [E. B. B.]

own caprices. Not one single engineer came to Minas Gerais to direct the mining operations. The miners learn from experience, but they are far from perfect because they follow no principles.

, For this reason they have dug mines which are useless and invested large sums with no return.

The mistake of mining on the top of the hill prior to excavating the gold at the foot of the hill is incomprehensible. Those lower sites became blocked with the dirt from the top of the hill, and the gold which existed in the lower sites remains forever buried beneath the earth where it cannot be reached.

It is amazing that the government created superintendents of agriculture for various regions of America and never appointed superintendents of gold mining to regulate the mines and the methods of their exploitation. This is a result of not informing His Majesty or his ministry of the aforementioned chaos.

These superintendents should be men with practical mining experience and given to such pursuits. The simple study of the laws of the Realm or of Roman law is not sufficient to make a superintendent of gold mining a useful man for a task which requires other knowledge.

If the miners of Rio das Velhas did not excavate on their own whims and if they were prohibited from working the mines without a minimum number of slaves, many of the mines would not fail to produce because of the lack of resources of the owners. Necessity would cause them to band together voluntarily to form one mining company capable of solving the problems which individually they could not solve, but there is no one in Minas Gerais who has jurisdiction to regulate the mining industry and to order others to work in it.

The results of all this are errors very prejudicial to public interests. Much of the gold is not extracted from the mines and many rich sites are covered up by other diggings.

The Lack of Police in the Captaincy of Minas Gerais and Some Injustices Which Need Prompt Remedy

The lack of police in the captaincy of Minas Gerais disturbs order there. The majority of the inhabitants of this captaincy either have come directly from Europe or are born of Europeans. They arrive here excited and with the hope of advancing their fortunes. The majority of them were either criminals or persons who at home had no more than what they earned with their hoe or by the offices they held. These men, who in Portugal were the scum of the masses and the despair of the elite, come to this enormous land of freedom to make themselves insolent and to play the role of nobles.

Governor Antônio de Albuquerque Coelho de Carvalho already

made this complaint in the letter he wrote to His Majesty on August 7, 1711. And what would he say if he could see the conditions in Minas Gerais today?

What sort of education can men of that kind give to their children? What virtues do they have which serve as examples for their own children? All of them refer to themselves as distinguished men and for that reason they deprecate work, living in idleness and thereby depriving the State of hundreds of workers.

In all the captaincy of Minas Gerais there is not one white man nor one white woman who wants to work, for they persuade themselves that to labor is to compete with the slaves. In such a way hundreds of male and female slaves must work at domestic tasks and abandon work in the mines or panning gold.

This presumption and idleness of the whites is being transferred to the mulattoes and Negroes because once they are freed they do not want to work anymore, and as necessity obliges them to look for sustenance by illicit means both the men and women take part in the vices characteristic of their different sexes.

Those mulattoes who are not total idlers find employment as musicians of whom there are so many in the captaincy of Minas Gerais that certainly they exceed the number in all Portugal. But what good is such an overabundance of musicians to the State?

The protectors of orphans,[3] following in every respect the pernicious practices already described, take no care to hire out and to apprentice the orphans in their districts, as they are required to do by law. They only take care to get hold of the gold which might belong to some of those orphans for their own coffers by using various tricks such as the testimony of third persons that the money is being spent for the upkeep of the orphans.

The Count of Valladares attempted to remedy these deep-rooted evils, but the lack of jurisdiction diminished his great zeal for the conservation and improvement of the captaincy.

The governor, who has a patriotic spirit and who wants to fulfill his obligations, ought to report these wrongs to His Majesty so that he could put a halt to these acts prejudicial to both the royal interests and those of the people.

I shall speak now of those judges who have jurisdiction over the property of the dead and those absent from the captaincy of Minas Gerais.[4] This is a subject which demands considerable discussion but I shall be brief and limit myself to pointing out only the most notable abuses of these judges.

The justices of the peace of the juridical districts of Minas Gerais

---

[3] Juiz dos orfãos. [E. B. B.]

[4] Juizos dos defuntos e ausentes. [E. B. B.]

serve as purveyors of the dead and absent in virtue of the authority granted to them by the Conscience Board.[5] The rules by which they govern are incomplete and the orders that have been decreed to make up for that lack are infinite and some contradictory.

This contradiction and diversity of orders causes some judges to use one rule sometimes and another at other times according to the case. The people feel the vexations of rapid legal action which is unfavorable to them, and being ignorant of the law they do not know that there also exist rules favorable to their side of the case.

The decisions of the High Court of Rio de Janeiro, which have been handed down in these matters, are famous and do little honor to the purveyors.

The poverty-stricken masses have no resources to dispute the jurisdiction of those justices when they are told that they will not receive custody of the inheritance. Even if they would appeal the decisions, the appeals are received only on the basis of restoration, and the sequestration of the goods of the inheritance proceeds pending a judgment on the competence of the judge.

The executors of a will or the administrators of inheritances are obliged in this manner to make compromises with the treasurers handling the property of the absent, giving to them certain means or certain sums necessary to disentangle the inheritances.

. . .

The Count of Vallardares wanted to stop these injustices. Such action, prompted by the extortions of the judges in charge of the affairs of those absent, is authorized by the clamors of the people. In one particular case, the Count knew perfectly well that the inheritance of the Franças of Congonhas do Campo was extremely important, and while it wasted away in custody by order of the judge, one of the heirs had to go around begging alms, which I saw with my own eyes, at the same time that his goods were in the hands of the treasurer because of a corrupt bribe.

I must mention another famous case which I witnessed. A keen-witted Negro slave was imprisoned in Mariana. He belonged to João da Silva Coura, an inhabitant in the vicinity of that city. He ended up in the court of the absent as an unclaimed property as it appeared that he belonged to no one. It was as if that slave were a cow or a beast or some animal that could not respond to questioning as provided by specific formalities of the law. But the Count of Vallardares learned of this matter after some time and he ordered that slave to be returned to his proper master who took him back into custody.

Besides this, the treasurers of the property of those absent from the captaincy have in their power for many months the slaves which form

---

[5] Mesa da Consciência. [E. B. B.]

part of an inheritance, and they do not hesitate to make use of them in domestic service or they put them to work mining or send them into the forests for firewood and into the pastures for hay, both of which are sold for profit. On top of this it is necessary to pay for the food and clothing of the slaves held in custody.

As to the furniture passed on as an inheritance, those same treasurers make use of them to decorate their homes or for other purposes, and in this way the goods deteriorate.

Those same treasurers, when they go with the secretaries of the courts to make inventories of the goods of the deceased, describe the furniture of greatest size and least importance and they do not mention the valuable pieces. This is an easy theft abetted by the purveyors who do not visit the homes of the dead at once prior to ordering an inventory of their goods.

There is yet another method by which the treasurers and the other officials with authority rob the goods left by the dead or the absent.

After making the inventories of the inheritances, it is necessary to appraise the goods described in them. The treasurers in collusion with the appraisers assign the lowest possible prices to the goods or furniture that they want for themselves. These evaluations are kept secret, and the bidders can get the goods only if they offer a price superior to the appraisal price, which the public does not know, and the bidders are never willing to offer very much. However, the treasurers who know which goods, farms, and furniture bear ridiculously low appraisals boldly bid a third more than the evaluated price and still buy cheaply. This is the reason for keeping the appraisals secret from the bidders.

.   .   .

As to the executors of wills one cannot count in the captaincy of Minas Gerais more than two who do not rob the inheritances in their care. I could make a catalogue of them because I know many of them but it is not necessary because these are known and public facts.

.   .   .

It is certain that there have been and are in this captaincy many honorable and disinterested judges, but not all of them are so. In order to avoid doubts and extortions it is best to issue some new regulations to prevent the evil and the ambitious from doing injustices and corrupting the good.

❧ 12 ❧

A *Bandeirante's* Odyssey

————— ◄◄◆►► —————

José Peixoto da Silva

The initial discovery of gold in Brazil was made by prospectors from São Paulo, whose hardy inhabitants, lacking a profitable export product, had turned instead to a search for gold and Indian slaves. For this purpose the Paulistas organized expeditions called bandeiras, *which frequently covered thousands of miles and lasted several years, penetrating deep into the territory that lay to the west and south of the settled portions of the colony. Beginning in 1628–1629, when the boundaries between Spanish and Portuguese America were blurred because of the fact that the king of Spain ruled Portugal,* bandeirantes *conducted numerous raids against the Jesuit missions of Paraguay, capturing thousands of Indians for their own use or for sale in other parts of Brazil. The hardships often experienced by the* bandeirantes *are graphically portrayed in this reading, an account of an expedition in 1722 from São Paulo to Belém in northern Brazil. The selection also illustrates the antipathy between the paulistas and Portuguese immigrants, disdainfully known as* Emboabas, *which had already resulted in a "War of the Emboabas" in Minas Gerais in 1708–1709.*

On July 3, 1722, I left the city of São Paulo in the company of Captain Bartholomeu Bueno da Silva, known by the nickname Fearless, who was in charge of a force consisting of 39 horses, two Benedictines, Brother Antônio da Conceição and Brother Luiz de Sant'Anna, a Franciscan, Brother Cosme de Santo André, and 152 soldiers along with twenty Indians given by Rodrigo Cézar, then captain-general of São Paulo, to Bartholomeu Bueno to carry burdens. Nearly all the whites were from Portugal. One was from Bahia and five or six were from São Paulo, with their Indians and Negroes.

Crossing the Tietê River, we stopped near the forest of Jundiahy, four leagues away from the city of São Paulo. The following morning we entered the forest and we spent four days in it. Leaving the forest,

From E. Bradford Burns (ed. and tr.), *A Documentary History of Brazil* (New York: Knopf, 1966), 102–116. Copyright © 1966 by E. Bradford Burns. Reprinted by permission of Alfred A. Knopf, Inc.

we crossed the Mogig River, which can be navigated by canoes, contains a variety of fish, and shows some signs of gold but of little value. We spent one day here and on the following, always headed northward, we came to another river also navigable by canoe, and we spent the night there. The relatively flat land has clumps of trees and good pasture and is well watered.

On the next day, we forded a stream whose water came up to our chests, and we marched on for three or four leagues and made camp in the middle of the fields. Traveling across these fields is easy. The pastures are good, and there are many animals to hunt. The streams contain many fish. We continued on about four leagues and camped near another stream which, like the others, flows into the Rio Grande. From here we moved on to the banks of another stream where we halted. The following morning we crossed it using poles and holding stout vines in order to prevent the strong force of the violent water from sweeping us away. We spent a day there because the soldiers were demanding that Fearless divide up the shares as he had promised to do at Mogig and as yet had failed to do. He excused himself with the promise that he would do so as soon as Captain João Leite da Silva Ortiz, his son-in-law, who was behind us with his own group, caught up, or, if he failed to arrive within a reasonable length of time, he would do it at Rio Grande.

With that hope, the troops marched again for seven or eight days through fields and thick woods, halting always at the banks of streams or rivers. There was game and fish. We came to the Rio Grande and in the morning crossed it in canoes made of the trunks of the kapok ceiba. We waited there for two days hoping he would make the promised division of shares, but as always Fearless failed to do so. We left that place somewhat discouraged and went another four leagues to camp by another stream which flowed into the Rio Grande. Here we began to feel a food shortage, and it was necessary to march five days living off of what our guns provided, birds and monkeys, as well as palm cabbage and some honey.

After five days we reached the Velhas River, which flows into the Rio Grande. It is torrential, full of fish, but without any signs of gold. We spent two days fishing and hunting in the nearby woods in order to get provisions for our trip. Here Fearless left us, going ahead with part of the group. The rest would follow him later. While he was gone, João Leite arrived with his men, and because of this, we delayed our departure one more day. On the following day, accompanied by João Leite, we followed Fearless and after a four-day march we found him in the forest with a camp already constructed. On the way we forded some streams which offered no difficulty because it is now the dry season.

After the men had had a talk with the chief, João Leite asked him to make the division of shares that he promised so many times to do, not only in São Paulo but in the backlands, because the way was far from certain. It was feared that the enterprise might fail despite the fact that both General Rodrigo Cézar and the sovereign himself had been assured of its success. He replied to them that he did not have to divide up the shares because the Emboabas, as those from Portugal are called, were not men who merited it. With that reply not only the Emboabas lost confidence but also the few Paulistas who accompanied us. They determined to return at once to São Paulo, but João Leite hurried to entreat them with pleas, with promises, and, what is more important, with his natural charm, not to abandon the expedition. The chief decided to push on, out of dislike of the Emboabas whose hope he was. The group followed and we spent the night near a stream which contained some fish. Good pastures and woods were near at hand. Here we lost confidence in everything Fearless had told us, and we believed that he wanted to get rid of us in the middle of this hinterland. Some resolved to stay right there and to cultivate the land by planting some corn that they still had, for food. But Captain João Leite once again spoke with them, encouraging and persuading them to move on with the rest of the group.

For some days we trudged onward, crossing rivers and streams with a good deal of risk and work. The water was high and we were hungry. We made camp near Meia Ponte, where there is a dangerous river with plenty of fish and with good pastures and woods in the vicinity. We made it across the river in some small canoes of tree bark. We slept on the opposite bank, under the downpour of a raging thunderstorm which lasted until the following morning. There was so much rain that we were unable to build any shelters, and I made good use of a canvas I had with me. Two days' journey from Meia Ponte, Brother Antônio left us, along with ten Indians, his nephew, a mulatto, and another white Paulista, in order to start farming. The group missed the priest. Fearless sent word to him to rejoin the expedition again and to go along with the rest. As a response, Brother Antônio told him that his lies and false promises prohibited him from rejoining the group and that he was determined to plant corn and gather the natives around him in order to Christianize them.

Fearless set off again with the troops and judging that by going north, as he had done up to that point, that Goiás would lay off in another direction, he changed course and went to the northeast.[1]

We continued on for more than one-hundred leagues in that direction without anything more to eat than the forest could give us, which was scanty. At that time eight Indians belonging to our leader fled,

---

[1] The direction taken should have been west-northwest. [E. B. B.]

but first they warned everyone that we were headed in the wrong direction because we had bypassed Goiás, which lay in another direction. Of these Indians only three were brought back after some days. João Leite, with two Negroes and four whites, captured them after a search. He also brought with him Brother Antônio whose little settlement was about eighty leagues away. But even though Brother Antônio came he did not abandon his settlement, because he left his nephew there with almost all the Indians. We then came onto some extensive plains which were destitute of all necessities, without trees or any food, although there were streams in which there were fish, dorados, lungfish, and small freshwater fish, which were our only salvation. We also found some palm cabbage which they call *jaguaroba,* which we ate roasted, and, although it is bitter, it nourishes more than the other varieties.

Here everyone in our group began to weaken. Among the whites and Indians over forty persons died from starvation. I owe it to my horse that I remained alive. He carried me in my extremely weak state. I had to grab hold of the first grass we came across in order to feed and to sustain the horse.

When our leader saw this misery and began to fear the death of his followers and even more when he realized his error in taking the direction in which we were now headed, he called upon Heaven; and it was the first time that I witnessed his remembrance of God. He promised and said some novenas to St. Anthony so that we might come across some Indians who, once subdued, would be able to furnish us food to satisfy the hunger from which we were dying. After two weeks of considerable hardship, we found a rough path in those plains. We followed it for nine days, finding along it some huts made of poles and branches with some shoots of corn just beginning to grow. At the end of nine days, we arrived at some mountains whose watershed gave rise to streams flowing northward. Sending ahead four Indians to hunt out the natives, we followed behind three days later. We were only sixteen with our leader as we had left the rest of the expedition and equipment behind with the sick.

On the night of the third day, we caught sight of the huts and fires of the Indians. We hid in the woods in order to await dawn, but their dogs, of which they had many and excellent ones, sniffed us out so that when we approached they received us with their bows and arrows.

On the order of our captain, we did not fire a single shot. It turned out that nearly all of the Indians fled from us. One of them attacked the nephew of the leader with much courage. Grabbing the bridle of his horse with one hand, he tore his gun from him with the other hand and took from his belt his sword with which he struck him on the shoulder and on the left arm and then fled carrying the weapons with him. Embarrassed by the Tapuya, the Paulista chased him without any more results than retrieving the gun the Tapuya took from him and recovering his sword.

At that same moment, another Tapuya in one of the hut doors slightly wounded Francisco Carvalho de Lordelo in the chest with an arrow. Another rushed up and hit him on the head with a club and, as he fell, still another Tapuya struck him with a club, and they left him for dead.

It is amazing that throughout all this conflict not one person did anything except our leader, who rushed around shouting and ordering us to fire only into the air in order not to terrorize the Indians.

It was God's will to give us the huts under a rain of arrows and clubs.

Fleeing into the woods, the Tapuyas always kept us within their sight. So much so that when we made efforts to bury Carvalho, persuaded that he was dead, they attempted, in two attacks, to seize him in order to eat him, and seeing themselves beaten back, they asked us by signs, since their language was different from the general Indian tongue, to give them at least half of the body to eat. Attending to the body of Francisco de Carvalho we found his mouth, nose, and wounds full of bugs, but finding that his heart still beat and that he gave other signs of life we put him into a hut and tended his wounds with urine and smoke and we bled him with the point of a knife for lack of a better surgeon's lancet. He responded so well to the cure that by night Carvalho was himself again. He opened his eyes but he could not speak until the following day. We fed him as best we could on porridge and some potatoes we found in the huts.

During all this time, the Indians did not leave us. They harassed those whom we sent to get some potatoes from the twenty-five large and excellent potato fields. They killed one of them as well as a horse. When our captain learned of this, he made one of the huts into a fortress. He ordered all the corn that could be found to be collected and stored in a corn crib over which he put guards, as he also did over the seven Indians whom we captured. He ordered iron chains put on all of them except one lame Indian, also a captive, to whom he later gave freedom. From his hut, Fearless ordered an expedition to set out in search of the sick and the rest of the baggage.

By then the Indians had become more pacific, following us and serving us without their bows and arrows, and they greatly admired our weapons. They offered us their clubs. One of those days they brought us sixteen young Indian maidens, light of skin and well shaped, as a sign of friendship. Against the wishes of the soldiers, the captain refused to accept them, and it was I who did the most to try to persuade him to accept them. I pointed out to him that in consideration that we were few in number, weak, and starved and that the

Indians were many, we ought not to offend them. We could use these maidens along with the Indians we had captured as a means of asking these tribes not only to have peace but to persuade them to give us some guide who could point out the right direction to Goiás. None of these arguments moved Fearless, who wanted to control all the Indians himself, the same motive which kept him from dividing up the shares. The Indians became suspicious and disappeared at once on the following day. We were afraid that these or other Indians would attack the huts containing the baggage and the sick in order to eat them up, and the Indians who were with us affirmed that that is just what they would do. Desperate at the absence of the Indians, the captain set the lame Indian free, giving him some knives, trinkets, and other gifts in order to persuade the others to return, but the lame one left and we never saw him again.

These Indians are known as the Quirixá. They live in villages; they use the bow, arrow, and war club. They are light skinned and well built; they go around completely naked, the men as well as the women. They have nineteen huts, completely round, quite high and covered with palm branches, with some openings near the ground instead of doors. In each of these twenty or thirty families live together. The beds are nets made of palm fiber which serves both as mattress and cover. They numbered about 600 souls. This entire village was situated next to a large stream that furnished many good fish. On the second day of our march in search of them, we came upon a large stream in which there were many fish. There was palm cabbage and the hunting was good, which was a great help to us. In the village we found corn, potatoes, macaws, and some parakeets which served both to feed and to amuse us. They also had a plentiful supply of gourds and pots and a tremendous number of dogs, which they killed when they fled, and they left everything behind so that they might not be heard by our forces, which went out to spy on them, as we discovered later in the bandeiras.

We stayed here three months, during which time the captain never once gave us any corn, reserving it all for himself and for his retinue and excusing his tyranny by telling us it was necessary to save it for the expeditions that had to be sent out, but even though two were ordered out he did not give them very much corn. However, his horses and his retinue never lacked this nor flour. I had the good luck of receiving seventeen ears of corn, and I got some more corn thanks to the effort and risk of harvesting it in the fields left behind by the fleeing Indians. The rest of them did the same thing including even the religious because if they wanted some they had to harvest it and carry it with their own hands, always escorted by others for fear of the Indians. Before we left, four of the Indians held by our leader fled and they were never seen again.

During our delay in this village, the men realized that the captain, by failing to make the division of the Indian shares so many times promised, bore the blame for the loss of the Indians, and they mutinied; two bastards and one Mameluco with some Paulistas wanted to take his life and to make his brother, Simão Bueno, the leader because he was considered better and more genial. I knew of their plans, and, although Fearless deserved no consideration, I did everything possible to dissuade them from their attempt by insinuating how much they owed to João Leite. Once the bastards and their followers had been dissuaded, we continued on our way by following the bank of the stream near the settlement or village until we came to a river which we also followed on the north bank in search of new Indians who could point out to us the way to Goiás. On this march we spent seventy-six days, two of them without finding any water so that when we did arrive at the bank of a river the joy among us was such that we took heart again and even the horses were so pleased to see water that we could not get them out of it no matter how many slaps we gave them. We stayed there twelve or fifteen days waiting for João Leite, who had remained behind in search of Indians, but he did not arrive.

At this place, having heard it said to the captain that we were near Maranhão, I decided to leave the expedition to move downstream in search of populated territory, in order not to perish from hunger and thirst in the middle of those forests. Three companions, José Alves, Francisco de Carvalho, his brother, Manoel de Oliveira, a Paulista, and João de Matta, a youngster from Bahia, accompanied me. José Alves, with a male and female Indian, his brother with one Indian, I with three and a mulatto were the only ones to escape from the expedition of Fearless. I had begun with six Indians and the mulatto, Alves with five, and his brother with three. The captain did not want the two brothers to leave with me without first paying a debt of forty-six *milreis,* which they owed to João Leite, who by this time had arrived with Brother Antônio. I paid for them because I saw no other solution. However, when João Leite saw that I was going to depart, he insisted, along with Brother Antônio (as much as he could), that we should not abandon them, but the insolence of Fearless, who publicly stated that he ought to hang all the Emboabas, forced me to go against the wishes of João Leite and Brother Antônio. It was certain that Fearless had given orders to one of his Tapuyas to kill Alves for some very insignificant reason and worse was the fact that when Fearless learned I was to leave him he took one of my Indians named Pascoal, a clever guide in the forest, and made him stay with him. When I noticed his absence, I returned to the captain, about half a league behind, and petitioned him to restore the Indian to me. He answered that the Indian was not in his power and that he knew nothing about him. I then went to Brother Antônio asking him that if he could get hold of the Indian to do so and to sell him and send the proceeds of the sale to my wife, Leonarda Peixoto, in the city of Braga. João Leite learned of this business, and being displeased with the action of his father-in-law, offered me, in place of my Indian, a boy named Estevão Mascaste Francez whom I immediately accepted because we needed more people to paddle the canoes. The captain spoke out saying that since we had gone and left him we would die in those rivers and forests and it would be better to kill us than to let us perish in those waters. I do not doubt that he wanted to inherit our Indians as he had done with those of our other companions.

We made two canoes, and I gave my horse to Brother Luiz, as his had died, so that he would say masses for me to Our Lady of Safe Journeys. We headed downstream where there was plenty of fish as well as good hunting. We spent a week's good journey and came upon the bar of another river which flowed in from the right hand, from Portuguese territory, every bit as large as the one on which we were paddling. We passed that bar and after four more days we caught sight of another bar of a smaller river that came from the right side also. Always seeking the north, which was the direction of our river, in another fifteen or twenty days we came upon a larger river that came from the left side in which we found many rafts made of vines, which was evidence that Indians were near. We pushed on, and after five or six days, we caught sight of some stone reefs and not a few rapids, which we passed near the right bank steering the canoes among the rocks but not with such caution that one did not avoid striking against a rock, and the canoe broke in two in the middle, and we lost two baskets with clothes, gold, silver, pans, guns, maps, hooks, cord, and other essential articles necessary for the back country. Among these, understandably, sank a package of lead weighing about sixty pounds, while another package of about the same weight was saved, as well as a small barrel of powder that came bobbing to the surface. We were able to rescue three of the eight guns we brought but all the rest was lost.

This danger past, we went in the other canoe to investigate the left bank below the rapids where the river made a backwash, with an excellent beach. On it we killed two wild pigs which served us as provisions for the trip, and we made another new canoe with three axes and two adzes, which we also had saved, our hands shedding blood because of the very hard wood we used. We spent days working on it, shaded by the trees of that forest, and since we lost the hooks and lines we were unable to fish and we made use of the palm cabbage of the Acrocomia palms, which after skinning and cutting into small pieces, we dried on the fire. After it was dry, we beat it on a stone, and we ate it in a mush using as a pan or pot a small alloy basin which we also had saved. The canoe finished, we continued our course and after three days we ran into a fallen tree along the edge of the river. We beached the canoes to search for some monkeys to eat to satisfy our great hunger, when we discovered the settlement of some Indians little more than one or two gunshots away. The settlement was large and had more than thirty or forty round huts. Having sighted this, we returned at once to embark; we fled with everyone paddling to escape being discovered by them. We went about four or five leagues downstream before stopping to sleep, constructing shelters in the forests on the left side where we found some palm cabbage. So great was the persecution of the bats that night that we slept little and it was very troublesome to free ourselves from them. By now we were naked and the minute we closed our eyes they bit into us to draw blood so that we awoke covered with blood, which caused us to leave that camp site much earlier than we normally would have.

From here we paddled downstream to where we came across a marmalade box genip whose fruit sustained us for two days. After we finished that fruit, our hunger was so great that we ate the seeds. But these affected us in such an adverse way that we thought ourselves dead and, using some small sticks, we aided nature in evicting the poison. We delayed at this point four or five days which we spent in search of some game to eat, and in order to get some fish we made a fine fishhook from the crossguard of a sword hilt, which we cut with the adze and sharpened with a stone. Using as a line a little wire, we pulled out quite a few fish. The fish were large, plentiful, and excellent and as abundant as in the sea. Here we also killed many saki monkeys, and roasted they served us as a new supply of food for the journey. We moved on downstream, and after some days the other canoe broke against a rock at the edge of a rushing current. Here we lost everything and since I did not know how to swim, I grabbed hold of the broken canoe and then taking firm hold on a vine I pulled myself up onto a rock reef. Something worse happened to one of my Indians who was pulled along by the rapids for more than two or three gunshots, and after we thought him to be dead, we found him seated on a large rock formation, at least a quarter of a league in length, which was in the middle of the river. Here we also lost our precious fishhook which a large and beautiful fish robbed from us and so we remained only with palm cabbage and the marmalade box genip— and these only when we could find them.

At this stop we repaired the canoe, and continuing downstream for two weeks, we were forced each night to sleep stretched out on the sands of the many islands in the river, also fearful of the innumerable Indians. What is worse, we could not fire a single shot to kill something to satisfy our hunger, which was not little. Here we saw various bars of other small rivers that from one or the other side flowed into the river on which we traveled. After passing these, we discovered, some leagues farther on, the bar of a great river which flowed from the right side. We slept that night between two bars. Leaving the following morning, we followed the shore of the river on the right side. The river here had an extraordinary width. We came upon a grove of babaçú palms and three Indians near the beach. One of my companions grabbed his gun, fired at one of them and wounded him. He also wounded the other Indians, who gave such screams and made such a horrible racket that it seemed to us as if Hell itself had opened up at that spot. We sought to avoid an attack, so we immediately crossed the river, fleeing while it was still possible. Here we feared to be lost again because the waves and tides were such, on crossing the current, that we very much feared they would submerge us. We arrived at an island very tired out and nearly dead. We pulled the canoes up on the sand at one point and then went to hide ourselves elsewhere so that if the Indians came looking for us they would not see us.

That danger over, we spent two days traveling without any sustenance other than the small coconuts and some palm cabbage which the palm trees provided us. Then we faced a new danger. We crashed against a rock reef in the middle of the river. The canoe in which I rode seemed lost because as it came off the rocks it was sucked into a whirlpool where, after seventeen or eighteen turns which the force of the water gave it, it spun free. The other had better luck and was thrown up against the shore. But everything came out all right. We slept that night on the shore of the same river next to a forest, very hungry and under a heavy rain that lasted all night. After two days of travel we killed a tapir that was so weak that it waited for the shot which killed it, and we ate it badly roasted. That night we found the trail of whites, which of course filled us with new courage. We saw a river, entering on the left side. Afterwards we learned it was the Araguaia because we were navigating the Tocantins. We followed the path because it ran along the edge of the river and from there we floated for three days among eight islands and we were perplexed because we could not locate the channel that we should follow. We searched for land, and we wanted to beach our canoes on some rocks near it but we could not because the water was so shallow.

We spent four days there searching for some palm cabbage or game, which was scarce, and, as our hunger increased, I sent my mulatto out to kill something to eat. He returned empty handed but with the certainty of having found a real path belonging to a white. I grabbed my gun and, nude as I was, I followed that path accompanied only by the Paulista, and less than four leagues away we caught sight of a recently constructed mission of the Reverend Fathers of the Jesuit Company. Seeing us naked and with arms, one of the fathers immediately fled and spread the news that the Manas Indians were there. These also use firearms which they obtain by trading with the Dutch, and they are our enemies. The officer in charge, who was stationed among the fathers, came running with all his men, armed and beating on boxes. Also, the mission Indians came hurrying with their bows and arrows. We threw our weapons on the ground and clapped our hands as a sign of peace. The Reverend Father Marcos Coelho, the superior of the mission, came to speak with us at once; and seeing that we were Portuguese, he took us with him, with extraordinary happiness and love; and when he heard us recount what we had endured, he could not hold back his tears. As soon as he learned that we had more companions, he ordered some of his Indians to go look for them in one of the canoes. When they arrived, we were received with three joyous clangs, caused by striking a piece of iron with a stone, because the small chapel had no other bell.

In this first and affectionate lodging, we began to satisfy our hunger. There was no lack of beans and fish, and as everything was seasoned, our stomachs did not stop reacting to it for a long time. This pleasantness lasted only two weeks because at the end of that time the officer in charge, Domingos Portella de Mello, sent us on to Pará, a journey of twenty days. When we arrived at Pará, Governor João da Maia de Gama learned of it, and he came down to the port to see us. Hearing us tell about the tragic events of the trip, he would not believe us. He intended to arrest us until we could prove whether or not the Indians that we brought with us were ours or were fugitives from the same expedition from which we had deserted. I answered him that I had catechized the Indians and that, if catechized they confessed they were not ours, he could punish us; and notwithstanding the misery in which he saw us because we were all naked with our skin clinging to our bones, he left us to stay on the same beach and canoe port without resolving anything and with no more sustenance and shelter than the chips of wood and tree bark of the royal boatyard could give us.

However, immediately the following morning, private citizens of the town, the Reverend Canon João de Mello and others, made up for the unkind behavior of their Governor by coming to find us on the beach of the boatyard. Taking pity upon the miserable condition in which they found us, they took us to their homes. I went to the home of the Reverend Canon João de Mello; José Alves went to the home of Manoel de Góes with his brother; Manoel d'Oliveira went with João de Souza, a native of Basto, and João da Matta went with João de Silva, a native of Guimarães. After some months in Pará I fell ill of a fever that threatened to take my life, and my condition was so badly degenerated by malaria that I was anointed. I remained sick for eight months and during that time two of my slaves died, one of bubo and the mulatto of a poison that a Tapuya Indian gave him. Thus I embarked for Maranhão with only two. Of these I still keep one because it was necessary to sell one in order to buy two horses to carry me to

Minas Gerais. I spent, on the road, just under ten months, and from the time we left the great Fearless until God brought us to Pará, four months and eleven days.

I recall that before we arrived at the whirlpool, when we fled from the Indians about whom I spoke above, because the river was so wide and we were nearly dead of exhaustion, we tied the two canoes together and let them drift. Everyone slept except me. Fearful and cautious, I kept vigil all night, and it paid off because, hearing a roar farther ahead in the same river, I woke up the men shouting that we were nearing a waterfall and for that reason we put in at an island. As soon as it was dawn, we saw the danger we escaped at night, because the waterfall was horrible and so high that it measured 500 palms and it fell among large rocks that made it even more formidable and with so many waves, mist, and splashing that it appeared like an inferno. We passed by it on the rocks and pushed the canoes through the channel. They came out below the falls, full of water and with holes. We took them from the water and mended them as best we could. We continued on our way. These are, Reverend Sir, the works, miseries, and the great advantages that I got out of the new mines of Goiás, etc.

❧ 13 ❦

Entry of a Viceroy into Lima

Jorge Juan and Antonio de Ulloa

In the Spanish colonies the viceroy was the personal representative of the king and enjoyed a handsome salary and the trappings of royalty as well as extensive, although not unlimited, administrative and military powers. This reading describes the entry of a new viceroy into Lima in the eighteenth century, an event which was the occasion for the ceremony and display of pomp that were so marked a feature of urban life in the Spanish colonies. This selection is an excerpt from A Voyage to South America *by Jorge Juan (1713–1773) and Antonio de Ulloa (1716–1795), members of the French scientific expedition to Quito (1735–1744), which had as its purpose the measurement of an arc of the meridian at the equator.*

On the landing of the viceroy at Paita, two hundred and four leagues from Lima, he sends a person of great distinction, generally some officer of his retinue, to Lima, with the character of an ambassador; and, by a memoir, informs his predecessor of his arrival, in conformity to his majesty's orders, who had been pleased to confer on him the government of that kingdom. On this ambassador's arrival at Lima, the late viceroy sends a messenger to compliment him on his safe arrival; and on dismissing the ambassador, presents him with some jewel of great value, and a jurisdiction or two which happen at that time to be vacant, together with an indulgence of officiating by deputy, if most agreeable to him. The corregidor of Piura receives the new viceroy at Paita, and provides litters, mules, and every other necessary for the viceroy and his retinue, as far as the next jurisdiction. He also orders booths to be built at the halting-places in the deserts; attends him in person, and defrays all the expences, till relieved by the next corregidor. Being at length arrived at Lima, he proceeds, as it were incognito, through the city to Callao, about two leagues and a half distant. In this place he is received and acknowledged by one of the

From Jorge Juan and Antonio de Ulloa, *A Voyage to South America*, the John Adams Translation (New York: Knopf, 1964), pp. 187–193. Reprinted by permission of Alfred A. Knopf, Inc. Footnotes deleted. Italicized bracketed note in text is by Helen Delpar.

ordinary alcaldes of Lima, appointed for that purpose, and also by the military officers. He is lodged in the viceroy's palace, which on this occasion is adorned with astonishing magnificence. The next day, all the courts, secular and ecclesiastical, wait on him from Lima, and he receives them under a canopy in the following order. The audiencia, the chamber of accounts, the cathedral chapter, the magistracy, the consulado, the inquisition, the tribunal de Cruzada, the superiors of the religious orders, the colleges, and other persons of eminence. On this day the judges attend the viceroy to an entertainment given by the alcalde; and all persons of note take a pride in doing the like to his attendants. At night there is a play, to which the ladies are admitted veiled, and in their usual dress; to see the new viceroy.

The second day after his arrival at Callao, he goes in a coach provided for him by the city, to the chapel de la Legua, so called from its being about half-way between Callao and Lima, where he is met by the late viceroy, and both alighting from their coaches, the latter delivers to him a truncheon as the ensign of the government of the kingdom. After this, and the usual compliments, they separate.

If the new viceroy intends to make his public entry into Lima in a few days, he returns to Callao, where he stays till the day appointed; but as a longer space is generally allowed for the many preparatives necessary to such a ceremony, he continues his journey to Lima, and takes up his residence in his palace, the fitting up of which on this occasion is committed to the junior auditor, and the ordinary alcalde.

On the day of public entry, the streets are cleaned, and hung with tapestry, and magnificent triumphal arches erected at proper distances. At two in the afternoon the viceroy goes privately to the church belonging to the monastery of Montserrat, which is separated by an arch and a gate from the street, where the cavalcade is to begin. As soon as all who are to assist in the procession are assembled, the viceroy and his retinue mount on horses, provided by the city for this ceremony, and the gates being thrown open, the procession begins in the following order:

The militia; the colleges; the university with the professors in their proper habits; the chamber of accompts [*tribunal of accounts—a court for the auditing of public accounts*]; the audiencia on horses with trappings; the magistracy, in crimson velvet robes, lined with brocade of the same colour, and a particular kind of cap on their heads, a dress only used on this occasion. Some members of the corporation who walk on foot, support the canopy over the viceroy; and the two ordinary alcaldes, which are in the same dress, and walk in the procession, act as equerries, holding the bridle of his horse. This part of the ceremony, though prohibited by the laws of the Indians, is still performed in the manner I have described; for the custom being of great antiquity, the magistrates have not thought proper to alter it, that the respect to the viceroy might not suffer any diminution, and no person has yet ventured to be the first in refusing to comply with it.

This procession is of considerable length, the viceroy passing through several streets till he comes to the great square, in which the whole company draw up facing the cathedral, where he alights, and is received by the archbishop and chapter. Te Deum is then sung before the viceroy, and the officers placed in their respective seats; after which he again mounts his horse and proceeds to the palace-gate, where he is received by the audiencia, and conducted to an apartment in which a splendid collation is provided, as are also others for the nobility in the antechambers.

On the morning of the following day, he returns to the cathedral in his coach, with the retinue and pomp usual in solemn festivals, and public ceremonies. He is preceded by the whole troop of horse-guards, the members of the several tribunals in their coaches, and after them the viceroy himself with his family, the company of halberdiers bringing up the rear. On this occasion all the riches and ornaments of the church are displayed; the archbishop celebrates in his pontifical robes the mass of thanksgiving; and the sermon is preached by one of the best orators of the chapter. From hence the viceroy returns to the palace attended by all the nobility, who omit nothing to make a splendid figure on these occasions. In the evening of this, and the two following days, the collations are repeated, with all the plenty and delicacy imaginable. To increase the festivity, all women of credit have free access to the halls, galleries, and gardens of the palace, when they are fond of shewing the dispositions of their genius, either by the vivacity of repartees, or spirited conversations, in which they often silence strangers of very ready wit.

This shew and ceremony is succeeded by bull-feasts at the city's expence, which continue five days; the three first for the viceroy, and the two latter in compliment to the ambassador who brought advice of his arrival, and the great honour conferred on him by the sovereign in the government of this kingdom.

This ambassador, who, as I before observed, is always a person of eminent quality, makes also a public entrance into Lima on horseback on the day of his arrival, and the nobility being informed of his approach, go out to receive and conduct him to the palace, from whence they carry him to the lodgings prepared for him. This ceremony used to be immediately followed by feasts and public diversions; but in order to avoid that inconvenience, just when the city is every where busied in preparing for the reception of the viceroy, they are deferred, and given at one and the same time as above recited.

The bull-feasts are succeeded by that ceremony, in which the university, the colleges, the convents and nunneries acknowledged him as their viceroyal protector. This is also accompanied with great splen-

dour; and valuable prizes are bestowed on those who make the most ingenious compositions in his praise. These ceremonies, which greatly
heighten the magnificence of this city, are so little known in Europe,
that I shall be excused for enlarging on them.

They are begun by the university, and the rector prepares a poetical
contest, adapted to display either the wit or learning of the competitors. After publishing the themes, and the prizes to be given to
those who best handle the subjects they have chosen, he waits on the
viceroy to know when he will be pleased to honour the university with
his presence; and, the time being fixed, every part of the principal court
is adorned with the utmost magnificence. The prizes which are placed
in order distinguish themselves by their richness, while the pillars and
columns are hung with emblematical devices, or pertinent apothegms
on polished shields, surrounded by the most beautiful mouldings.

The reception is in the following order. On the viceroy's entering the
court he is conducted to the rectorial chair, which, on this occasion,
glitters with the magnificence of an Eastern throne. Opposite to it sits
the rector, or, in his absence, one of the most eminent members of that
learned body, who makes a speech, in which he expresses the satisfaction the whole university feels in such a patron. After this the viceroy
returns to his palace, where, the day following, the rector presents him
with a book, containing the poetical contest, bound in velvet, and
plated at the corners with gold, accompanied with some elegant piece
of furniture, whose value is never less than eight hundred or a thousand
crowns.

The principal end of the university in this ceremony being to
ingratiate itself with the viceroy and his family, the rector contrives
that the poetical pieces which gain the prizes, be made in the name of
the principal persons of his family, and accordingly the most distinguished prizes are presented to them; and there being 12 subjects in
the contest, there are three prizes for each, of which the two inferior
fall to those members, whose compositions are most approved of. These
prizes are pieces of plate, valuable both for their weight and work-
manship.

The university is followed by the colleges of St. Philip and St.
Martin, with the same ceremonies, except the poetical contest.

Next follow the religious orders, according to the antiquity of their
foundation in the Indies. These present to the viceroy the best theses
maintained by students at the public acts.

The viceroy is present at them all, and each disputant pays him some
elegant compliment, before he enters on his subject.

The superiors of the nunneries send him their congratulatory compliments, and when he is pleased in return to visit them, they enter-
tain him with a very fine concert of musick, of which the vocal parts
are truly charming: and at his retiring they present him with some of

the chief curiosities which their respective institutes allow to be made by them.

Besides these festivities and ceremonies, which are indeed the most remarkable; there are also others, some of which are annual, in which the riches and liberality of the inhabitants are no less conspicuous. Particularly on new-year's day, at the election of alcaldes, who being afterwards confirmed by the viceroy, appear publickly on horseback the same evening, and ride on each side of him, in very magnificent habits ornamented with jewels, and the furniture of their horses perfectly answerable. This cavalcade is very pompous, being preceded by the two companies of horse-guards, the halberdiers, followed by the members of the tribunals in their coaches, the viceroy's retinue, and the nobility of both sexes.

On twelfth-day in the morning, and the preceding evening, the viceroy rides on horseback through the town, with the royal standard carried in great pomp before him. This is performed in commemoration of the building of the city, which, as we have already observed, was begun on this day; solemn vespers are sung in the cathedral, and a mass celebrated; and the ceremony is concluded with a cavalcade, like that on new-year's day.

The alcaldes chosen for the current year, give public entertainments in their houses, each three nights successively; but that the feasts of one might not interfere with those of another, and occasion resentments, they agree for one to hold his feasts the three days immediately succeeding the election, and the other on twelfth-day and the two following. Thus each has a great number of guests, and the entertainments are more splendid and sumptuous. The other feasts in the course of the year, are not inferior to these either with regard to numbers or expence; at least the number of them must excite a high idea of the wealth and magnificence of Lima.

~§ 14 §~

The Colonial *Audiencia*

John Leddy Phelan

Despite the viceroy's powers and prestige, no institution of government in the Spanish Indies was more important than the audiencia. *Like its peninsular antecedent, the audiencia was essentially a judicial body, but in the New World it performed major administrative functions as well. The recruitment and training of the members of colonial audiencias, especially in the seventeenth century, are discussed here by John Leddy Phelan of the University of Wisconsin. In* The Kingdom of Quito in the Seventeenth Century, *from which this selection is taken, Professor Phelan effectively demonstrates that the imperial system of the Hapsburgs was not as highly centralized or monolithic as is often asserted and that the colonial bureaucracy could and did exhibit considerable flexibility and independence.*

The most important elements of government in the Indies were the smaller territorial units known as audiencias rather than the larger, more prestigious viceroyalties. Like most colonial institutions, the audiencias had a Castilian prototype. Ferdinand and Isabella reorganized the audiencias of Granada and Valladolid as the next-to-highest judicial tribunals in the kingdom of Castile. The jurisdiction of Granada included all the territory south of the Tagus River, and that of Valladolid extended north of the Tagus. In time the audiencias in the New World acquired extensive administrative, political, and military functions that their prototypes in the peninsula never exercised. The latter remained exclusively law courts. There were eleven audiencias overseas: Santo Domingo (1526), Mexico (1527), Panama (1535), Lima (1542), Guatemala (1543), Guadalajara (1548), Santa Fe de Bogotá (1549), Charcas (1559), Quito (1563), Manila (1583), and Chile (1609); Buenos Aires (1661) was suppressed within a few years.

The audiencias were not equal in status or prestige. The audiencias

From John Leddy Phelan, *The Kingdom of Quito in the Seventeenth Century: Bureaucratic Politics in the Spanish Empire* (Madison: University of Wisconsin Press, 1967), pp. 119–141, *passim.* Copyright © 1967 by the Regents of the University of Wisconsin. Reprinted by permission of the publisher and the author. Italicized bracketed notes in text are by Helen Delpar.

in Mexico City and Lima, as the capitals of the two viceroyalties, were the highest in rank. There were two distinct categories among the nonviceregal audiencias. The superior or pretorial audiencias had as their presiding officer a president who was not a lawyer. He exercised supreme military command in his capacity as captain general. Although one of the two viceroys exercised nominal supervision over the superior audiencias, the chief magistrates of the latter enjoyed by right a considerable measure of autonomous military and political authority.

The presidents of the inferior or subordinate audiencias were *letrados,* i.e., lawyers. *De jure* the inferior audiencias were merely judicial tribunals. With time they acquired widespread, *de facto* authority in political, administrative, fiscal, and military matters but only by delegaton from the viceroy. The viceroys exercised a tighter supervision over the inferior audiencias than they did over the superior tribunals. The viceroys also exercised much more patronage in filling local and provincial offices in the inferior audiencias than they did in the superior audiencias. In the viceroyalty of New Spain, which embraced all of Spanish North America north of the isthmus and also included the Philippines, Guadalajara was the only inferior audiencia. In the viceroyalty of Peru, the inferior audiencias were Quito and Charcas, and the superior tribunals were Bogotá, Panama, and Chile.

The juridical ties uniting the overseas settlements to the peninsula were not, strictly speaking, those of colony and mother country. Each audiencia was in law a separate kingdom, united in a personal union with the crowns of Castile and León. Indicative of the sovereign status of the audiencias, those tribunals in their corporate capacity enjoyed the rank, title, and style of Highness. Prior to the election of Charles V as Holy Roman emperor, the kings of Castile were addressed as "Highness" and not "Majesty." All the audiencias in the Indies enjoyed the superior status of supreme courts, *cancillerías,* from whose verdicts appeals were strictly limited. In Spain itself the only cancillerías were those of Valladolid and Granada, the capitals of the ancient kingdoms of Castile and Granada. The Council of the Indies alone exercised jurisdiction over the kingdoms of the New World, to the total exclusion of the other territorial councils. Functional councils such as those of finance, war, and the Inquisition, on the other hand, had competence in all the dominions of the king.

. . .

If the viceroys constituted the political layer of the imperial bureaucracy, the *ministros superiores,* i.e., the presidents, the *oidores,* and the *fiscales,* formed the professional echelon. During the two centuries of Habsburg rule [*1516–1700*], some 1,000 superior magistrates held office in the audiencias. The number of these posts was about ninety-four. More than any other group, these men were the real rulers of the Spanish empire. Serving indefinite terms of office, in contrast to the viceroys whose tenure seldom exceeded five years, they provided the viceroys with day-to-day technical and administrative assistance. In the nonviceregal audiencias, they were the highest agency of political administration. The audiencias performed the complex task of acting as intermediaries between the central authorities in Madrid and the king's vassals in the Indies. Few decisions in the New World came to pass without the heavy imprint of the audiencias.

Among the superior magistrates, there were distinctions of rank and privilege, with the president at the top. Although he possessed a vote equal to that of the oidores, the president, like the viceroy vis-à-vis his own audiencia, exercised considerably more influence than the other oidores. How much more depended on his political skill.

That seniority was highly prized is indicated by the frequency of litigations on this question. Ordinarily seniority was determined from the date the officeholder actually took possession of his office. Hence oidores took great risks, in an age when travel under even the best conditions was hazardous, in order to arrive at their posts a few days before their colleagues. An oidor lost his seniority when transferred from either an inferior or a superior audiencia. One of the advantages of the viceregal audiencias was that oidores transferred from Mexico to Lima retained their seniority. The judges of the audiencias of Granada and Valladolid also enjoyed this privilege.

Disputes about seniority arose from the conviction of many jurists that length of service ought to be determined from the date of appointment by the king if an appointee were performing official business elsewhere which made it necessary for him to postpone his departure for his new post. On occasion the crown followed this procedure. Antonio Rodríquez de San Isidro Manrique, who was appointed oidor in Quito on February 20, 1630, was then serving as visitor general of the audiencia of Bogotá. The King issued a cedula on February 20, 1630, granting him possession of the office in the audiencia of Quito as of the date of his appointment. He did not take actual possession of his new office until January 7, 1636. Another oidor, Lic. Alonso Castillo de Herrera, arrived in Quito without a duly notarized royal cedula. The audiencia would not allow him to take office for over a year, nor could he apply time toward seniority until the proper documents arrived from the peninsula.

This was a hierarchal society in which status and rank in the corporations to which one belonged counted a great deal. The junior oidor often received some of the onerous assignments. The rank of senior oidor was prized, since that magistrate became acting president of the audiencia in the event of the death of the proprietary president. These interim presidencies occurred frequently. They might last as long as two years, until the new appointee arrived from Spain. There are very few cases of the senior oidor's receiving the proprietary appointment.

Because of the greater volume of business, the viceregal audiencias had eight oidores, in contrast to the other tribunals whose usual complement was four or five judges. In Lima and Mexico City a separate inferior court, attached to the audiencia proper, exercised criminal jurisdiction. The four *alcaldes de crimen,* who formed the *sala de crimen,* were subordinate in status to the oidores. In the nonviceregal audiencias criminal jurisdiction was also the responsibility of the oidores.

In Mexico City and Lima there were two fiscales, the junior serving in the sala de crimen and the senior being attached to the audiencia proper. The fiscal was a state attorney. His primary responsibility was to defend the interests of the royal fisc [*treasury*], hence the origin of the title. He also had special duties to defend the Indians and the *real patronato.* In the early decades of the sixteenth century, the junior oidor acted as fiscal, but in time a separate office emerged. Although his salary was the same as that of the oidores, he ranked below the junior oidor. He could not vote in those cases to which he was party as crown attorney, but, in those cases to which he was not, he could vote only to break a tie. The fiscal deliberated but could not vote, *con voz pero sin voto,* in the political and administrative actions of the tribunal.

The machinery for filling audiencia appointments illustrates the quasi-professional character of this layer of the imperial bureaucracy. When a vacancy occurred, the Council of the Indies drew up a consulta, listing three or four candidates. Always brief, these consultas included four types of information. One was the educational background, since a law degree, either a licentiate or a doctorate, was an indispensable qualification for these judicial offices. There were, of course, no competitive examinations as such. The British pioneered this procedure in the mid-nineteenth century for entrance into the Indian Civil Service. Even without competitive examinations, a law degree from a seventeenth-century Spanish university was not an insignificant professional qualification. Furthermore, the council lent much weight to the previous administrative and judicial experience of the candidates. Virtually every person listed on a consulta had held some minor judicial office in the peninsula. Inexperienced and uneducated youths seldom received consideration. The moral character and the family background of the candidates also received some attention in the consultas. The council ranked the candidates in terms of suitability.

The king usually appointed the first name on the list; however, sometimes he chose the third or fourth name. An aspiring bureaucrat who enjoyed the support of a powerful nobleman might use that influence with those around the king. Although an element of favoritism entered into the selection of magistrates, it should not be forgotten that virtually all the names presented to the king possessed solid professional qualifications. Thus recruitment on the oidor level was based on a mixture of modern professional qualifications with overtones of medieval patrimony, by which officeholders were members of the king's household and hence office was viewed as an expression of royal favor and royal largesse. Yet the principles of permanence in the service and promotion on the basis of merit and experience were deeply embedded in the Spanish political theory of the seventeenth century. This theory profoundly influenced practice.

.   .   .

There was no set term for the offices of president and oidor. Attempts were made to establish limits, but they were never enforced. On the political level and on the provincial layer also, there were set terms. Viceroys and corregidores both served for five years. The Council of the Indies opposed a proposal of Olivares to restrict the term of professional magistrates to five years. Juan de Solórzano y Pereira [*seventeenth-century Spanish jurist and official*] argued that the term of office should be at the pleasure of the prince. He was willing that the less professional presidents of the superior audiencias, who did not need a law degree, should serve for fixed terms of eight years. Since the oidores acquired their offices on the basis of their academic studies and their magisterial service, in his opinion they should not be deprived of their posts unless they were guilty of proven malfeasance. He feared that a time limit would make these posts less desirable and hence make it more difficult to recruit men of ability.

In practice there was considerable rotation on the audiencia level. The axiom that no magistrate should have personal or economic ties in his district encouraged this trend. The oidores themselves were restless. They often pleaded for a change of assignment. The presidents of Quito in the seventeenth century served for an average period of five years. The term of Dr. [*Antonio de*] Morga [*president of the audiencia of Quito from 1615 to 1636*], spanning twenty-one years, was an exception that resulted in some measure from the duration of the *visita general* [*of the audiencia of Quito begun in 1624*]. Of the nineteen oidores serving between 1598 and 1636, eight served for more than ten years, six between five and ten years, and the remaining five for periods of less than five years. Of the three fiscales during the same period, one served for nine years, another for eleven years, and Lic. Melchor Suárez de Poago held office for a record-breaking twenty-eight years.

The Council of the Indies consciously sought to encourage professionalization by promoting magistrates from lesser to higher audiencias. Thus they tried to provide a system of incentives which would motivate officials to perform their duties effectively and conscientiously. Positions in the inferior audiencias, such as Guadalajara, Quito, and Charcas, were considered less prestigious than those in the superior audiencias. To be sure, some of the superior audiencias were regarded as undesirable, for example, the audiencias of Manila, Panama, Chile, and Santo Domingo. Manila and Panama were undesirable for their hot and humid climates, Chile for its isolation, and Santo Domingo for its lack of importance. Hence many oidores considered it a promotion to be transferred from one of those superior audiencias to tribunals such as Quito or Charcas where the climate was thought to be more healthy or agreeable. Although Quito enjoyed the reputation of a climate of eternal spring, most magistrates subsequently complained about the hardships of the altitude. Among the bishops there was also an informal system of promotion in which the relative prestige of an episcopal see was equivalent to that of the corresponding audiencia.

In the hierarchy of promotions, every oidor yearned for an appointment to one of the viceregal audiencias, with Lima outranking Mexico. Not only were the climates in both capitals moderately healthy, but also both cities possessed some of the creature comforts and a way of life reminiscent of what they had known in the peninsula. In fact, the overwhelming majority of oidores in both Lima and Mexico City had seen previous service in one of the other audiencias in the Indies.

Most professional magistrates nostalgically yearned to return to Spain itself. Few attained the goal, but it did exist as the highest promotion in the service. Between 1523 and 1600, only one oidor from an American audiencia received an appointment to the Council of the Indies. None was promoted from the Indies for the period between 1629 and 1700. Yet during the years from 1600 to 1629 six oidores from the New World received seats in the Council of the Indies. The most illustrious of them was, of course, Juan de Solórzano.

. . .

The preponderance of the oidores were Spaniards from the peninsula and not Spaniards born in the Indies, i.e., creoles. Discrimination against the creoles had no basis in law. The crown repeatedly urged that properly qualified Spaniards from the Indies be given consideration. Juan de Solórzano urged recruitment of the bench from the bar, that is, from among the lawyers, many of them creoles, who were licensed to practice before the audiencias. Encomenderos and the descendants of the conquerors and the first settlers constituted a social grouping, *los beneméritos de las Indias,* who, according to repeated royal cedulas, should be given consideration for appointment to offices in conformity with their abilities and qualifications.

The crown and the council in practice gave preference to Spanish-born lawyers. They were closer to the seat of power. Few creoles could enlist the patronage of powerful nobles or bureaucrats at Court, since the former had no personal ties with the latter. Another factor inhibiting creoles from becoming oidores was the principle that no judge could own property in the kingdom where he exercised jurisdiction.

Hence any would-be creole oidor had to be prepared to leave the American kingdom where he was born and reared in order to undertake the peripatetic existence normal to such magistrates. A creole of means faced with obvious distaste the prospect of leaving his and his wife's property in the hands of an administrator. If he did not have some property, the chances were that he lacked the minimum social and educational qualifications for consideration as a candidate.

The *de facto* exclusion of the creoles from the ranks of the professional magistracy prevented the development of a tradition in which several generations of a family would enjoy bureaucratic careers in the New World. The children and the grandchildren of oidores joined the ranks of the creoles. Thus the oidores never became a hereditary *noblesse de la robe* like that which developed under the ancien régime in France. It is possible that such a development did occur in the Spanish peninsula, but further study needs to be done. In British India, on the other hand, the children of Indian civil servants received their education in England. Admission into the service was by competitive examination. Consequently there developed a tradition, especially among some Scottish families, in which several generations served in the Indian Civil Service.

The social origins of the professional bureaucracy were middle-sector, in contrast to the political bureaucrats on the viceregal level, who were of the landed and titled aristocracy. The oidores came from the urban middle groups or the country gentry for whom a university education was not merely an ornament, as it was for the nobility, but a necessary prerequisite to earn their kind of living. While some of them may have inherited modest means from their parents or their wives, as a group they were not independently wealthy. Many of them were not destitute, however. The first wife of Dr. Morga, for example, brought him a dowry of 10,000 ducats. Dr. Morga's father, don Pedro de Morga, was one of the leading bankers in Seville until the failure of his bank during the second royal bankruptcy of 1576. Hence Dr. Morga inherited nothing from his father. In any case, few bureaucrats had enough property in the peninsula to make it worth their while to stay there. Accordingly they depended for their livelihood in large measure on the salaries they earned.

These men were not middle class in the modern sense of belonging to a class with self-identity and aspirations autonomous from those of other classes. Rather they lived in the orbit and by the favors of the monarchical and aristocratic society whose cornerstones were institutionalized inequality and hereditary privilege. It was, after all, a combination of aristocratic patronage, academic training, and previous experience which enabled them to acquire entrance into and promotions inside the professional bureaucracy in the Indies.

❧ 15 ❧

Inquisitorial Inspection of Books

————◆❖◆————

Irving A. Leonard

*The task of preserving political and religious orthodoxy in Spanish
America was entrusted by the crown to the Holy Office of the Inquisition, which was established in Lima in 1570 and in Mexico City in
1571. In its efforts to extirpate heresy, the Inquisition was empowered
to exercise close supervision over books imported into the colonies.
However, in this reading, Irving A. Leonard, Professor Emeritus of the
University of Michigan, indicates that the vigilance of the Inquisition
was perfunctory and ineffectual. The implication of Professor Leonard's
conclusions in this and other writings is that the colonies did enjoy
considerable intellectual freedom despite the restrictions of Church
and state. The degree to which writings deemed subversive by the
authorities were able to enter the colonies in the eighteenth century is
of special significance in determining the role of the Enlightenment in
the independence movements of the early nineteenth century.*

The profound conviction of both the Crown and the Church that
the propagation of the Catholic faith in the newly acquired realms
must be safeguarded at all costs from the schismatic dissensions of contemporary Europe stimulated their unremitting, if somewhat unsuccessful, efforts to prevent the circulation of heretical books in the Indies.
These rulers made earnest attempts not only to choke off the exportation of such literature from Spain itself but also to exclude from
entrance to the ports of debarkation any works of subversive character
which might evade the vigilance of the officials in the homeland. The
preventive measure adopted for the American side of the Atlantic
service was a *visita,* or customs inspection, of all incoming ships. A
decree of 1556 required the treasury officers at these terminal points to
exercise extreme care in checking the cargoes of arriving vessels with

From Irving A. Leonard, *Books of the Brave: Being an Account of Books and
Men in the Spanish Conquest and Settlement of the Sixteenth-Century New
World* (Cambridge, Mass.: Harvard University Press, 1949), pp. 166–182, *passim.*
Reprinted by permission of the author. This article appears as reprinted in
Fredrick B. Pike (ed.), *The Conflict Between Church and State in Latin America*
(New York: Knopf, 1964), pp. 65–77.

the sealed registers they brought in order to note the possible inclusion of books on the Inquisition *Index*; any listed works discovered must be turned over promptly to the archbishops or their duly appointed representatives. The lax enforcement of this command—the fate of so many in the sixteenth century and later—soon obliged the authorities to consider the establishment of a special agency to perform this and other functions, since the menace of heresy was growing alarmingly. Thus it was decided to install in the New World itself branches of the secular arm of the Church, known as the Holy Office of the Inquisition, to supervise and coordinate all activities designed to protect the purity and integrity of the one True Faith.

Until 1570 the inquisitorial powers in the colonies rested mainly in the hands of the archbishops or their appointed subordinates. Prior to this date there was some censorial activity but it was, on the whole, sporadic and unsystematic. The Lutheran revolt in Europe was spreading even as the *conquistadores* were overrunning the New World and as the pioneer missionaries were attempting the spiritual conquest of its aboriginal inhabitants. The long-drawn-out sessions of the historic Council of Trent, which met intermittently from 1545 to 1563, were dominated by the ultra-conservative elements of the Church, and hence they failed to arrive at any formulae of reconciliation with the dissident Protestants. The great schism widened as official Spanish Catholicism clung fanatically to a rigid orthodoxy which inevitably placed it on the defensive. In an effort to purify itself within its doctrinal frame and to exclude what were regarded as pernicious influences, it resorted to practices of censorship which, on the whole, proved more potent for evil than for good. In the last of its long sessions the Council of Trent drew up a series of ten rules "as a guide and instruction for all ecclesiastics or other authorities who might thereafter be charged with the duty of literary censorship." These laws applied to theological and religious works almost exclusively, though the seventh commandment dealing with "books professedly treating of lascivious or obscene subjects, or narrating, or teaching these" clearly opened the door to banning secular literature of a lighter character.

The increasing dread of Protestantism and the fear of heretical books steadily invading the overseas dominions of Spain spurred a prompt compliance with the directives of both secular and ecclesiastical councils, but the machinery of enforcement was invariably defective. To remedy the situation inquisitional tribunals similar to those existing in Spain were authorized for the colonies, and they began to operate in Lima and Mexico City on January 29, 1570, and on November 4, 1571, respectively. It was anticipated that these local branches would be more efficient in hunting down and eradicating growing evils. Books immediately claimed the special attention of the transplanted Inquisition, but only those works, it should be emphasized, which were regarded as so inimical to the faith or to good morals that they gained a place on the official *Index*. The bishops in the viceroyalties had had some discretion in discharging their duties of this sort and they were occasionally arbitrary, but their interference with the circulation of books other than those officially proscribed by the home office of the Inquisition in Spain was infrequent. Indeed, these high dignitaries showed a surprising indifference to the literature of recreation, considering the tirades directed against it during the sixteenth century from their own pulpits and the fact that these *"libros profanos"* were specifically and repeatedly prohibited in the Spanish Indies by secular decrees of the Crown.

On January 3, 1570, Dr. Pedro Moya de Contreras, then serving as Inquisitor of Murcia in the Peninsula, was notified of his designation as presiding executive of the projected Tribunal at Mexico City. Though he started for the New World late that year, delays of one sort or another, including shipwreck off the coast of Cuba, prevented him from setting up this new branch of the Holy Office until near the end of 1571. One of his first official acts was to publish a long edict which stipulated, among other matters, that booksellers and private persons receiving shipments of printed material from Spain must present invoices or lists for the scrutiny of the Inquisition before claiming delivery. After this checking, the owners would receive instructions on the disposition they could make of their books.

The bureaucratic meddling with individual enterprise, theretofore relatively unrestricted, promptly drew the fire of a small group of bookdealers of Mexico City. The commissioner of the Inquisition had stopped delivery of a shipment of breviaries and missals, and the aggrieved merchants protested that this act was an obvious injustice and amounted to a virtual confiscation of their property. This incident was symptomatic of the conflicts and disagreements which disturbed the relations of the representatives of the State, the Holy Office, and the commercial elements throughout the colonial period, and these irritations largely nullified the carefully devised efforts of authorities, ecclesiastical and secular alike, to control contraband and the black-market operations of the period. The first point of contact where friction developed was at the port of entry on the occasion of the customs inspection, which was aggravated by the separate inquisitorial *visita*.

Earlier royal decrees had required specially appointed treasury officials to inspect for the Crown all incoming ships, whether single or in fleets, at the terminal ports of the Indies. No goods or persons could go ashore until this indispensable formality was completed. The inspectors must uncover by careful search any unregistered goods and detect any unlicensed persons seeking entry into the colonies. Carelessness, indifference and, probably as often, flagrant corruption characterized the execution of these commands. The task of opening all the containers in the cargoes, checking their contents, and closing them again was too laborious and time-consuming, and it delayed far too long the disembarkation of sea-weary travelers. The crews and officers naturally resented such excessive exertions at the end of a tiring voyage, and the merchants were disgruntled by the resulting disarrangement of their wares. And, in the end, all this bother did not stop petty thieving, fraud, or contraband. Soon the more convenient method was instituted of summoning sailors, officers, and passengers on deck and demanding from them an oral statement under oath. This procedure saved a vast amount of trouble, but lent itself even more effectively to evasion and deceit; swearing to the truth of an allegation quickly became mechanical and in no way prevented private deals by faithless officials with merchants and peddlers on the incoming vessels. With such malpractices general, contraband trade flourished even before the Conquistador had finished his work in the New World, and these abuses largely nullified the carefully contrived regulations governing commerce and navigation between Spain and its colonies.

Considering the opportunities for private gain enjoyed by the Crown inspectors and the merchants alike, the evident resentment and hostility of both to the added inquisitorial *visita* are understandable. A parallel inspection for ecclesiastical purposes had various disadvantages. In the first place, it amounted to a division of authority, and the treasury officials were always jealous of their prerogatives, but more important still, it meant a menace to or, at least, a sharing of the illicit traffic they found so remunerative. Consequently, the second and concurrent *visita* intended to ferret out prohibited books and images thus instituted by the newly appointed Inquisitor created a new source of conflict, wrangling, and confusion in the disorder associated with the arrival of the fleet and the period during which the ships remained in port. The effect of this situation is reflected in the frequency with which the Holy Office urged its representatives at Vera Cruz to exercise the utmost tact in their dealings with their fellow inspectors, the treasury officials of the Crown, and to take extreme care in restoring books and other objects examined to the original cases and in such good condition that their owners should have no legitimate cause for complaint. The fear of vexing merchants, clearly evident in these written orders of the Inquisition, indicates that this dread institution did not enjoy the oppressive sway over all elements of colonial society traditionally ascribed to it.

When the General of a fleet put into port his first duty was to notify the customs officers of the Crown stationed there and then stand by until their work was done. Both the secular and the inquisitorial inspectors were cautioned by their respective superiors to be punctual in meeting the fleets and individual vessels so that the debarkation of passengers and freight should be delayed as little as possible—another indication of the healthy respect that the allegedly tyrannical Crown and Church had for the business elements of the colonial society over which these authorities are presumed to have exercised despotic sway. Both of the delegations put out from the shore in small boats provided by the government and soon they clambered up the sides of the anchored ships. Since the books of the Conquistador and his descendants are of primary interest here, only the routine of the inquisitorial *visita* will be described.

Accompanying the deputy of the Holy Office were a notary and an *alguacil,* or constable, or occasionally a fellow official of the Inquisition who bore its emblem of authority. Into the stern cabin or some other these inspectors summoned the shipmaster, the pilot, and one or two passengers, who represented all the rest. In the absence of the latter, since some of the ships conveyed merely freight or slaves, a pair of the more intelligent members of the crew were brought together and each one of this group was constrained to answer eight questions and to swear to speak the truth, under penalty of the severest anathema of the Church.

If nothing worthy of note developed out of this cross-examination, the deputy with his assistant and the notary were to search the stern cabin and others he thought necessary; he should have a few boxes, chests, or bales opened that might possibly conceal banned books or other prohibited articles since it was the "ordinary fashion of heretics" to smuggle printed volumes among legitimate goods. Obedience to this instruction doubtless irked the owners and shippers most, and their vigorous protests moved the Holy Office to instruct the agents to perform their functions with great circumspection, carefully restoring the contents of each inspected case to their original place.

The entire procedure seems ordinarily to have been exceedingly perfunctory, with the questioning a hasty, mechanical mumbling which fulfilled the letter rather more than the spirit of the regulations. Even the directing heads of the Inquisition acknowledged that a full compliance in writing "would be a lengthy and laborious task for those in charge of it" and recommended that the questions and answers be given orally; only in the event that the cross-examination produced evidence of a serious infraction was a detailed record necessary. If there was nothing untoward the scribe made a few notations of a summary character, which included indications of the place of the *visita,* the port from which the ship sailed, the date of arrival, the names of the inspectors, the *maestre,* pilot, passengers or sailors quizzed, and the gist of the information elicited. While these data were jotted down the deputy had a few cases opened and, after this cursory examination, he stated that, so far as the Holy Office was concerned, disembarkation of passengers and freight could proceed at once. The completed report in its short, terse form was then signed by the representative of the Inquisition, the shipmaster, the pilot, and the other witnesses if they were able to write, and finally the whole was countersigned by the notary.

When the inquiry brought unsatisfactory replies or suspicious findings a more extensive document was obligatory. But even where questionable literature was uncovered experience appears to have taught the Holy Office in Mexico City not to place too much reliance on the discretion of its own representatives at Vera Cruz. An edict of 1572 declared that if, on opening cases or boxes, *any* books of sacred writings, philosophy, or related subjects were noticed, the inspectors must promptly close the containers in question without attempting to read or even glance through such printed works. It was then their duty to place the seal of the Holy Office on the shipment and forward it directly to Mexico City for checking at the head office of the Inquisition before the owners could take possession. Even books consigned to other parts of the vast viceroyalty must be routed in the same way.

One other aspect of the Inquisition's instructions to its subordinates at Vera Cruz invites attention. The *visitas* in which they participated not uncommonly degenerated into more or less convivial meetings, with the shipmaster acting as host. Food was liberally dispensed and wine flowed freely. No doubt merchants on the incoming vessels contributed to these festivities for certain ulterior motives of their own. Where the fleet was large the necessity of visiting so many of its units must have been a severe test of the bibulous proclivities of the deputies and their assistants. Under these circumstances bargains and agreements of a private nature affecting the entry of books and other articles of possibly contraband character into the realm were doubtless consummated. Conceivably, the agents of the Holy Office were induced to *hacer la vista gorda,* as the Spaniards so expressively put it; that is, like their fellow inspectors of the Crown, they overlooked certain irregularities in the clearing of cargoes at the port. The stern and repeated admonitions of the chief Inquisitors to their deputies against accepting gratuities, gifts, or presents from anyone on the incoming ships amply confirm the existence of these abuses. Subordinates were expressly forbidden at the time of the *visita* to dicker or attempt to buy anything on shipboard—"not even something to eat"—for themselves or for a third party because, indeed, such an act would be "a bad example and *desedificación.*" Thus it is clear that the purposes of the inquisitorial inspection were often defeated by flagrant flouting of its regulations, and by the connivance of the representatives of the Holy Office itself with arriving passengers or crew.

Relations between the examiners and the examined were sometimes badly strained, however. During the 1585 *visita* the commissioner of the Inquisition had occasion to send for the shipmaster of *La Trinidad.* When the messenger of the dread institution came aboard to apprise its master of his errand, he found that worthy in shirt sleeves and underdrawers engaged in a friendly game of poker, or its equivalent. He was playing for stakes of silk stockings at seven pesos a pair and, as he had a hand or two more to play, this crusty seaman refused to heed the summons at once and growled that he would show up later in the afternoon. Pressed by the troubled messenger to come right away as ordered, the exasperated *maestre* bellowed loudly enough to be heard by everyone in the immediate vicinity, telling the inquisitorial emissary, with particularly lurid epithets, to get out. Such a shocking disregard of the expressed command of so august a corporation as the Holy Office was an indignity not to be tolerated, especially as this sort of thing was becoming distressingly common, and the offending shipmaster soon found himself clapped into jail and obliged to put up a heavy bail to defray the expenses of trial. The shortage of seamen in the port, however, was great and there was a pressing need to prepare the fleet to resume its voyage—facts which possibly explain in part this mariner's independence and insolence. The urgency of the naval situation at the moment was much too severe to spare any member of the crews and, when word of the shipmaster's plight reached the General of the fleet an hour or so later, he hurried to plead personally for the release of the culprit. The high authority and the indispensability of the shipmaster's services provided irresistible pressure, and the deputy of the Holy Office promptly acceded to the General's request. When the matter was reported later to the chief Inquisitor in Mexico City, that official wrote back that the commissioner had done entirely right in jailing the disrespectful skipper; instead of locking him up for only an hour, however, he should have done so for a week!

There were doubtless many similar clashes between the inspectors and the inspected, and numerous occasions when injured vanity, jealous resentment, and tactless acts on both sides caused friction and delay. Officious inquisitors, overconscious of their importance as guardians of the one True Faith, sometimes adopted an imperious manner at which equally individualistic shipmasters and pilots, accustomed to absolute command on their own vessels, did not fail to take umbrage. Well aware, too, of the manifest hypocrisy of these deputies, who were not averse to bribery in one form or another, both the crew and the passengers accorded them scant courtesy. As a consequence, arriving voyagers were sometimes subjected to petty annoyances by these pompous and too meticulous officials who searched their cabins and baggage for banned books and other contraband with excessive zeal. In 1575, for example, the deputy of the Holy Office and his assistants boarded the good ship *La Candelaria* where they found copies of prayer books and other devotional works, *Amadis,* and several other romances of chivalry, a *Life of St. Francis,* and also a *Life of Julius Caesar,* which had diverted some of the passengers during the crossing. The last-mentioned volume was in the possession of a student named San Clement, a somewhat indiscreet youth, apparently. On finding this book among the young man's personal effects the inquisitorial inspector felt called upon to emit a literary judgement on the youthful traveler's reading tastes. Departing from the ritualistic interrogations of the *visita* the official queried the student as to why he did not read something better, such as the life of St. Francis, who was a Christian? Why did he waste his time perusing a volume about Julius Caesar who had gone to hell, anyway, because, you know, that hero of ancient Rome was never baptized? This impertinent intrusion into the young scholar's reading preferences quite naturally irritated him and, not having reached full maturity, he was so injudicious as to engage in a heated argument with the censorious representative of the Inquisition. This unwise reaction to bureaucratic interference resulted in the drawing up of a judicial brief against him, in which this admirer of Julius Caesar was placed in the category of one suspect in the faith. How this rash youth emerged from his embarrassing predicament the existing records do not reveal. But the reiterated admonitions of the executive officers of the Holy Office in Mexico City to their subordinates in Vera Cruz and elsewhere to perform their duties with courtesy and tact indicate that incidents of this sort did not increase the popularity of the *visita,* and that secular complaints from influential sources were so numerous that even the powerful institution of the Inquisition could not ignore them. Such excess of zeal on the part of their employees was likely to be self-defeating, particularly when it operated in conjunction with other factors tending to foster resistance to vexatious restrictions.

Between the obvious unpopularity of the Inquisition's efforts to intervene in the commercial importation of books into the colonies and the prevalence of corruption among its own servitors, it is not surprising that the precautions and measures taken to prevent smuggling were largely ineffectual. Even if, as is so often alleged, the Holy Office had sought to exclude the romances of chivalry and other forms of light fiction—which it clearly did not do—some of these books, doubtless many, would have slipped through the barriers just as forbidden works actually did. The fact that superiors of the Inquisition issued edict after edict and command after command, demanding the utmost care and vigilance in the inspection of incoming vessels, offers convincing evidence that the attempt to suppress truly contraband literature, such as Lutheran tracts and Bibles, frequently failed. The smuggling of heretical works was continuous and even members of the religious communities themselves participated in this illegal traffic.

The choice of colonial book buyers in entertaining literature was as wide as that of their relatives in Spain itself. Depite the long delays caused by the slowness of the means of transportation and by the bureaucratic routines of the House of Trade and the Holy Office, the time lag in obtaining copies of the more recent literary successes of the Peninsula was remarkably short. Even if these agencies, particularly the Inquisition, had sought to keep the fiction works out of the hands of the overseas readers—and, of course, early royal decrees had endeavored to do just this—resourceful bookdealers would doubtless have found means to supply the lucrative demand. That they were often able to do so even with the clearly forbidden religious and theological writings is evident from the need of the Holy Office to make periodic rounds of the city shops in an effort to detect the source of contraband literature that continued to find its way into colonial hands. Now and then bookdealers were obliged to submit inventories of their stock to the authorities of the Inquisition, and now and then one found himself in serious difficulties with this censorious corporation which, in its self-imposed task of protecting the moral and spiritual welfare of the community, took upon itself the functions of municipal police. Its officers even resorted to raids on the bookstores under pressure from Spain or from local sources, but the intervals between these forays were usually long, during which the sale of printed works of all kinds proceeded quietly as a legitimate part of the commercial activity of colonial society. The fiction, poetry, and drama of Spain's great writers stirred the hearts and minds of the Spanish-speaking peoples on both sides of the Atlantic throughout the centuries of imperial glory and national decline.

Eighteenth-Century Commercial Reforms

C. H. Haring

The death of Charles II without issue in 1700 marked the end of Hapsburg rule in Spain and resulted in the accession of Philip V, grandson of Louis XIV of France. During the reigns of the first Bourbon kings, and especially that of Charles III (1759–1788), Spain experienced an economic and intellectual revival, and numerous reforms affecting the administration and trade of the colonies were introduced. The administrative reforms, the most notable of which was the establishment of the intendant system, were designed to rationalize colonial government and to increase royal revenue from the colonies. The commercial reforms, which were aimed primarily at liberalizing trade within the empire in order to curb foreign inroads on the Spanish monopoly, are discussed in this selection by Clarence H. Haring who was Professor of Latin American History at Harvard University for many years.

The black night of Spain's weakness and humiliation under Charles II was to usher in the dawn of recovery under the princes of the House of Bourbon. The speculative ideas of the Enlightenment that came to prevail among philosophers and publicists in eighteenth-century Europe penetrated as well into official circles in Spain, and resulted in important innovations in political administration and in trade. Serious attempts were made to balance the Spanish budget, to suppress the centrifugal forces of regionalism in the peninsula, to revive the navy, and to encourage trade both with Europe and with the provinces overseas. Colonial reforms did not begin as early, nor were they as complete or as well-rounded as those in Spain. Spanish traditionalism, and obstruction from those entrenched in the American trade, were hard to overcome. But especially after the middle years of the eighteenth century, under a series of intelligent and far-sighted ministers—Campillo, Aranda, Floridablanca, Gálvez—many of the old Hapsburg restrictions were gradually removed.

The system of *Galeones* and *Flotas,* in the last stages of decay at the death of Charles II, disappeared altogether during the early years of the War of the Spanish Succession. During the first five years no fleet at all sailed to the Caribbean; between 1706 and 1712 only four to New Spain and one to the isthmus, under convoy of French frigates. The needs of the colonists were meantime met by Spain's maritime foes, the English and the Dutch; also after 1703 by French merchant ships, chiefly from St. Malo, which a complacent allied government in Madrid permitted to sail around the Horn to the Pacific ports of Chile and Peru. French traders soon dominated the commerce of the South Sea, and their goods were sold in Lima from 60 to 80 per cent cheaper than those which arrived by way of the fair at Portobello. Havana, Vera Cruz, Cartagena, and other West Indian ports were also centers of extensive French operations. Everywhere French and Spanish vessels went together almost indistinguishably, often under the auspices of the French Guinea Company which in 1701 secured from Spain the *asiento* to supply during ten years 42,000 Negroes to the Spanish American colonies. In fact it seems that the cost of the war on both sides, French and Anglo-Dutch, was met largely with the gold and silver which came from the Spanish colonies by way of contraband trade.

After the Peace of Utrecht these French activities gradually ceased, and the old Spanish *flota* system was revived, at first it seems under separate contract for each fleet with the Cadiz merchants. Finally by the well-known *Projecto para galeones y flotas* of 5 April 1720, an effort was made to standardize it again. Fleets were to sail under convoy at stated intervals, and must depart promptly on the day announced whether all ships licensed to accompany it were ready or not. Sailing times were prescribed, for the Galleons or Tierra firme fleet early in September, for the Vera Cruz fleet early in June; and a maximum was set for the number of days the fleets might tarry in each of the American ports, Cartagena, Portobello, Vera Cruz, and Havana. In an attempt to improve communications and keep the trade informed of current market conditions, the *consulado* agreed to provide each year eight *avisos* or dispatch boats, two sailing every three months to New Spain and the isthmus, and supported by an additional 1 per cent on gold and silver from the Indies.

A small fleet sailed to New Spain at intervals of two or three years between 1715 and 1736, and then because of war or threat of war in Europe there was none at all for twenty years. Only five fleets were dispatched in the same period to Tierra firme. Indeed a royal order of 21 January 1735 suspended the Galleons altogether until goods sent out on the fleet five years earlier were disposed of and contraband activities curtailed. Single merchant vessels (*registros sueltos*) might be dispatched to Cartagena and Portobello when justified by market conditions, but thereafter the Galleons would be sent out only at a time and under circumstances agreed upon by representatives of the Lima merchants at the court. A fleet of seven merchantmen and two frigates did sail in 1737 for the isthmus, but war intervened, and in 1740 all fleets were suspended. Thereafter vessels departed alone under individual license from the crown for various ports in the Indies. Some of those which sailed to Buenos Aires had the right of *internación,* i.e., the privilege of dispatching goods over the Andes to Peru and Chile. The Galleons were never revived, the Portobello fair disappeared, and with it the prosperity and revenues of the Presidency of Panama. After 1740 ships were permitted to sail round the Horn directly to Peru, and thereafter scarcely a dozen vessels arrived annually on either side of the isthmus. In 1751 the *Audiencia* of Panama was suppressed.

The abolition of the fleets did not diminish frauds and other abuses. Contraband trade still flourished in America, to the prejudice as always of the export of goods via Cadiz. Indeed there were times when colonial markets were overstocked by the interlopers to their own disadvantage. So the Cadiz merchants, seeing no remedy but the restoration of trade on the old basis, actually welcomed the re-establishment of the Vera Cruz fleet and the limitation of supply to the colonies which this implied. The Flota was restored by royal orders of 11 October 1754, on the basis of biennial sailings, although this regularity was never achieved. The first fleet was dispatched three years later, and occasional departures occurred till 1789 when the fleet system was again and finally abandoned. Thereafter New Spain enjoyed the same freedom which had been extended to the other American colonies decades earlier.

The monopoly enjoyed by the mercantile oligarchy of Cadiz and Seville was also curtailed by the organization of several privileged trading companies in the north of Spain. The first and most important was the *Real Compañía Guipuzcoana de Caracas,* created in 1728 with the privilege, later the monopoly, of trade with the coasts of Venezuela. In 1734 a Company of Galicia was permitted to send two ships a year to Campeche, in 1740 was organized a Havana Company, and in 1755 a Barcelona and Catalan Company for trade with Hispaniola, Puerto Rico, and Margarita.

Even before 1700 the Spanish government had been increasingly concerned over the prostration of American trade, and listened to many and strange devices for its recovery. Subjects of the crown had advanced a number of projects for chartered companies on the model of the English and Dutch East India Companies, some of them providing for the retention of the fleet system unchanged, with the administration of colonial trade and navigation centered in a single private corporation. A project of this sort, to which even foreigners were to be admitted, had been proposed in or about 1672 in the Council of the Indies. In 1687 and for a decade thereafter the Council had considered a proposal for a company in Flanders, to be granted the sole right to trade with Hispaniola and Puerto Rico, together with considerable political and judicial powers there. It might be open to all the king's vassals and even to capitalists of other friendly nations. None of these proposals had any real chance of acceptance under the Hapsburg regime. Lack of capital, or of confidence by prospective investors in the vagaries of Spanish officialdom, and the unremitting opposition of the Seville *consulado,* made failure inevitable. Not until two decades later, under a new dynasty and a new breed of royal advisers, was this foreign device of the chartered company accepted.

In the second quarter of the eighteenth century, with the support of accomplished statesmen like José Patiño, the concept of the privileged trading corporation became very popular with business men and in the government. It seemed to be the one device capable of restraining the inroads of foreign trade with the colonies. Most of the companies were organized with capital from Catalonia and the Biscay provinces, and they were generally permitted to send ships to and from some specified northern port, the vessels calling at Cadiz on the return voyage. They were frequently obligated to build ships in their yards for the royal navy, arm small vessels to repress contraband, and transport supplies or furnish other small services without charge to the government. And in every case they received special privileges, if not a monopoly, in the trade with one of the more backward, less developed, areas of the American empire—areas with which Spanish trade was almost nil as the result of the old, canalized system of colonial commerce, and where the foreign interloper dominated the situation.

The government therefore appealed to the private interests of a limited group of capitalists, offered them commercial, and sometimes governmental, privileges in a certain region, in return for maintaining a police or coast guard service to eliminate the smuggler; hoping also that they would develop the latent resources of these backward areas in order to make their privileges more lucrative. Incidentally the device served also to stop the clamors of capitalists outside Andalusia for a share in colonial commerce.

All of the companies were financial failures, often because of bad management or government interference, except the Caracas Company, which lasted until the eve of the French Revolution. In some respects its results were remarkable. Caracas at that time was the chief producer of cacao, and Spain was the largest consumer. Yet as most of the Venezuelan trade was in the hands of Dutch interlopers based upon the island of Curaçao, Spain had to buy much of her cacao from Holland. Not a single ship from Spain had entered the ports of La Guaira, Puerto Cabello, or Maracaibo during the years from 1706 to 1721, while eighteen or twenty Dutch ships regularly traded along that coast. The new company by policing the neighboring waters succeeded in eliminating a large part of the smuggling. The Spanish cacao trade doubled in volume, while the price in Spain fell by nearly a half. Before the eighteenth century only cacao had been grown in Venezuela for export; but other staples were introduced through the efforts of the Guipuzcoa Company: cotton in 1767, and indigo shortly thereafter. Tobacco, which had long been planted there, was increasingly cultivated, and became, with dyewoods, hides, and indigo, an important article of export. Some vested interests in the colony were doubtless hurt, and the company at times abused its monopolistic position. Nevertheless the prosperity of Venezuela as a Spanish American community really dates from the creation of this privileged company, whatever may have been the complaints of the colonists against it. The government of the province, formerly dependent upon an annual subsidy from the treasury of New Spain, almost immediately enjoyed a fiscal surplus.

Trade within the Spanish empire was still far from free, however. Most of it was still concentrated at Cadiz to the prejudice of other ports and other provinces of Spain, and at a few major seaports in America. In the colonies the contraband activities of Spain's rivals continued unabated. Neither private trading companies nor tinkering with small details of the old commercial system had succeeded in eradicating this evil, or in appreciably improving either Spanish trade or the royal revenues. Slowly the conviction spread that free exchange among Spanish subjects on equal terms was the only means of lowering prices to meet the competition of the foreign interloper. Under Charles III in the second half of the century many of the remaining limitations were gradually removed. Possibly the crown was influenced by the example of what happened at Havana under English control in 1762. Till then the European trade of the island of Cuba had been almost nil, often confined to five or six ships a year. When the English captured Havana in the Seven Years' War, they threw the port open to all English vessels, and in less than a year nearly a hundred ships entered the harbor. The need of imperial reorganization and defense, to which reference has been made in another connection, and consequently of increasing the prosperity and revenues of the empire, made this object lesson the more impressive.

Many of the major economic reforms under Charles III were foreshadowed in the celebrated work attributed to José Campillo y Cossío, *Nuevo Sistema de gobierno económico para la América,* apparently written just before his death in 1743, although not appearing in print until a half century later. Campillo, economist, statesman, minister of war and finance in 1741, bitterly criticized the economic backwardness of America, the miserable state of the Indians, and the small share that Spanish products had in colonial trade. Some of his proposals were a bit naïve, and more theoretical than practical in their approach to the problem, but his "system" as a whole reflected a thoughtful study of the colonial experience of competing nations. Although urging that colonial manufactures be strictly limited in the interest of the mother country, he advocated distributing lands to the Indians tax free on condition that they were cultivated; training the natives as farmers and artisans, and providing agricultural credits; diminishing the widespread contraband traffic by freeing Spanish commerce from heavy taxation, by reducing customs duties on foreign goods, and by encouraging trade between the colonies; organizing a frequent overseas mail service; and limiting or abolishing the Cadiz monopoly and the system of periodically convoyed fleets. These recommendations of Campillo were later substantially repeated by a royal commission which reported to the king early in 1765.

The first step had already been taken in 1764 when there was organized a monthly mail-packet service between Coruña and Havana, followed shortly by a bi-monthly service to Buenos Aires. In the following year trade with the West Indian islands (Cuba, Hispaniola, Puerto Rico, Trinidad, and Margarita), one of the most backward regions of the American empire, was thrown open to a number of important seaports of Spain. Special license from the crown was no longer required, and the many old taxes on trans-Atlantic trade were replaced on most articles by a single payment in Spain of 6 or 7 per cent *ad valorem* to the crown. Evidently the results exceeded expectations, for concessions of a similar nature were gradually extended to other parts of the empire: in 1768 to Louisiana, in 1770 to Campeche and Yucatan, in 1776–7 to Santa Marta and Rio de la Hacha on the coast of New Granada, and by the famous *Reglamento* of 1778 to all other American provinces except New Spain and Venezuela. Moving forward with characteristic caution, regarding the new freedom as still in the experimental stage, the Spanish government apparently held these two prosperous areas in reserve in the interest of the royal exchequer. A certain number of tons for Vera Cruz were assigned each year to each qualified Spanish port from 1784 to February 1789, when special licenses and apportioned tonnage were abolished, and commercial relations with New Spain and Venezuela (the Caracas Company having disappeared) were made identical with those of the other American provinces. Meantime, in a series of decrees beginning in 1772, there had been further reduction of duties, and an increasing number of articles, Spanish and American, were placed on a free list.

What was more, many of the restrictions on intercolonial trade were at the same time removed. By 1774 Peru was permitted to trade more freely, although in American products only, with New Spain, Guatemala, and New Granada, and two years later Buenos Aires with Chile and the provinces of the interior. Thus by the time of the death of Charles III, although American commerce was still reserved to Spain and to Spaniards, it was open to all important seaports and to all Spanish subjects. It was not free trade in our sense of the term, but thereafter any Spaniard might trade directly from any part of Spain with any part of the Indies. Finally in 1790 the *Casa de Contratación* at Cadiz was abolished, after a continuous and not undistinguished history of 287 years.

The results in general were remarkable. The trade of Cuba, which in 1760 required five or six vessels a year, in 1778 employed over two hundred. The export of hides from Buenos Aires rose from 150,000 to 800,000 a year. And in the decade between 1778 and 1788 the value of the whole trade with Spanish America is said to have increased about 700 per cent.

The most noteworthy concession to the new spirit animating government policy was made in 1782. Louisiana, acquired two decades earlier from France, with a preponderantly French population accustomed to French goods, menaced at the same time by Anglo-American encroachment from the north, could not be adequately supplied by the commerce of Spain. If the prosperity of the province was to be maintained, to say nothing of its loyalty to the Spanish crown, commercial intercourse with some foreign nation seemed essential. And for many reasons trade with France was the natural choice. In fact during the war with England the colonial authorities in Louisiana had been forced to acquiesce in it. A royal decree of 22 January 1782, therefore, permitted ships belonging to Spanish subjects in Spain or Louisiana to sail with cargoes to New Orleans or to Pensacola directly from any port in France where a Spanish consul was resident, and to return with American products except gold and silver. The trade was subjected to a 6 per cent export and import duty in America, and 2 per cent additional on Spanish goods re-exported to other colonies. Trade was also permitted with some of the French West Indian islands in order to encourage the importation of Negro slaves. The concession was to last for ten years. As a matter of fact two years earlier, to meet the demands of the sugar planters while the war was on with Great Britain, Spanish colonists about the Caribbean Sea and the Gulf of Mexico had received permission to buy Negroes from neighboring French colonies; and from 1789 even foreigners were allowed to supply Negroes free to the Spanish islands and later to the other colonies as well. War in Europe in the last decades of the colonial era forced the Spanish government more than once to suspend temporarily the Spanish trade monopoly. Because of the increasing difficulty of supplying the colonies in Spanish ships during hostilities with England, a royal order of 18 November 1797 lifted the ban on trade in foreign vessels of neutral origin. The order was revoked in April 1799, but was renewed again in the years 1805–09.

The increasing freedom of commercial movement within the empire in the second half of the eighteenth century not only produced a greater volume of business; it operated to reduce prices in the colonies, discourage contraband trade, and probably to effect a wider distribution of wealth. The older monopolistic commercial houses, controlling imports on occasional fleets, had rested content with an understocked market, and expected to reap enormous profits from what was virtually a noncompetitive business. With the increase of maritime traffic, especially in seaports earlier debarred from an active trade with Spain, a new class of merchants arose—both in Spain and in America—more numerous and endowed with enterprise and foresight not called for under a monopolistic regime, "investing smaller sums [and] content with smaller profits." When vessels sailed alone at any time of the year, merchants could adapt themselves to meet the changing requirements of the American market more nearly as they arose, something impossible when supply was confined to fleets sailing at long intervals. And due to a more rapid turnover, they could sell more cheaply. Doubtless monopolistic practices persisted within the merchant fraternity, especially among commission agents in the seaports—as may happen even today. But the results of the new freedom in general must have been salutary for the community at large. Many lesser merchants who came out from Spain, moreover, used their profits to move into the domestic trade, and established themselves in the interior towns, to the mortification of the older vested interests.

BIBLIOGRAPHY

A general work on the early stages of Spanish colonization remarkable for its lucidity and objectivity is E. G. Bourne, *Spain in America, 1450–1580,* first published in 1904 and reissued (New York: Barnes and Noble, 1962) with an introduction by Benjamin Keen. More recent works are C. H. Haring, *The Spanish Empire in America* (New York: Harper & Row, 1947); Charles Gibson, *Spain in America* (New York: Harper & Row, 1966); and J. H. Parry, *The Spanish Seaborne Empire* (New York: Knopf, 1966). Bailey W. Diffie, *Latin-American Civilization: Colonial Period* (Harrisburg, Pa.: Stackpole Sons, 1945; reissued, New York: Octagon, 1967) traces the social and economic evolution of both the Spanish colonies and Brazil.

Julian H. Steward (ed.), *Handbook of South American Indians,* 7 vols. (Washington, D.C.: Government Printing Office, 1946–1959) is a standard source of information on the aboriginal cultures of Latin America, as is its companion series, Robert Wauchope (ed.), *Handbook of Middle American Indians* (Austin: University of Texas Press, 1965—), of which eight volumes have been published to date. John H. Rowe, "Inca Culture at the Time of the Spanish Conquest" (in Steward, *op. cit.*, vol. 2, pp. 183–330) is still considered the best treatment of this subject. Other basic works are Sylvanus G. Morley, *The Ancient Maya*, rev. ed. (Stanford, Cal.: Stanford University Press, 1956); J. Eric S. Thompson, *The Rise and Fall of Maya Civilization*, 2nd ed. (Norman: University of Oklahoma Press, 1966); Michael D. Coe, *The Maya* (New York: Praeger, 1966); George C. Vaillant, *Aztecs of Mexico: Origin, Rise, and Fall of the Aztec Nation*, rev. ed. (Garden City, N.Y.: Doubleday, 1962); J. Alden Mason, *The Ancient Civilizations of Peru* (Baltimore: Penguin Books, 1957); and Edward P. Lanning, *Peru Before the Incas* (Englewood Cliffs, N.J.: Prentice-Hall, 1967). Robert Wauchope (ed.), *The Indian Background of Latin American History* (New York: Knopf, 1970) is a collection of readings.

An excellent introduction to conceptual and historiographical problems related to the Spanish and Portuguese roots of Latin American civilization is Julian Bishko, "The Iberian Background of Latin American History: Recent Progress and Continuing Problems," *Hispanic American Historical Review,* 36 (1956), 50–80. The Iberian antecedents of specific Spanish American institutions are discussed in Robert S. Chamberlain, "Castilian Backgrounds of the Repartimiento-Encomienda," *Carnegie Institution of Washington Publication,* No. 509 (1939), 19–66, and "The *Corregidor* in Castile in the Sixteenth Century and the Residencia as Applied to the *Corregidor*," *Hispanic American Historical Review,* 23 (1943), 222–257; and in Julian Bishko, "The Peninsular Background of Latin American Cattle Ranching," *ibid.,* 32 (1952), 491–515. The Spanish background of Latin American history can be further explored in Américo Castro, *The Structure of Spanish History* (Princeton, N.J.: Princeton University Press, 1954); Jaime Vicens Vives, *An Economic History of Spain* (Princeton, N.J.: Princeton University Press, 1969); John H. Elliott, *Imperial Spain, 1469–1716* (New York: St. Martin's Press, 1963); John Lynch, *Spain Under the Hapsburgs, Volume 1: Empire and Absolutism, 1516–1598* (New York: Oxford University Press, 1964) and *Spain Under the Hapsburgs, Volume 2: Spain and America, 1598–1700* (New York: Oxford University Press, 1969); and Ruth Pike, *The Genoese in Seville and the Opening of the New World* (Ithaca, N.Y.: Cornell University Press, 1956). On the Portuguese background see Charles E. Nowell, *A History of Portugal* (Princeton, N.J.: Van Nostrand, 1952); Bailey W. Diffie, *Prelude to Empire: Portugal Overseas Before Henry the Navigator* (Lincoln: University of Nebraska Press, 1960); C. R. Boxer, *The Portuguese Seaborne Empire, 1415–1825* (New York: Knopf, 1969); and Emílio Willems, "Portuguese Culture in Brazil," *Proceedings of the International Colloquium on Luso-Brazilian Studies* (Nashville, Tenn.: Vanderbilt University Press, 1953), pp. 66–78. Selections from several of the works listed above appear in H. B. Johnson, Jr. (ed.), *From Reconquest to Empire: The Iberian Background to Latin American History* (New York: Knopf, 1970).

General works dealing with the perennially controversial topic of the Black Legend are Rómulo D. Carbia, *Historia de la leyenda negra hispano-americana* (Madrid: Consejo de la Hispanidad, 1944); Sverker Arnoldsson, *La leyenda negra: Estudios sobre sus origenes* (Göteborg: Elanders Boktryckeri Aktiebolag, 1960); and Charles Gibson (ed.), *The Black Legend* (New York: Knopf, 1971). For a reply to the article by Benjamin Keen reprinted in this volume, see Lewis Hanke, "A Modest Proposal for a Moratorium on Grand Generalizations: Some Thoughts on the Black Legend," *Hispanic American Historical Review*, 51 (1971), 112–127; for Keen's rejoinder to Hanke, see "The White Legend Revisited," *ibid.*, pp. 336–355.

Hanke has written numerous works which deal with sixteenth-century Spanish concern over the theological, legal, and social questions raised by the discovery of America and its native inhabitants and which also serve to shed light on the Black Legend. Among these are: *The First Social Experiments in America* (Cambridge, Mass.: Harvard University Press, 1935), *The Spanish Struggle for Justice in the Conquest of America* (Philadelphia: University of Pennsylvania Press, 1949), and *Aristotle and the American Indians* (Chicago: Henry Regnery, 1959). However, most works treating the interaction of Spaniards and Indians in colonial America pose, at least implicitly, the problem of evaluating the Spanish record in America. Those that may be cited here include Charles Gibson, *The Aztecs Under Spanish Rule: A History of the Valley of Mexico, 1519–1810* (Stanford, Cal.: Stanford University Press, 1964); George Kubler, "The Quechua in the Colonial World," *Handbook of South American Indians*, 2 (1946), 331–410; John H. Rowe, "The Incas Under Spanish Colonial Institutions," *Hispanic American Historical Review*, 37 (1957), 155–199; and Eugene H. Korth, *Spanish Policy in Colonial Chile: The Struggle for Social Justice, 1535–1700* (Stanford, Cal.: Stanford University Press, 1968). On the proselytization of the Indians by the religious orders, see Robert Ricard, *The Spiritual Conquest of Mexico* (Berkeley: University of California Press, 1966) and Antonine Tibesar, *Franciscan Beginnings in Colonial Peru* (Washington, D.C.: Academy of American Franciscan History, 1953). Magnus Mörner, *The Political and Economic Activities of the Jesuits in the LaPlata Region: The Hapsburg Era* (Stockholm: Library and Institute of Ibero-American Studies, 1953) is a dispassionate account of the Jesuit missions in Paraguay.

Mörner is also the author of a concise survey of miscegenation, *Race Mixture in the History of Latin America* (Boston: Little, Brown, 1967). The closely related topics of racial mixture and class structure can be examined in the following: C. E. Marshall, "The Birth of the Mestizo in New Spain," *Hispanic American Historical Review*, 29 (1939), 161–184; Woodrow Borah, "Race and Class in Mexico," *Pacific Historical Review*, 23 (1954), 331–342; and Lyle N. McAlister, "Social Structure and Social Change in New Spain," *Hispanic American Historical Review*, 43 (1963), 349–370.

An indispensable work on the *encomienda* is the pioneering monograph by Leslie Byrd Simpson, *The Encomienda in New Spain*, first published in 1929. The revised third edition (Berkeley: University of California Press, 1950) is discussed in a review article by Robert S. Chamberlain, "Simpson's *The Encomienda in New Spain* and Recent *Encomienda* Studies," *Hispanic American Historical Review*, 34 (1954), 238–250. Other works on the same topic include F. A. Kirkpatrick, "Repartimiento-Encomienda," *Hispanic American Historical Review*, 19 (1939), 372–379 and "The Landless Encomienda," *ibid.*,

22 (1942), 765–774; Silvio Zavala, *De encomienda y propiedad territorial en algunas regiones de la América Española* (Mexico: Antigua lib. Robredo de José Porrúa e hijos, 1940); Elman R. Service, "The *Encomienda* in Paraguay," *Hispanic American Historical Review*, 31 (1951), 230–252; and Eduardo Arcila Farías, *El régimen de la encomienda en Venezuela* (Seville: Escuela de Estudios Hispano-Americanos de Sevilla, 1957).

A classic study of the hacienda in New Spain is François Chevalier, *Land and Society in Colonial Mexico* (Berkeley: University of California Press, 1963). An important new book on a related subject is Ward Barrett, *The Sugar Hacienda of the Marqueses del Valle* (Minneapolis: University of Minnesota Press, 1970). Various aspects of colonial mining are examined in Arthur P. Whitaker, *The Huancavelica Mercury Mine* (Cambridge, Mass: Harvard University Press, 1941); Robert C. West, *The Mining Community in Northern New Spain* (Berkeley: University of California Press, 1949); and Walter Howe, *The Mining Guild of New Spain and Its Tribunal General* (Cambridge, Mass.: Harvard University Press, 1949). Lewis Hanke, *The Imperial City of Potosí: An Unwritten Chapter in the History of Spanish America* (The Hague: Martinus Nijhoff, 1956) is a vivid sketch of life in that turbulent boom town.

The institutions of Spanish American government are discussed in Lillian Estelle Fisher, *Viceregal Administration in the Spanish-American Colonies* (Berkeley: University of California Press, 1926); J. H. Parry, *The Audiencia of New Galicia in the Sixteenth Century* (Cambridge, Eng.: Cambridge University Press, 1948); Guillermo Lohmann Villena, *El corregidor de indios en el Perú bajo los Austrias* (Madrid: Ediciones Cultura Hispanica, 1957); and John P. Moore, *The Cabildo in Peru Under the Hapsburgs* (Durham, N.C.: Duke University Press, 1954) and *The Cabildo in Peru Under the Bourbons* (Durham, N.C.: Duke University Press, 1966). Studies devoted to individual viceroys include Arthur S. Aiton, *Antonio de Mendoza, First Viceroy of New Spain* (Durham, N.C.: Duke University Press, 1927) and Bernard E. Bobb, *The Viceregency of Antonio María Bucareli in New Spain, 1771–1779* (Austin: University of Texas Press, 1962).

The close relationship between the crown and the Catholic Church in the Spanish colonies is discussed in the first part of J. Lloyd Mecham, *Church and State in Latin America*, rev. ed. (Chapel Hill: University of North Carolina Press, 1966); W. E. Shiels, *King and Church: The Rise and Fall of the Patronato Real* (Chicago: Loyola University Press, 1961); and Nancy M. Farriss, *Crown and Clergy in Colonial Mexico, 1759–1821: The Crisis of Ecclesiastical Privilege* (London: Athlone Press, 1968). On the Inquisition see Henry Charles Lea, *The Inquisition in the Spanish Dependencies* (New York: Macmillan, 1908) and Richard E. Greenleaf, *The Mexican Inquisition of the Sixteenth Century* (Albuquerque: University of New Mexico Press, 1969).

Developments in Spain after the accession of the Bourbon dynasty are traced in Richard Herr, *The Eighteenth-Century Revolution in Spain* (Princeton, N.J.: Princeton University Press, 1958). Administrative reforms in the Spanish colonies are treated in Lillian Estelle Fisher, *The Intendant System in Spanish America* (Berkeley: University of California Press, 1929); John

Lynch, *Spanish Colonial Administration, 1782–1810* (London: Athlone Press, 1958); and John Fisher, "The Intendant System and the Cabildos of Peru, 1784–1810," *Hispanic American Historical Review,* 49 (1969), 430–453. Magnus Mörner (ed.), *The Expulsion of the Jesuits from Latin America* (New York: Knopf, 1965), considers the causes and effects of the suppression of the order in both Spanish America and Brazil. Other aspects of eighteenth-century Spanish America are explored in Lyle N. McAlister, "The Reorganization of the Army of New Spain, 1763–1766," *Hispanic American Historical Review,* 33 (1953), 8–32; Roland D. Hussey, *The Caracas Company, 1728–1784* (Cambridge, Mass.: Harvard University Press, 1934); and Lillian Estelle Fisher, *The Last Inca Revolt, 1780–1783* (Norman: University of Oklahoma Press, 1966). Jorge Juan and Antonio de Ulloa, *A Voyage to South America,* Irving A. Leonard (ed.) (New York: Knopf, 1964) is an abridged version of the English translation of this well-known travel account. For a brief biography of Ulloa see Arthur P. Whitaker, "Antonio de Ulloa," *Hispanic American Historical Review,* 15 (1935), 155–194.

Source materials dealing with colonial Brazil can be found in E. Bradford Burns (ed.), *A Documentary History of Brazil* (New York: Knopf, 1966). Burns has also compiled "A Working Bibliography for the Study of Brazilian History," *The Americas,* 12 (1965–1966), 54–88, which covers the colonial as well as the imperial and republican periods. Alexander Marchant, *From Barter to Slavery* (Baltimore: Johns Hopkins Press, 1952; reissued New York: Peter Smith, 1966) analyzes the economic relations between Indians and Portuguese during the initial phases of colonization. João Lúcio de Azevedo, *História de António Vieira,* 2nd ed., 2 vols. (Lisbon: Livraria Clássica Editora, 1931) is the standard Portuguese biography of the gifted seventeenth-century Jesuit, while C. R. Boxer, *A Great Luso-Brazilian Figure: Padre António Vieira, S.J., 1608–1697* (London: Hispanic and Luso-Brazilian Councils, 1957) is a short biography in English. Richard M. Morse (ed.), *The Bandeirantes: The Historical Role of the Brazilian Pathfinders* (New York: Knopf, 1965) offers a variety of readings as well as an excellent introduction by the editor. Works on Brazil in the mining era include C. R. Boxer, *The Golden Age of Brazil, 1695–1750* (Berkeley: University of California Press, 1962) and Manoel S. Cardozo, "The *Guerra dos Emboabas:* Civil War in Minas Gerais, 1708–1709," *Hispanic American Historical Review,* 22 (1942), 470–492 and "The Brazilian Gold Rush," *The Americas,* 3 (1946–1947), 137–160. Among other important volumes dealing with colonial Brazil the following may be mentioned here: C. R. Boxer, *Salvador de Sá and the Struggle for Brazil and Angola, 1602–1686* (London: Athlone Press, 1952) and *The Dutch in Brazil, 1624–1654* (Oxford: Clarendon Press, 1957); Caio Prado, Jr., *The Colonial Background of Modern Brazil* (Berkeley: University of California Press, 1967); Dauril Alden, *Royal Government in Colonial Brazil, with Special Reference to the Administration of the Marquis of Lavradio, Viceroy, 1769–1779* (Berkeley: University of California Press, 1968); and A. J. R. Russell-Wood, *Fidalgos and Philanthropists: The Santa Casa de Misericórdia of Bahia, 1550–1755* (Berkeley: University of California Press, 1968).

❧ TWO ❧

THE INDEPENDENCE
OF LATIN AMERICA

The spark that kindled the revolution for independence in Spanish America was the French invasion of Spain in 1807 and the subsequent deposition of the King of Spain, Ferdinand VII, by Napoleon Bonaparte (who awarded the vacant throne to his own brother Joseph). Although the Napoleonic wars were also a cause of the independence of Brazil, the emancipation of the Portuguese colony was achieved without bloodshed and under the leadership of the heir to the Portuguese throne, who became Pedro I of Brazil.

Although historians agree that the Napoleonic invasion of Spain can be considered the immediate cause of the Spanish American revolutions, attempts to identify the more basic causes of the independence movement and to determine the relative importance of each have frequently produced disagreement. It can be argued, of course, that without the French invasion the independence of the colonies would not have taken place or would have at least been delayed and that the achievement of independence was in fact premature since subsequent events showed that the colonies had not been ready for self-government. If these arguments are accepted, then the importance of determining the fundamental causes of the revolution is considerably diminished.

In any discussion of the possible causes of dissatisfaction with Spanish rule, a prominent place must be assigned to the grievances of Creoles, who, though equal in law to Spaniards born on the Iberian peninsula (*peninsulares*), were virtually excluded from high office in both Church and state. Another source of dissatisfaction lay in the economic policies of the Spanish government. The reforms of Charles III had greatly liberalized commerce within the empire, but trade remained a Spanish monopoly that in America, as in Spain, was controlled by Spanish merchants. In addition, Spanish efforts during the eighteenth century to increase royal revenue from colonial sources aroused discontent and occasionally violent resistance, notably in the Indian rebellion launched by Tupac Amaru in Peru in 1780 and in the Creole and mestizo uprising of the *comuneros* in New Granada (1781). Even so, it has been pointed out that "the empire, at the time of the death of Charles III in 1788, had never been better governed, nor had its people ever enjoyed a greater prosperity or well-being." [1] However, prosperity and well-being may have aggravated Creole grievances instead of diminishing them. In his well-known study *The Anatomy of Revolution* Crane Brinton found that the four prerevolu-

---

[1] R. A. Humphreys and John Lynch (eds.), *The Origins of the Latin American Revolutions, 1808–1826* (New York: Alfred A. Knopf, 1965), p. 6.

tionary societies that he analyzed were "on the whole on the upgrade economically before the revolution came, and the revolutionary movements [seemed] to originate in the discontents of not unprosperous people who [felt] restraint, cramp, annoyance, rather than downright crushing oppression." [2]

Finally, partly because the revolutionaries justified their rebellion against the mother country as an assertion of their natural rights against tyranny, historians have been concerned with the intellectual origins of the independence movement, particularly the extent to which it may have been influenced by Enlightenment thought. However, even if it is conceded that the works of the French philosophes and other writers of the Enlightenment were brought into the colonies despite official efforts to exclude material that might undermine political and religious orthodoxy, it is by no means certain that the new ideas encouraged revolutionary tendencies on the part of the Creoles who were exposed to them.

In any case, Creole desire to supplant the peninsulares was not necessarily accompanied by a commitment to political democracy or to fundamental social and economic reform on behalf of the "castes" or other nonwhite segments of society. Although the revolutionary era offered opportunities for upward mobility to many nonwhites, and although some of the liberators supported progressive policies that were often enacted into law, the social and economic structure of the former colonies remained essentially intact in 1830.

---

[2] Crane Brinton, *The Anatomy of Revolution*, rev. and expanded ed. (New York: Vintage Books, 1965), p. 250.

❧ 17 ❧

The Independence of Brazil

C. H. Haring

*The first link in the chain of events that would culminate in the inde-
pendence of Brazil was forged when a French army invaded Portugal
in 1807 after the Prince Regent, Dom João, had antagonized Napoleon
by rejecting a French ultimatum to declare war on England. The flight
of the Portuguese royal family to Brazil and its long residence there
gave the colony de facto independence years before it was finally declared in 1822. In this selection, Professor Haring traces the consequences of the exodus of the royal refugees and their entourage.*

Among all the newborn nations of the American hemisphere in the
nineteenth century, only Brazil was able successfully to preserve the
institution of monarchy. From 1822, the year in which the Brazilians
separated from the mother country, Portugal, until 1889, they were
governed by emperors under a constitutional regime.

Brazilians were not alone in this desire to retain in the New World
the institutions with which they had been familiar in the Old. Other
Latin American communities in their struggle for independence
harbored the idea of setting up a native or American monarchy. One
actually made the experiment—Mexico—without success. Brazil alone
accomplished it. In Chile, Argentina, and Peru many of the conservative, landowning class thought along similar lines. Most of them
wanted political independence—that is, escape from the political,
economic, and social inferiority imposed upon them by their colonial
status. But many believed that monarchy was what the popular masses
really understood and respected. To many it seemed to be the only
guarantee of political and social stability. It would commend itself

From C. H. Haring, *Empire in Brazil: A New World Experiment with Monarchy* (Cambridge, Mass.: Harvard University Press, 1958), pp. 1–2, 3–18.
Copyright, 1958, by the President and Fellows of Harvard College. Reprinted
by permission of the publisher. This article appears as reprinted in R. A.
Humphreys and John Lynch (eds.), *The Origins of the Latin American Revolutions, 1808–1826* (New York: Knopf, 1965), pp. 207–220. Deletions in text
are by R. A. Humphreys and John Lynch. Italicized bracketed note in text is
by Helen Delpar.

more readily to the monarchical governments of Europe whose diplomatic recognition they devoutly hoped for. It would also preserve the aristocratic framework of society with which their personal interests, economic and social, were identified.

In Chile and Peru the patriot leaders never got so far as to set up a king, or even to invite one to rule over them. In Argentina they tried for several years to find a European prince, and conceivably might have succeeded, had not the government in Buenos Aires been defeated and scattered by the presumably more democratic, rural, provincial forces in the interior.

The Mexicans, in default of a Spanish prince from Europe, accepted somewhat reluctantly one of their own number, Agustín de Iturbide, By Divine Grace First Emperor of the Mexicans. But he survived for only a year, 1822–23. One really couldn't accept or respect one's next-door neighbor as king or emperor, especially if he displayed more concern for the trappings of royalty than intelligent understanding of the critical problems facing a brand new nation. As for real princes—men who, however unworthy they might be personally, bore in the minds of their contemporaries the ineffable stamp of birth if not of breeding—they were not especially attracted by the prospect of rule over distant, unruly, half-Indian communities. It was in Brazil, and Brazil only, that, after a revolt from the Portuguese crown, monarchy survived—largely because a prince of the ruling Portuguese dynasty happened to be at hand. And it endured until near the close of the nineteenth century.

. . .

Brazil repudiated Portuguese rule in 1822, when upper-class Brazilians decided that the time had come to fend for themselves as an independent nation. The masses, for the most part illiterate, were scarcely yet a segment of the body politic. A nationalistic sentiment, a feeling of separateness from Europe and Europeans, had been growing in Brazil for a long time. Brazilian historians carry it back at least to the middle of the seventeenth century, when the Dutch West India Company seized and held for a quarter-century the coastal area in the northeast around Pernambuco; just as contemporaneously they established themselves in North America in the valley of the Hudson River. These Dutch intruders were ultimately expelled from Brazil by the efforts, almost unaided, of the colonists themselves. And this achievement gave to the Portuguese Americans an enhanced sense of their own self-sufficiency, and some disillusionment perhaps with their Portuguese cousins in Europe.

On several occasions in the following century and a half there were armed conflicts between American-born and European-born Portuguese; protests usually against the privileged position occupied by the latter in government and trade, or against the social inferiority in

which Americans were held by Europeans generally. There is no doubt
that the example of the thirteen English continental colonies in
achieving independence from Great Britain had considerable influence on the minds of contemporary Brazilians, as had the new concepts
of liberty and equality released by the French Revolution. Cultural
relations were intimate between Portugal and France, and the cat-
astrophic course of events in Paris was followed closely by intellectual
circles in Brazil. In short, the early years of the nineteenth century
were a time of conflicting ideologies, of social turmoil and change,
under any regime old or new. The parallel with our own age is obvious enough. And the Portuguese Brazilians, with their own special
grievances, responded to the spirit of the times.

These forces were at work in all the American colonies, Spanish
and Portuguese, and in both Portuguese and Spanish America the
course of events culminating in political independence was occasioned
and fashioned by the situation in Europe, more specifically by the
seizure in 1807–1808 of both Portugal and Spain by the armies of
Napoleon Bonaparte. In Spanish America the effect was a bitter military struggle of some fifteen years' duration before independence of
the continental colonies was finally achieved. In Brazil the course of
events was very different. The first impulses to independence were
in fact received from the Portuguese royal family itself.

When a French army under General Junot approached Lisbon near
the end of November 1807, the royal family and the court fled overseas to Brazil under the protection of a British fleet. Portugal for a
century had been to all intents and purposes an economic protectorate
of England, and in the gigantic struggle then involving all of Europe,
a choice had to be made between the military imperialism of Napoleon and the economic imperialism of Great Britain. At the Portuguese court there were sharply opposing currents, one English, the
other French. In this painful dilemma, the Portuguese crown and its
chief advisers, after last-minute hesitations, chose to remain loyal to
their traditional allies. The sovereign at this time was Maria I, but
she was insane, and the actual government was in the hands of her
son and heir, the prince regent Dom João. When Junot approached
the city gates, the royal flight had the appearance of a panic, but it
evidently had been discussed and decided upon in detail, for treasure,
archives, and all the apparatus of administration were on board the
fleet when the hesitant prince regent finally embarked.

After a brief sojourn in the ancient city of Bahia, the exiles sailed
on to Rio de Janeiro in March 1808. Rio became the temporary
capital of the Portuguese empire. As [*Brazilian historian Manuel de*]
Oliveira Lima has remarked, the event was unique: the emigration of
a European court overseas, the transfer across the Atlantic of the seat
of one of the great empires of the Old World, an empire that still

included, besides Brazil, the islands of Cape Verde, Madeira, and the Azores, the vast unexplored territories of Angola and Mozambique in Africa, and establishments in India, China, and Oceania.

The change was a great boon to Brazil. The old mercantile monopolies of Portugal associated with colonialism were swept away. On the advice of the governor of Bahia, the Conde da Ponte, and of José da Silva Lisboa, devoted follower of Adam Smith and Brazil's most distinguished economist of his time, Brazilian ports were immediately thrown open to the trade of all friendly nations—to the special advantage of England, it need scarcely be added, especially when a treaty of trade and navigation two years later gave British merchants tariff concessions greater than those accorded to Portugal itself.[1] The step in any case was inevitable, for trade with the metropolis occupied by French armies was impossible, and foreign commerce was essential to sustain what was now the head of the empire.

A variety of other reforms in Brazilian economic and cultural life were sanctioned, freeing them from old colonial restrictions: promotion of communications by land and water between the widely separated population centers; some improvement of the administration of justice and taxation; establishment of the first bank, mercilessly exploited by the government, and of a naval academy and a college of medicine and surgery; opening of the royal library of 60,000 volumes to the public; establishment of a botanical garden, or garden of acclimatization, of especial interest to the prince regent, and visited by tourists today; even a printing press was acquired for the first time in Brazil, in the beginning for official use only, but the first step toward the emergence of a public press. Measures were at the same time taken for the improvement of agriculture. It was in this period that the production of coffee began to expand under royal protection, and in the botanical garden was introduced the cultivation of oriental tea. A Brazilian iron industry had its beginnings at this time, as well as the production of textiles, which was to be Brazil's most important manufacture in the nineteenth century.

Rio de Janeiro especially prospered and grew rapidly. Many foreigners were attracted to Brazil, scientists and technicians, often invited by the crown. The development of the fine arts was accelerated by the increase of urban life and the brilliance of court functions. The arrival of a mission of French artists in 1816, at the suggestion of the Conde da Barca, minister of João VI—painters, sculptors, architects and musicians—became the nucleus of the later Academy of Fine Arts. Facilities were accorded to distinguished foreign naturalists—botanists and zoologists—who traversed great stretches of this vast territory, and

---

[1] The treaty also included the right of British subjects to be tried by their own judges, and the promise to abolish the African slave trade with Brazil.

whose writings are classics in the history of Brazilian scientific literature: Martius, Spix, Auguste de St. Hilaire, Eschwege, Prince Max
of Wied-Neuwied. Brazil, in short, no longer an exploited colony,
became a convergence of European culture.[2]

But there was another side to the picture. With the crown came a
host of exiled aristocrats, courtiers, officials, generals, hangers-on, who
had lost their properties in Portugal, some fifteen thousand, it is said.
Many of them arrogant, avaricious, they monopolized the offices and
sinecures in the government. Rio de Janeiro, a squalid, unhealthy
tropical city of 130,000 inhabitants, without waterworks or sewers,
where daily life had been simple and uneventful, had suddenly to
lodge and maintain a throng of strangers accustomed to a much more
sophisticated existence. Even the housing of these newcomers was a
problem, and many Brazilians were constrained to vacate their residences in Rio to make room for them. Discomforts and grumblings
on both sides were inevitable. Taxation too was necessarily heavier,
for now it was left to Brazil alone to support a royal court and an
army. In earlier days the occupation of Brazil had never been a military one. It had been practically impossible for the metropolis to
maintain a numerous garrison in the widely scattered overseas provinces, and such forces as there were had been mostly Brazilian, a well-
organized system of local militia. So many of the native Americans
were gradually alienated. A latent hostility between Creole and Portuguese, between American and European, was intensified. And it appeared even among army officers.

It was also in part a racial question, for most of the Brazilians, even
of the upper class, were of mixed ancestry. The mingling of races had
been a characteristic of Brazilian society from the early days of the
colony. In the beginning, when European women were few, Indian
women became the mothers of the children of the Portuguese adventurers. And very soon Negroes were brought in as slaves from Portuguese possessions across the Atlantic in west Africa. Negro slaves became very numerous on the plantations in the sugar-growing area of
Pernambuco and Bahia, and far outnumbered the whites. The white
planter, besides his white family, often had a numerous colored
progeny as well, who were frequently treated as the sons of their
father and sometimes were educated. The Portuguese, in fact, have
displayed little or no aversion to the so-called colored races, biologically

[2] Karl Friedrich Philipp Martius and Johann Baptist von Spix were members of a Bavarian scientific mission that came out to Brazil in 1817 with the
Archduchess Maria Leopoldina, daughter of the emperor Francis I of Austria
and bride of Dom Pedro de Alcantara, heir to the Portuguese crown. Among
them was a Viennese artist, Thomas Ender, whose many drawings and water
colors of Brazil have only in recent years received adequate appreciation in
exhibitions and books.

or socially. Racial prejudice of the sort common among Anglo-Saxons has never existed in Portuguese countries.

The consequence was that most Brazilians, to a slight or greater degree, were of mingled European and Indian or African extraction, and the racial complexion varied from one region to another. In Amazonia the prevailing element was Indian, in the pastoral area of the northeast and the interior provinces of Mato Grosso and Goiás it was *mameluco* (Indian and white), along the sugar-producing coast from Rio de Janeiro to Pernambuco and Paraíba and in the mining region of Minas Gerais it was Negro and mulatto, and south of Rio there was a mingling of all three races with an increasing predominance of the European. The Portuguese who followed the court to Brazil were inclined to look down upon these Americans as mere colonials, but also as Indian or African, and jealousy and hostility between them was only aggravated.

The prince regent and the court had been driven from Portugal by the onslaught of the armies of Napoleon. After the reconquest of the Iberian peninsula by the forces of the Duke of Wellington and the exile of Napoleon, the Portuguese royal government might have been expected to return to Lisbon. But Dom João elected to remain in Brazil, despite the urgings of Lord Strangford, the British minister, that he restore normalcy in the old country and rejoin the galaxy of restored sovereigns in Europe. Dom João liked Brazil. Indeed he seems to have fallen under the influence of his American environment to a degree surprising in a sovereign born to absolute rule. In correspondence with Thomas Jefferson, President of the United States, he alluded to the "well-founded liberal principles, religious as well as political, that we both possess," and to the "most perfect union and friendship which I hope will continue without interruption between the nations that occupy this new world." Rio de Janeiro itself, before it was embellished with wide avenues, manicured beaches and ultra-modern skyscraper apartments, although less healthful than today, must with its incredible natural environment have possessed even greater fascination and charm.

The Brazilians, as might be anticipated, bitterly opposed Dom João's departure, for fear that they might lose all that they had gained by the presence of the crown. Indeed Dom João in December 1815, in order to normalize the situation in the eyes of the European sovereigns meeting at the Congress of Vienna, was persuaded to elevate the colony to formal and legal equality with the mother country. In the following year the mad queen died, and the prince became king as João VI of the "United Kingdom of Portugal, Brazil, and the Algarve." Meantime Portugal was administered by a council of regency presided over by the British minister, Sir Charles Stuart, while a British general, Marshal Beresford, was commander-in-chief of the Army. If the

Brazilians feared that the king would return to Europe, the Portuguese in Europe were as profoundly discontented at seeming to remain an appendage of their former colony and under alien rule. Moreover, the disappearance of the old colonial trade monopoly had grievously affected Portugal's economic prosperity. Commercial treaties following that with Great Britain in 1810 had induced an active correspondence of Brazil with Europe and the United States, and the balance of trade with Portugal, formerly very favorable to the metropolis, was sharply reversed. Here was a dangerous dichotomy which the crown was never able satisfactorily to resolve.

In America the most serious international problem of the reign of Dom João VI was a conflict with Buenos Aires over possession of the eastern bank of the Río de la Plata, a conflict from which ultimately emerged the Republic of Uruguay. It involved on the one hand territorial ambitions of Portugal in America that harked back to the sixteenth century; on the other, the aspiration of Buenos Aires to constitute itself the heir of the Spanish viceroyalty of the Río de la Plata; and both crossed by the desire of the natives of the *Banda Oriental* for political autonomy, if not independence. . . .

A domestic conflict—the republican revolt in 1817 in the province of Pernambuco—revealed the continued smoldering of discontent among native Brazilians, especially in the northern provinces which shared few of the benefits enjoyed by the capital. Swayed to some extent by the example of the United States and by the struggle for independence in the Spanish colonies, it was sparked by antagonisms between Portuguese and native officers of the garrison, resulting in personal encounters and assassinations. Masonic influences were also involved, but fundamentally the outbreak was an expression of a deep-seated regionalism that has always been an important factor in the history of Brazil. A secret society had existed since 1814 aiming at the establishment of a republican government, and early in 1817 it was forced prematurely to resort to arms. Envoys were sent to the United States and England to obtain material aid if not official recognition, but disciplined forces were promptly dispatched from Bahia under the Conde dos Arcos, and the revolt was suppressed without difficulty and with unnecessary harshness. Its leader, Domingos José Martins, and several of his followers were executed, and others were banished or imprisoned. But the episode remains today a patriotic landmark in the history of Brazilian independence.

As circumstances in Napoleonic Europe had started a course of events that culminated in the emergence of Brazil from its former colonial status, so it was again political developments in Europe that gave occasion for the complete separation of Brazil from the mother country.

The year 1820 was a time of political upheaval in southern Europe. In Spain, Portugal, Italy, and Greece there were armed protests against the monarchical absolutisms that prevailed generally after the fall of Napoleon. In Portugal the liberal elements, fired by the example of revolution in next-door Spain, irritated by their continued bondage to an "English" regency, demanded a constitution and the return of their king. Uprisings first in Oporto and later in Lisbon, during the temporary absence of Beresford in Brazil, forced the regency to summon a national parliament or *côrtes*, which took steps to elaborate a modern democratic constitution, by which Brazilians were to be accorded representation in the parliament.

The liberal movement, although not anti-Brazilian in the beginning, with the continued postponement of the king's return became the medium of the pent-up resentments of the Portuguese. It soon appeared that the Portuguese liberals, once they had their king back and their own liberties secure, were determined to reduce the American realm to its former condition of an exploited dependency. In Brazil the news of these events of 1820 produced a profound repercussion. Both groups, the Portuguese and the native American, displayed strong sympathies with the revolution in Lisbon. The Portuguese courtiers felt no strong attraction to a liberal constitution, but were intensely interested in returning with the king to their estates in Europe. The Brazilians hailed the constitution, but wanted to retain their king. Many preferred separate constitutions for the two kingdoms under the same crown, i.e., home rule for Brazil. And so there were demonstrations in all the principal cities, while in some of the provinces liberal *juntas* were chosen to replace the old captains-general.

Dom João, well-meaning but temperamentally timorous and irresolute, knew not which way to turn. He was an old man, who by education and inheritance possessed little understanding of the constitutionalism fashionable at that time. But if he returned to Portugal, it was clear enough that he might lose Brazil. If he remained in Brazil, he would certainly lose Portugal. Meantime, although some representative Brazilians appeared in the Lisbon assembly and eloquently upheld their cause, all attempts at conciliation failed. The new constitution sharply repudiated the system of dual monarchy devised by Dom João VI.

In February 1821, the king, pressed by the Portuguese about him and by his son, the crown prince Dom Pedro, and threatened by mutiny in the garrison at Rio, issued a decree approving the Portuguese constitution (although it was unfinished and its exact terms were unknown), and a fortnight later announced his approaching departure. The British government threw its influence on the side of departure, and even prepared to send a squadron to Rio to convey him back to Europe.

Dom João also summoned Brazilian electors to a meeting in Rio to choose deputies to the *côrtes* in Lisbon. This assembly met on April 21, but it immediately proceeded, *ultra vires,* to announce a separate constitution for Brazil—the celebrated Spanish Constitution of 1812—and to insist on the king's remaining in Brazil. These decisions the king, who so far had clutched at any pretense to avert the dreaded voyage back to Portugal, accepted next day. However on the following day the military stepped in, dispersed the assembly, and forced the unhappy monarch to re-proclaim the Portuguese constitution. To complete the confusion, some believe that Dom João was himself privy to the whole stratagem. At any rate, on April 24 he boarded a warship and two days later sailed for Europe, taking with him most of the cash in the Bank of Brazil and all the jewels he could collect, and accompanied, it is said, by some three thousand of the Portuguese party. He left behind his son and heir, Dom Pedro, as regent in his place. In a famous letter addressed to Dom Pedro he anticipated the secession of Brazil, and advised him to take the crown for himself before some adventurer seized it.

Dom João VI was a genial, democratic, if rather weak and vacillating autocrat, but in general his government was enlightened and liberal. Although born to rule as an absolute sovereign, he was tolerant, clairvoyant, and fortunate in his choice of ministers. He "had the rare quality of being able to discover merit, and the rarer quality of not being jealous." He left Brazil with regret, and Brazilians remember him with affection and gratitude as the ruler who, by raising Brazil out of its colonial abasement, made national independence inevitable.

A peculiar role was played in these episodes by the crown prince Dom Pedro, then twenty-four years of age. He was the favorite son of his father, to whom he was generally devoted, but of very different personality. Ardent, impulsive, courageous, with considerable native intelligence but with little formal education, he liked to identify himself with the liberalism then current. But temperamentally he was a child of eighteenth-century absolutism. In the incidents of February and April 1821, he is suspected of complicity with the Portuguese party in forcing the king's departure, although it was contrary to the desires of the Brazilian liberals. He was ambitious to remain behind as regent, as actually transpired. In fact, there is considerable evidence that Dom João VI had an understanding with his son that continued to the day of the king's death in 1826: that the only way the House of Braganza could retain control of the two countries was by Brazilian secession under Dom Pedro's leadership, with the expectation that the latter, retaining his right of succession in Portugal, would ultimately reunite the two crowns.

Thereafter events moved rapidly, impelled by the actions of the *côrtes* in Lisbon, which increasingly betrayed the intentions of even the liberals in Portugal to subject Brazil to its former colonial bondage. Decrees were issued abolishing the organs of central government at Rio and making the provinces individually responsible to Lisbon, with the obvious intention of playing upon interprovincial jealousies and rivalries and preventing unity of action among the Brazilians. Another decree peremptorily ordered Dom Pedro to return at once to Portugal and prepare for a tour of Europe to complete his political education. At the same time Brazilians were by edict excluded from political and military offices. Dom Pedro in letters to his father noted the universal popular discontent, the profound agitation throughout the country, and the danger that extremists would conspire to establish a republic whether he was present or not. In Portugal the old king, completely intimidated by the liberals, spied upon, in fear of his life, his correspondence violated, gave way to their least demands.

The instructions from Lisbon Dom Pedro, after some hesitation, refused to honor. And on January 9, 1822, in response to memorials and petitions from the provinces of São Paulo and Minas Gerais and from the municipality of Rio de Janeiro urging him to remain with them in Brazil, he gave his celebrated promise: "As it is for the good of all and the general felicity of the nation, say to the people that I will remain." This is the famous *Fico* of Brazilian annals. It was a formal, public rejection of Portuguese authority and avowal of alliance with the American patriots, "the turning of a page in Brazilian history."

Two days later the Portuguese garrison in Rio retorted by demanding the regent's compliance with the orders from the *côrtes* and threatening to bombard the city. Citizens and militia rushed to arms. The Portuguese commander, intimidated by the crowd, capitulated next day and moved the regiments across the bay to Niteroi. And a month later, for a price, he sailed with the garrison back to Europe.

At the same time Dom Pedro called into a newly formed council of ministers perhaps the most distinguished Brazilian of his day, José Bonifácio de Andrada. José Bonifácio was a native of São Paulo. He had studied at the Portuguese university of Coimbra and with eminent scientists elsewhere in Europe and had become a scholar and mineralogist of note. He lived for many years in Portugal, where he held important official positions. He was a professor at Coimbra, perpetual secretary of the Academy of Sciences in Lisbon, and a member of many other European learned societies. He returned to Brazil in 1819 and soon rose to be the political leader of his native province. Early in 1822 he came to Rio de Janeiro to urge Dom Pedro to defy the Portuguese parliament and remained to be his chief minister. And it was his experience, energy, and statesmanship that guided the last steps to independence.

As remarked above, events moved rapidly. In February 1822 Dom Pedro published a decree creating a consultative council or *junta* to consist of representatives of all the provinces. In May he accepted from the municipality of Rio the title: "Perpetual and Constitutional Defender of Brazil." In June he issued a call for a constituent assembly for Brazil in order to "establish the bases on which should be erected its independence." In August, in a series of proclamations, he urged the people to resist coercion, forbade the landing of Portuguese troops without his permission, and addressed a circular to the diplomatic corps announcing that Brazil was almost ready to proclaim its independence under the Braganzas. The final step was taken on September 7. While on a journey through São Paulo to unify resistance in that province, as he had already done successfully in the province of Minas Gerais, Dom Pedro was overtaken near a small stream called Ipiranga by a messenger from the council in Rio with the latest Portuguese dispatches. The *côrtes* had revoked as rebellious the orders for the assembly of representatives of the provinces, had annulled all the acts of the regent, and declared his ministers guilty of treason. There also arrived letters from his wife, the Princess Leopoldina, and from José Bonifácio insisting that the decisive moment had come.

Dom Pedro read the dispatches, and before his escort and with show of great indignation, crumpled them and ground them under his heel, drew his sword, and cried out: "The hour has come! Independence or death! We have separated from Portugal!" This was the famous "Cry of Ipiranga" of Brazilian history. There was no official act confirming this gesture. In fact, several earlier dates, in January, May, June, and August, were almost equally significant. But September 7 remains the Independence Day for all Brazilians.

❧ 18 ❧

"Americanism" in New Spain

———◆◀◉▶◆———

Alexander von Humboldt

Hostility between Creoles and peninsulares *in the Spanish colonies had existed at least as early as the seventeenth century but became more marked in the decades before independence. In this reading, the antipathy between Creoles and Spaniards in New Spain and the development of a feeling of "Americanism" among the Creoles are described by the Prussian scholar Alexander von Humboldt (1769–1859), the most distinguished of the foreign scientists who visited the Spanish colonies in the eighteenth century. The investigations conducted by Humboldt during his five years in America (1799–1804) constituted a major contribution to scientific knowledge about the New World.*

Amongst the inhabitants of pure origin the whites would occupy the second place, considering them only in the relation of number. They are divided into whites born in Europe, and descendants of Europeans born in the Spanish colonies of America or in the Asiatic islands. The former bear the name of *chapetones* or *gachupines,* and the second that of *criollos.* The natives of the Canary Islands, who go under the general denomination of *isleños* (islanders), and who are the *gérans* [*managers*] of the plantations, are considered as Europeans. The Spanish laws allow the same rights to all whites; but those who have the execution of the laws endeavor to destroy an equality which shocks the European pride. The government, suspicious of the Creoles, bestows the great places exclusively on the natives of Old Spain. For some years back they have disposed at Madrid even of the most trifling employments in the administration of the customs and the tobacco revenue. At an epoch when everything tended to a uniform relaxation in the springs of the state, the system of venality made an alarming progress. For the most part it was by no means a suspicious and dis-

———

From Alexander von Humboldt, *Political Essay on the Kingdom of New Spain,* John Black (tr. and ed.), 4 vols. (London, 1811), Vol. 1, pp. 204–206, 209–211. This article appears as reprinted in R. A. Humphreys and John Lynch, (eds.), *The Origins of Latin American Revolutions, 1808–1826* (New York: Knopf, 1965), pp. 269–274. Deletions in text are by R. A. Humphreys and John Lynch. Italicized bracketed note in text is by Helen Delpar.

trustful policy, it was pecuniary interest alone which bestowed all employments on Europeans. The result has been a jealousy and perpetual hatred between the *chapetones* and the Creoles. The most miserable European, without education, and without intellectual cultivation, thinks himself superior to the whites born in the new continent. He knows that, protected by his countrymen, and favored by chances common enough in a country where fortunes are as rapidly acquired as they are lost, he may one day reach places to which the access is almost interdicted to the natives, even to those of them distinguished for their talents, knowledge, and moral qualities. The natives prefer the denomination of *Americans* to that of Creoles. Since the peace of Versailles, and, in particular, since the year 1789, we frequently hear proudly declared: "I am not a *Spaniard,* I am an *American!,*" words which betray the workings of a long resentment. In the eye of law every white Creole is a Spaniard; but the abuse of the laws, the false measures of the colonial government, the example of the United States of America, and the influence of the opinions of the age, have relaxed the ties which formerly united more closely the Spanish Creoles to the European Spaniards. A wise administration may reestablish harmony, calm their passions and resentments, and yet preserve for a long time the union among the members of one and the same great family scattered over Europe and America, from the Patagonian coast to the north of California. . . .

It would be difficult to estimate exactly how many Europeans there are among the 1,200,000 whites who inhabit New Spain. As in the capital of Mexico itself, where the government brings together the greatest number of Spaniards, in a population of more than 135,000 souls, not more than 2,500 individuals are born in Europe, it is more than probable that the whole kingdom does not contain more than 70 or 80,000. They constitute, therefore, only the 70th part of the whole population, and the proportion of Europeans to white Creoles is as one to fourteen.

The Spanish laws prohibit all entry into the American possessions to every European not born in the peninsula. The words European and Spaniard have become synonymous in Mexico and Peru. The inhabitants of the remote provinces have, therefore, a difficulty in conceiving that there can be Europeans who do not speak their language; and they consider this ignorance as a mark of low extraction, because, everywhere around them, all, except the very lowest class of the people, speak Spanish. Better acquainted with the history of the sixteenth century than with that of our own times, they imagine that Spain continues to possess a decided preponderance over the rest of Europe. To them the peninsula appears the very center of European civilization. It is otherwise with the Americans of the capital. Those of them who are acquainted with the French or English literature fall easily into a contrary extreme; and have still a more unfavorable opinion of the mother country than the French had at a time when communication was less frequent between Spain and the rest of Europe. They prefer strangers from other countries to the Spaniards; and they flatter themselves with the idea that intellectual cultivation has made more rapid progress in the colonies than in the peninsula.

This progress is indeed very remarkable at Mexico, the Havanah, Lima, Santa Fe, Quito, Popayan, and Caracas. Of all these great cities thé Havanah bears the greatest resemblance to those of Europe in customs, refinements of luxury, and the tone of society. At Havanah the state of politics, and their influence on commerce, is best understood. However, notwithstanding the efforts of the *Patriotic Society of the Island of Cuba,* which encourages the sciences with the most generous zeal, they prosper very slowly in a country where cultivation and the price of colonial produce engross the whole attention of the inhabitants. The study of the mathematics, chemistry, mineralogy, and botany is more general at Mexico, Santa Fe, and Lima. We everywhere observe a great intellectual activity, and among the youth a wonderful facility of seizing the principles of science. It is said that this facility is still more remarkable among the inhabitants of Quito and Lima than at Mexico and Santa Fe. The former appear to possess more versatility of mind and a more lively imagination; while the Mexicans and the natives of Santa Fe have the reputation of greater perseverance in the studies to which they have once addicted themselves.

No city of the new continent, without even excepting those of the United States, can display such great and solid scientific establishments as the capital of Mexico. I shall content myself here with naming the School of Mines, directed by the learned Elhuyar . . . ; the Botanic Garden; and the Academy of Painting and Sculpture. This academy bears the title of *Academia de los Nobles Artes de Mexico.* It owes its existence to the patriotism of several Mexican individuals, and to the protection of the minister Galvez. The government assigned it a spacious building, in which there is a much finer and more complete collection of casts than is to be found in any part of Germany. We are astonished on seeing that the Apollo Belvedere, the group of Laocoön, and still more colossal statues, have been conveyed through mountainous roads at least as narrow as those of St. Gothard; and we are surprised at finding these masterpieces of antiquity collected together under the torrid zone, in a tableland higher than the convent of the great St. Bernard. The collection of casts brought to Mexico cost the king 200,000 francs. The remains of the Mexican sculpture, those colossal statues of basalt and porphyry, which are covered with Aztec hieroglyphics, and bear some relation to the Egyptian and Hindu style, ought to be collected together in the edifice of the academy, or rather in one of the courts which belong to it. It would be curious to see these monuments of the first cultivation of our species, the works of a semi-barbarous people inhabiting the Mexican Andes, placed beside the beautiful forms produced under the sky of Greece and Italy.

The revenues of the Academy of Fine Arts at Mexico amount to 123,000 francs, of which the government gives 60,000, the body of Mexican miners nearly 25,000, the *consulado,* or association of merchants of the capital, more than 15,000. It is impossible not to perceive the influence of this establishment on the taste of the nation. This influence is particularly visible in the symmetry of the buildings, in the perfection with which the hewing of stone is conducted, and in the ornaments of the capitals and stucco relievos. What a number of beautiful edifices are to be seen at Mexico! nay, even in provincial towns like Guanaxuato and Queretaro! These monuments, which frequently cost a million or a million-and-a-half of francs, would appear to advantage in the finest streets of Paris, Berlin, and Petersburg. M. Tolsa, professor of sculpture at Mexico, was even able to cast an equestrian statue of King Charles the Fourth; a work which, with the exception of the Marcus Aurelius at Rome, surpasses in beauty and purity of style everything which remains in this way in Europe. Instruction is communicated *gratis* at the Academy of Fine Arts. It is not confined alone to the drawing of landscapes and figures; they have had the good sense to employ other means for exciting the national industry. The academy labors successfully to introduce among the artisans a taste for elegance and beautiful forms. Large rooms, well lighted by Argand's lamps, contain every evening some hundreds of young people, of whom some draw from *relievo* or living models, while others copy drawings of furniture, chandeliers, or other ornaments in bronze. In this assemblage (and this is very remarkable in the midst of a country where the prejudices of the nobility against the castes are so inveterate) rank, color, and race is confounded: we see the Indian and the *mestizo* sitting beside the white, and the son of a poor artisan in emulation with the children of the great lords of the country. It is a consolation to observe, that under every zone the cultivation of science and art establishes a certain equality among men, and obliterates for a time, at least, all those petty passions of which the effects are so prejudicial to social happiness.

Since the close of the reign of Charles the Third, and under that of Charles the Fourth, the study of the physical sciences has made great progress, not only in Mexico, but in general in all the Spanish colonies. No European government has sacrificed greater sums to advance the knowledge of the vegetable kingdom than the Spanish government. Three *botanical expeditions,* in Peru, New Granada, and New Spain, under the direction of MM. Ruiz and Pavon, Don José Celestino Mutis, and MM. Sesse and Mociño, have cost the state nearly two millions of francs. Moreover, botanical gardens have been established at Manilla and the Canary Islands. The commission destined to draw plans of the canal of *los Guines* was also appointed to examine the vegetable productions of the island of Cuba. All these researches, conducted during twenty years in the most fertile regions of the new continent, have not only enriched science with more than four thousand new species of plants, but have also contributed much to diffuse a taste for natural history among the inhabitants of the country. The city of Mexico exhibits a very interesting botanical garden within the very precincts of the viceroy's palace. Professor Cervantes gives annual courses there, which are very well attended. This *savant* possesses, besides his herbals, a rich collection of Mexican minerals. M. Mociño, whom we just now mentioned as one of the coadjutors of M. Sesse, and who has pushed his laborious excursions from the kingdom of Guatemala to the northwest coast or island of Vancouver and Quadra; and M. Echeveria, a painter of plants and animals, whose works will bear a comparison with the most perfect productions of the kind in Europe, are both of them natives of New Spain. They had both attained a distinguished rank among *savants* and artists before quitting their country.[1]

---

[1] The public is as yet only put in possession of the discoveries of the botanical expedition of Peru and Chili. The great herbals of M. Sesse, and the immense collection of drawings of Mexican plants executed under his eye, arrived at Madrid in 1803. The publication of both the Flora of New Spain and the Flora of Santa Fe de Bogota is expected with impatience. The latter is the fruit of 40 years' researches and observations by the celebrated Mutis, one of the greatest botanists of the age.

A Plea for Freedom of Trade

◆◀◆▶◆

Mariano Moreno

In the decades before independence Creole landowners in the agricul-
tural regions of Spanish America became increasingly convinced of the
desirability of opening American ports to the ships of all nations. This
belief was especially strong in the Río de la Plata area, which had
briefly enjoyed freedom of trade during the short-lived British occupa-
tion of 1806. The landowners' point of view was ably expressed by a
young Creole lawyer, Mariano Moreno (1778–1811), in his famous
Representación, en nombre de los labradores y hacendados de las
Campañas del Río de la Plata, *a summary of which appears here.*
Moreno had been moved to take up his pen on behalf of freedom of
trade after a request in 1809 by two British merchants to be allowed
to dispose of their goods in Buenos Aires had provoked strong objections
from the attorney of the consulado *(merchants' guild) of Cadiz, despite*
the fact that commerce between Spain and the colonies had been
virtually paralyzed by the Napoleonic wars. In 1810 Moreno became a
key member of the provisional junta set up in Buenos Aires on May
25 to rule the provinces of the Río de la Plata.

The resources of the royal treasury being exhausted by the enormous
expenditure which has lately been required, Your Excellency, on as-
suming the reins of government, was deprived of the means of providing for the safety of the provinces committed to your charge. The
only mode of relieving the necessities of the country appears to be
to grant permission to the English merchants to introduce their manufactures into the town, and to re-export the produce of the interior,
by which the revenue will be at once increased, and an impulse given
to industry and trade.

Your Excellency possesses powers sufficient for the adoption of any
measures that the safety of the country may require, but a natural de-

---

From "Extracts from a Representation, addressed to the Viceroy of Buenos
Aires, by the Apoderado (Agent) of the Landlords of the Province," in H. G.
Ward, *Mexico in 1827,* 2 vols. (London, 1828), vol. 1, pp. 479–483. This article
appears as reprinted in R. A. Humphreys and John Lynch (eds.), *The Origins
of the Latin American Revolutions, 1808–1826* (New York: Knopf, 1965), pp.
185–189.

sire to ensure the result of these measures, by adapting them to the peculiar situation of the viceroyalty, induced Your Excellency to consult the *cabildo* of this city, and the *Tribunal del Real Consulado,* before any definitive resolution was taken.

The intentions of Your Excellency had barely transpired, when several of the merchants manifested their discontent and dissatisfaction. Groups of European shopkeepers were formed in all the public places, who, disguising their jealousy and personal apprehensions under the most specious pretenses, affected to deplore, as a public calamity, the diminution of the profits which they have hitherto derived from the contraband trade. At one time, with hypocritical warmth, they lamented the fatal blow which the interests of the mother country were about to receive, and at another, they predicted the ruin of the colony, and the total destruction of its commerce: others again announced the universal distress that the free exportation of the precious metals would bring upon us, and pretended to feel a lively interest in the fate of our native artisans (whom they have always hitherto despised), endeavoring to enlist in their cause the sacred name of religion, and the interests of morality.

Never, certainly, has America known a more critical state of affairs, and never was any European governor so well entitled as Your Excellency to dispense at once with the maxims of past ages; for if, in less dangerous times, the laws have often been allowed to sleep, when their observance might have checked the free action of the government, surely Your Excellency cannot now be condemned for the adoption of a measure, by which alone the preservation of this part of the monarchy can be effected.

Those should be doomed to eternal infamy, who maintain that, under present circumstances, it would be injurious either to Spain, or to this country, to open a free intercourse with Great Britain. But even supposing the measure to be injurious, still it is a necessary evil, and one which, since it cannot be avoided, ought at least to be made use of for the general good, by endeavoring to derive every possible advantage from it, and thus to convert it into a means of ensuring the safety of the state.

Since the English first appeared on our coasts, in 1806, the merchants of that nation have not lost sight of the Río de la Plata in their speculations. A series of commercial adventures has followed, which has provided almost entirely for the consumption of the country; and this great importation, carried on in defiance of laws and reiterated prohibitions, has met with no other obstacles than those necessary to deprive the custom house of its dues, and the country of those advantages which it might have derived from a free exportation of its own produce in return.

The result of this system has been to put the English in the exclusive possession of the right of providing the country with all the foreign merchandise that it requires; while the government has lost the immense revenues which the introduction of so large a proportion of foreign manufactures ought to have produced, from too scrupulous an observance of laws, which have never been more scandalously violated than at the moment when their observance was insisted upon by the merchants of the capital. For what, Sir, can be more glaringly absurd than to hear a merchant clamoring for the enforcement of the prohibitive laws, and the exclusion of foreign trade, at the very door of a shop filled with English goods, clandestinely imported?

To the advantages which the government will derive from the open introduction of foreign goods may be added those which must accrue to the country from the free exportation of its own produce.

Our vast plains produce annually a million of hides, without reckoning other skins, corn, or tallow, all of which are valuable, as articles of foreign trade. But the magazines of our resident merchants are full; there is no exportation; the capital usually invested in these speculations is already employed, and the immense residue of the produce, thrown back upon the hands of the landed proprietors, or purchased at a price infinitely below its real value, has reduced them to the most deplorable state of wretchedness, and compelled them to abandon a labor which no longer repays them for the toil and expense with which it is attended.

The freedom of trade in America was not proscribed as a real evil, but because it was a sacrifice required of the colonies by the mother country. The events which led to the gradual increase of this exclusive commerce, till it became a monopoly of the Cádiz merchants, are well known.

Well-informed men exclaimed in vain against a system so weak, so ruinous, and so ill-judged; but inveterate evils are not to be cured at once. Minor reforms had paved the way for a system founded upon sounder principles, when the late extraordinary events, changing entirely the political state of Spain, destroyed by one unforeseen blow all the pretexts by which the prohibitory laws had been previously supported.

The new order of things which the mother country has proclaimed as the happy commencement of national prosperity has completely changed the motives for the prohibitory system, and demonstrated, in their fullest extent, the advantages that must result to the country from a free trade. Good policy, therefore, and the natural wish to apply a remedy to pressing evils, are converted into a positive duty, which the first magistrate of the state cannot, in reason, or justice, neglect.

Is it just that the fruits of our agricultural labors should be lost, because the unfortunate provinces of Spain can no longer consume them? Is it just that the abundant productions of the country should rot in our magazines, because the navy of Spain is too weak to export them? Is it just that we should increase the distress of the mother country, by the tidings of our own critical and vacillating state, when the means are offered to us of consolidating our safety upon the firmest basis? Is it just, that, when the subjects of a friendly and generous nation present themselves in our ports, and offer us, at a cheap rate, the merchandise of which we are in want, and with which Spain cannot supply us, we should reject the proposal, and convert, by so doing, their good intentions to the exclusive advantage of a few European merchants, who, by means of a contraband trade, render themselves masters of the whole imports of the country? Is it just, that when we are entreated to sell our accumulated agricultural produce, we should, by refusing to do so, decree at the same time the ruin of our landed proprietors, of the country, and of society together?

If Your Excellency wishes to diminish the extraction of specie, which has taken place latterly to so great an extent, there is no other mode of effecting it than to open the ports to the English, and thus to enable them to extend their speculations to other objects. It is one of the fatal consequences of the contraband trade, that the importer is absolutely compelled to receive the value of his imports in the precious metals alone. His true interest, indeed, consists in exchanging them at once for articles that may become the objects of a new speculation; but the risks with which the extraction of bulky commodities must be attended, under a system of strict prohibition, induce him to sacrifice this advantage to the greater security which exports in specie afford, and to deprive himself of the hope of new profits, and the country of the sale of its most valuable produce.

Yet the *apoderado* [attorney] of the Cádiz monopolists maintains, "that a free trade will be the ruin of our agriculture." This luminous discovery is worthy of his penetration. The free exportation of the produce is declared to be detrimental to the interests of the producer! What, then, is to be the mode of encouraging him in his labors? According to the principles laid down by our merchants, the agricultural produce should be allowed to accumulate—purchasers are to be deterred from entering the market, by the difficulties of exporting the articles bought up to countries where they might be consumed; and this system is to be persevered in until, after ruining the landholders by preventing them from disposing of the fruits of their labors, the superfluous produce itself is to be disposed of, in order to fill up the ditches and marshes in the vicinity of the town.

Yes, Sir, this is the deplorable state to which our agriculture has been reduced during the last few years. The marshes around the town have been actually filled up with wheat; and this miserable condition, which forms a subject of lamentation with all true friends to their country, and scandalizes the inhabitants of the whole district, is the natural fate of a province in which, as soon as an inclination is shown to apply a remedy to these evils, men are found daring enough to assert "that by giving value, or, in other words, a ready market, to the agricultural produce, agriculture will be ruined."

The Enlightenment and Latin American Independence

Charles C. Griffin

During the eighteenth century members of the literate colonial minority could become acquainted with the philosophical and political ideas of the Enlightenment through their own trips abroad or through the officials, merchants, visiting scientists, and others who traveled to America. However, as this selection makes clear, "the Enlightenment influenced Latin American political behavior in a wide variety of ways, among which innovation in political theories and principles was only one." The author of the essay is Professor Charles C. Griffin of Vassar College, a veteran student of the revolutions for independence, especially in northern South America.

In the course of the Latin American independence movement, country after country, at various times and in different words, based its declaration of independence on claims to natural rights of which each complained it had been unjustly deprived by the mother country. Though far from being unanimously held when the first Spanish American revolts occurred in the wake of Napoleon's invasion of the Peninsula in 1808, this view was already clearly manifest in the propaganda of the Hidalgo revolt of 1810 in New Spain and the contemporaneous uprisings in northern South America. Many rebel leaders justified their revolt on much less sweeping grounds, and subsequently they were echoed by conservative historians like the Mexican Lucas Alamán. Nevertheless, the political success of the rebel governments tended to win acceptance of the "natural rights" view of the antecedents of revolution. It was natural, therefore, that it should have

---

From Charles C. Griffin, "The Enlightenment and Latin American Independence," in Arthur P. Whitaker (ed.), *Latin America and the Enlightenment*. Second edition © 1961 by Arthur P. Whitaker. Reprinted by permission of Cornell University Press. This article appears as reprinted in R. A. Humphreys and John Lynch (eds.), *The Origins of the Latin American Revolutions, 1808–1826* (New York: Knopf, 1965), pp. 38–51. Italicized bracketed notes in the text are by Helen Delpar.

been adopted and perpetuated by the early historians of the independence movement.

This emphasis on the assertion of natural rights against tyranny involved assigning a major role to the political ideas of the Enlightenment as a cause of revolution. The writings of Montesquieu, Voltaire, and Rousseau were held to be at the root of the revolutionary movement, for from what other source could the notion have reached Latin America that man was born free, that he had natural rights, that governments not based on popular consent and not respectful of these rights were tyrannies?

With this in mind, diligent search was made for evidence of the transmission of these subversive principles during the last colonial generations—a search which met with considerable success. It was found that throughout Spanish and Portuguese America in the latter eighteenth century there were numbers of men who were familiar with notorious and officially prohibited books of the *philosophes,* including the highly inflammatory work of the Abbé Raynal. The dangers to such readers owing to Spanish regulation of the book trade and the activities of the Inquisition were emphasized.

Once the importance of the ideas of the Enlightenment as a cause of revolution was accepted, it followed that the popularization of these ideas in the previous revolutionary movements in the United States of America and in France was a significant means by which the fundamental ideas came to be transmitted to Latin America. The French Declaration of the Rights of Man and of the Citizen, it could be shown, had been published in Spanish and circulated in Spanish America. North American revolutionary documents had also served as models for South America. To top it all, there were the precursors: the Chilean friar Camilo Henríquez, the Peruvian Jesuit Viscardo y Guzmán, the New Granadan publicist Antonio Nariño, and most important of all, the eminent Venezuelan Francisco de Miranda. All these men could be shown to have exhibited in their writings in one way or another a debt to the enlightened thought of their time. The propaganda activities of these men and others like them reinforced the direct influence of foreign writers and provided a channel through which their ideas could be directed to literate Creoles.

In recent decades the pendulum of historical interpretation has swung away from the earlier emphasis on the Enlightenment as the cause of the Latin American independence movement. This tendency is the result of two major changes of historical outlook. First, thanks to the studies of Ernst Cassirer, Carl Becker, and others, the stress has been shifted from the political to the philosophical and scientific aspects of the Enlightenment, from Montesquieu, Voltaire, and Rousseau to Descartes, Locke, and Newton. And it has been shown that insofar as the Enlightenment had a political influence, this was by no means always favorable to revolution but quite as often to reform within the established order, and even at times to enlightened despotism. While findings of this kind have not yet been thoroughly applied to the impact of the Enlightenment in Latin America, they have shaken the faith of many present-day historians in the simplistic version of its impact there that prevailed up to a generation ago.

The other major change has been the growing preoccupation of the twentieth century with economic and social history. The study of economic conditions in the immediately pre-revolutionary period has made it possible to show the conflicting interests of groups of merchants, plantation-owners, and stockmen in various colonial regions and how these were affected by colonial laws and administrative practices. Marxian interpretations of Latin American independence have also appeared. Other authors have stressed the importance of cleavages among colonial social and racial groups and the effects of tensions of this nature in some parts of Latin America, while still others have traced the activities of the new learned societies of the *amigos del país* type in promoting useful knowledge.

Another reason for the recent downgrading of the importance of the political teachings of the *philosophes* has been a new emphasis on the limited objectives of the revolts in Spanish America in their early stages. One school of historians explains the beginning of the revolutions, in southern South America at least, as the result of a constitutional crisis in the empire in which the idea of independence had no place at all. Spaniards in America claimed, in view of the captivity of the monarch, Ferdinand VII, the right to the autonomous pursuit of the cause of resistance to Napoleon, just as the nationalists in Spain itself did. It was only later, it is claimed, as a result of the bitterness engendered by war, that the ideal of independence appeared. In some regions it was not dominant for many years.

Still another point of view which minimizes the Enlightenment as a direct cause of independence in Spanish America has recently been put forward by certain Hispanizing authors. It is not based on any questioning of the importance of ideas, but rather on some new notions as to their sources. This view began with an effort to show that the ideas of the Enlightenment reached Spanish America at least as much through Spanish authors as they did from foreigners. The Spanish liberals of the constitutional era from 1810 to 1814 were also held to have influenced Spanish thought by transmitting liberal principles to the New World even though they were politically at odds with the Americans.

But this was only a beginning. Of late there has been a new emphasis on the essentially liberal and anti-autocratic character of the medieval Spanish tradition. Royal authority was limited and contractual; the liberties of the municipalities of Castile did not end until the final defeat of the *comuneros* at Villalar in the reign of Charles I. Under the façade of absolutism created by the Habsburg and Bourbon monarchs, it is claimed, the spirit of the medieval *fueros* lived on and manifested itself anew both in Spanish liberalism and constitutionalism after the Napoleonic invasion and in the revolution in the American colonies.

This view, though strongly asserted and not lacking in plausibility, is difficult to prove by direct evidence. The same can be said about the attempt of certain authors to magnify the importance of the political theories of the seventeenth-century Jesuit writer Francisco Suárez for the thought of the revolutionary generation in Spanish America. There can be no doubt that Suárez, like other Jesuit theologians, stressed the duties of the monarch to his subjects and denied the principle of the divine right of kings. Royal power came from God but was exercised through popular consent. This version of Catholic political thought, however, had not been generally accepted in the Spanish universities and even less by writers on Spanish or colonial law. Since the expulsion of the Jesuits in the reign of Charles III there had even been a requirement enforced by royal order on all university professors in the Indies to deny under oath that they were teaching the objectionable political principles of the Jesuits. In these circumstances the importance of *Suarecismo* may be seriously questioned.

What can be said, in the light of our present knowledge, and of the various revisionist interpretations which have been mentioned, about the relation between the Enlightenment and the independence of Latin America? In the first place, it might be well to eschew any attempt to carry forward the debate as to the relative importance of ideas and of other factors as "causes" of the independence movement. Modern social science and modern historiography alike frown on the somewhat oversimple concept of causation which appeared in much of the earlier historical literature devoted to Latin American independence. As Crane Brinton has noted: "Ideas are always a part of the pre-revolutionary situation, and we are quite content to let it go at that. No ideas, no revolution. This does not mean that ideas cause revolution. . . . It merely means that ideas form part of the mutually dependent variables we are studying." If we accept this view we shall avoid the attempt to determine causal relationships. The task before us, then, becomes one of bringing out the ways in which the ideas of the Enlightenment manifested themselves in Spanish and Portuguese America in the era of independence.

What recent historical research has brought out very clearly is that the Enlightenment influenced Latin American political behavior in a wide variety of ways, among which innovation in political theories and principles was only one. Far more important than these in its effects on the revolutionary age may have been a faith in reason as the guide for the human spirit in its search for truth, without regard for the principle of authority, whether it was invoked on behalf of the philosophy of Aristotle, the theology of the Roman Catholic Church, or royal absolutism.

Faith in reason lay at the roots of a general intellectual revolution in the universities of Spanish America which was far more important than has generally been realized until recently. In every country *letrados* trained in institutions as far apart as San Carlos of Guatemala and San Francisco Xavier of Chuquisaca in Upper Peru were being accustomed to the questioning of the accepted and to solving problems by rational and empirical methods. As [*historian John Tate*] Lanning has pointed out in his study of the Enlightenment in Guatemala, university graduates played a significant role in the independence movement. He states: "The modernization of the colonial mind through perfectly normal and unpolitical channels was more basic to this role than any verbal Bastille-storming. We have already seen that American youth was not in darkness about any essential advance in the world. A student who knew everything leading up to and from Newton and embraced popular sovereignty could deny a Corsican usurper 'spontaneous consent' and make casual use of encyclopedists and *philosophes* when they became available."

A generation whose world view was changed by the study of science and modern philosophy in the eighteenth-century universities in Spanish America did not have to read Rousseau or Voltaire in order to be able to cope with the political crisis of its time. The list of men trained in such ways of thinking and who were influential in the revolutionary period is a long one, for almost all the civilian leaders of the revolution in Spanish America were products of the colonial universities. José Bonifácio de Andrada, the chief collaborator of Pedro I in the establishment of the Brazilian empire, was a graduate and one-time teacher at the Portuguese university of Coimbra, for there were no colonial universities in Brazil, but his intellectual formation in modern science and philosophy was essentially similar to that of the leaders in Spanish America.

Also prominent among the characteristics of the Enlightenment was a zest for the acquisition and dissemination of practical and useful knowledge. This is widely exemplified among the statesmen of the revolutionary period. Closely related to the general interest in the spread of knowledge was the effort to promote public primary education. In the midst of the struggle for independence decrees founding new schools and reorganizing old ones were frequent in all parts of Spanish America. Many of these were established in Mexico and South America on the system promoted by the English Quaker Joseph Lancaster, which involved the teaching, step by step, of older children as monitors who would in turn teach other children what they learned.

They were promising projects, and if they often came to naught it was not because of any lack of interest among the Latin American leaders, but rather because of the almost constant state of bankruptcy of national treasuries.

Equally representative of the thought of the Enlightenment is the philanthropic sentiment which brought about, at least in theory, a recognition of the rights of Indians by the revolutionary leaders. In part this was a mere reflection of the romantic cult of the noble savage in Europe, but it had practical consequences. [*Mexican revolutionary leader Miguel*] Hidalgo abolished the tribute which weighed so heavily on Indians and *castas* in Mexico. In Colombia new republican legislation attempted to create freer conditions for Indian citizens. [*José de*] San Martín [*revolutionary leader in South America; see Article 24*] exhibited his interest by seeing that Quechua translations of his proclamations were issued in the attempt to win the good will of native populations in Peru.

Progress in the emancipation of Negro slaves was an even more important example of the philanthropy encouraged by the Enlightenment than any changes in the status of Indians. Slavery was ended during the revolutionary period in Mexico, Río de la Plata, and Chile. Steps were begun toward gradual emancipation in Colombia. The institution survived only in regions where it was strongly entrenched, as in Peru and Brazil. The slave trade was almost entirely eliminated, persisting on any large scale only in Brazil.

Finally, the Enlightenment bequeathed to the era of revolution in Latin America the belief in progress that was all but universal in the latter period. In earlier ages men had been the victims of ignorance and error; in the future they would inherit an earthly millennium toward which the progress of the human mind would lead them. This belief had animated some of the enlightened bureaucrats of the last days of colonial rule like the second Count of Revillagigedo in New Spain or Ambrosio O'Higgins in Chile and Peru. Many royalists of the early period of revolution were also devotees of progress, especially some of the men who, in America and Europe, worked with the *cortes* of Cádiz. Abad y Queipo, the bishop-elect of Michoacán, Antonio Larrazábal, the Guatemalan representative to the *cortes,* and even some Spanish generals like Canterac and La Serna belonged to this type. Lastly, almost all the patriot leaders were believers in progress. It is true that San Martín, weighed down at last by illness and the harassment of administrative work, became a pessimist; Bolívar too, at the end, wondered whether he and his associates had done anything more than plow the sea, but these views were exceptional. By and large it was necessary for revolutionary leaders to believe in the bright future in the midst of suffering and poverty, and they did so.

The patriot governments of Spanish America in the era of the wars of independence were usually too busy with military operations against the royalists, too much concerned with challenges from domestic factions, too greatly handicapped by empty treasuries and exhausted credit to do much more than maintain themselves precariously. A few regimes, however, during the decade and a half of war and revolution, were briefly in a position to illustrate the continuing vitality of the ideas of the Enlightenment. These were paralleled by the enlightened rule set up by the regency of Dom João in Brazil.

In the first place, we see the continuation of the idea that the state should assume responsibility for developing economic resources. Rivadavia, as minister of the province of Buenos Aires (1821), attempted to establish new towns on the southern Indian frontier, improved the facilities of the port, studied the betterment of the city's water supply, and made plans for bringing immigrants from Europe in order to improve agriculture and industry. O'Higgins, as supreme director of Chile, showed a similar interest in bringing in skilled workmen from Europe and in improving the sanitation, paving, and lighting of Santiago. In Colombia, Vice-President Santander, while charged with the administrative duties of the presidency, studied the possibility of canals and railways for his country and established in Bogotá a school of mathematics and of mines in order to stimulate that industry. He too sought to encourage the immigration of skilled and industrious foreigners. Similar policies were followed by the government of the regent João after his arrival in the New World. The production of coffee was stimulated by royal protection; the iron and textile industries were also encouraged. The effort of O'Higgins to do away with the system of entail in Chile was characteristic of this aim to free and to stimulate economic activity. Of course, the general adoption of liberal commercial policies opening ports to the ships of all nations by all Latin American governments was in harmony with the development policies mentioned above.

Equally similar to the policies of enlightened despots of the preceding century were steps taken in all of the regimes referred to above to improve education and culture. Rivadavia founded the University of Buenos Aires in 1821; O'Higgins re-established the Instituto Nacional in Santiago in 1819; Santander was responsible in 1826 for the adoption of a general plan of education for Colombia that provided for new universities in Bogotá, Caracas, and Quito. Soon after the Portuguese court arrived in Brazil new military and naval academies were founded; instruction in medicine was established both in Rio de Janeiro and in Bahia, to say nothing of a number of other special technical chairs and courses. Parallel to these educational institutions were the new museums and libraries which appeared on the scene. Santander established a museum in Bogotá. National libraries were founded in Brazil, Buenos Aires, and Santiago.

There is also a similarity between the secular viewpoint of the European Enlightenment and the attitudes of some of these regimes of the revolutionary period toward the Church. Perhaps most extreme in this respect was the Buenos Aires regime under the leadership of Rivadavia which launched itself upon an anti-clerical program involving the abolition of the *fueros* of the clergy, the abolition of some monastic establishments, and the setting up of charity on a secular basis in the *Sociedad de Beneficencia*. O'Higgins also clashed with the clergy. Santander, though he was cautious, was *persona non grata* to the clergy because of his masonic affiliations and his regalist position on the question of ecclesiastical patronage. In Brazil it cannot be said that there was anti-clericalism in this period, but the government did strongly support the supremacy of the crown over the Church. This was also a period of extreme political radicalism among the clergy and one in which the clergy itself was somewhat secular in its interests.

The mere recitation of these manifold civic activities recalls the programs of European states in the era of the Enlightenment and indicates how in the midst of war and revolution efforts were continued to encourage economic and cultural progress.

Although it is proper to stress the pervasive influence of a whole gamut of ideas, it must be admitted that the revolutions for independence had a particularly close relation to political ideas and theories because they were political movements. There is a real difficulty in analyzing these relationships because, as already noted, there were divergent elements in the political ideas of the Enlightenment. On the one hand, insistence on rationality as a justification for political institutions called into question traditional authority in church and state, but was not democratic. It could manifest itself in the idea of enlightened absolutism as well as in admiration for the oligarchical constitutionalism of England. On the other hand, a current stemming from Rousseau and carried forward by such authors as Thomas Paine stressed the social contract, the sovereignty of the people, and theoretical democracy.

Before 1808 the chief influence of the political ideas of the Enlightenment on Latin America was to encourage rational and efficient administration. This was primarily apparent in the activities of the Spanish and Portuguese imperial authorities and in such conspicuous figures among them as the Marqués de Pombal and José de Gálvez. These men and their subordinate associates in colonial administration attempted to rationalize government. In these efforts they won some conspicuous successes, but their total accomplishments have lately been judged to have been limited. But it was not the colonial administrators alone who were influenced by this current of ideas. Many Creoles in this period took a public-spirited interest in the improvement of government in their respective countries and distinguished themselves in civic activities. Among them were Manuel Salas (Chile), Antonio Alzate (Mexico), Francisco Espejo (Quito), Hipólito Unánue (Peru), and Manuel Belgrano (Buenos Aires). Some of these men whose political experience began in colonial days were also leaders in the early stages of revolution.

The revolutionary influence of the thought of the Enlightenment in this period was a minor current. We cannot disregard the long and notorious career of Francisco de Miranda [*Venezuelan plotter against Spanish rule*], but it is necessary to realize that subversive propaganda had surprisingly little effect in Latin America before 1808. There can be little doubt that the general reaction to the French Revolution and its ideas was strongly negative. One must remember, too, that Miranda's ideas were not particularly democratic, as his draft scheme for Spanish American government clearly indicates.

Without meaning to do so, it is possible that the political principles of the Bourbon monarchs of Spain may have helped to promote revolution in America. The expulsion of the Jesuits has been held by some to have alienated many subjects of the crown, though the political activities in this field of the exiled Jesuits themselves seem to have been very minor. It has also been maintained that the colonial *cabildos*, previously in decay, were strengthened by the reforming zeal of royal intendants and were thus enabled to assume a more effective revolutionary role in 1810.

We come next to the early years of revolution following the Napoleonic invasion of the Iberian peninsula. In this period there seems to have been a very sharp difference in the character and inspiration of revolts in the different parts of the Spanish empire. Although there were all sorts of other factors involved, it would seem that in Mexico during the Hidalgo revolt and in northern South America about the same time there was a tendency to accept the principles of 1789 with little or no reservation. This was, at least, the style of language, if not of actual behavior. On the other hand, the influence of such ideas was smaller in the southern part of the continent. Brazil remained quiet under the rule of Prince Regent João. In Buenos Aires and in Chile the influence of a Creole aristocracy with reformist, autonomist, but not necessarily democratic ideas was dominant. There were some powerful voices raised in support of independence, republicanism, and liberal democracy, but the general acceptance of the need for independence was slow to develop, in spite of the speeches and newspaper articles of such men as Mariano Moreno (who translated Rousseau), Bernardo Monteagudo, and Camilo Henríquez. The leader of the Uruguayan *orientales*, José Gervasio Artigas, was a steadfast supporter of democratic republicanism, but he had little power during most of these years. However, if the voice of revolutionary democracy was largely stifled by the more powerful forces of oligarchy and by the rivalries and conflicts of ambitious generals and politicians, it must be remembered that the articles of Moreno in the *Gaceta de Buenos Aires* and of Camilo Henríquez in the *Aurora de Chile* expressed a democratic idealism to which the revolution would return for inspiration in later years.

In the years following 1815 there was a general retreat from radical democracy throughout the whole of Latin America. The quasi-constitutional dictatorship in Buenos Aires under Juan Martin de Pueyrredón, the dictatorship of O'Higgins in Chile, the protectorate of San Martín in Peru, and the power exercised by Simón Bolívar in Venezuela and Colombia until 1821 in no case denied the principle of popular sovereignty, but they did not operate under it. In practice they did not differ from frankly authoritarian governments and their behavior stems more closely from the earlier enlightened despotism than from revolutionary ideology. The shift in thought is well illustrated by the changes in the political ideas of Simón Bolívar. The enthusiastic Jacobin of 1810 and 1811 gave way rapidly to the more cautious and hard-headed author of the Cartagena manifesto and to his still liberal but less democratic principles communicated to the Congress of Angostura in 1819. Republics were unstable and weak. The executive of a republic must be strengthened to avoid the danger of anarchy. Especially, in view of the lack of racial, social, or geographical homogeneity, it was important to hold tendencies toward disorder in check by creating strong centralized power.

In Brazil one can see the same moderating and centralizing tendency at work. Though radical republican ideas flared briefly in the northeast in 1817, independence was won only when Pedro I declared himself emperor in 1822 by the will of his people. He rejected the constitutional draft evolved by the constitutional assembly and handed down from the throne the Constitution of 1824 which kept the imperial power predominant over the legislature and weakened the popular principle.

In Mexico there was not only a chastening moderation in the assertion of the ideas of popular government, there was even a negation of it. The chief supporters of Iturbide's revolution of 1821 were conservatives who rejected the ideas of 1789 and reasserted the values of a hierarchical order for an independent Mexico. Throughout the remaining years of the revolutions for independence the flickers of democratic radicalism were fitful and short-lived.

Any attempt to analyze the political ideas of the final years of revolution merges with the study of post-independence conflict between liberals and conservatives and between centralism and federalism. It becomes more and more difficult to trace clearly the relation between the ideas of the Enlightenment and those of the new era. There was a steady evolution which transformed what had been "enlightened" or what had been "Jacobin" into "liberal." Further, there was often a merging of principles which had earlier been opposed. One example of this kind of change is that represented by the regime of Bernardino Rivadavia in the United Provinces in the mid-twenties. It was highly enlightened in a number of ways, promoting education, economic progress, and good administration. It even had some of the anti-clerical prejudices of the *philosophes*. At the same time, it represented an oligarchical faction in the city of Buenos Aires which was very far from popular or democratic. At the same time, the federal party, which opposed Rivadavia's regime, was at once theoretically democratic and in practice barbarous and tyrannical in the character of its leadership. In dealing with this period it is no longer very profitable to make connections between political groups and the sources of their inspiration, for all these groups had been in one way or another influenced by the Enlightenment.

The foregoing consideration of the Enlightenment and the movement for Latin American independence differs from the usual treatment of this subject in that it is not concerned primarily with the evaluation of the Enlightenment as a "cause" of the later revolutionary movement. It attempts, rather, to show the continued presence of various characteristics of the Enlightenment in the latter era. A rational approach to learning and to the solution of human problems, a concern for economic development and progress, interest in education and useful knowledge, and a tendency to clash with the principle of authority in church and state—these were all manifest at different times and places in Latin America between 1808 and 1826. The variant forms of enlightened political theory were also manifested in different ways, as we have noted, in the pre-revolutionary, early, and later years of the struggle for independence. The influences noted here in brief were a part of a movement which continued for the greater part of the century between 1750 and 1850, during which Latin America, a provincial colonial preserve of the Iberian states at the beginning of the period, was incorporated into the cultural world of the West. From that incorporation has stemmed the economic and social progress that has since taken place in Latin America.

◄§ 21 §►

British, French, and American Influences

━━━━━◄◆►━━━━━

Sir Charles Kingsley Webster

*The Enlightenment was, of course, but one of many foreign develop-
ments that strongly influenced the revolutionary movements of Latin
America. British and North America, as well as French, influences on
the independence of the colonies are described and evaluated here by
Sir Charles Kingsley Webster (1886–1961), for many years Stevenson
Professor of International History at the University of London. He is
best known for his works on* The Foreign Policy of Castlereagh *(2 vols.,
London: G. Bell and Sons, Ltd., 1925–1931) and* The Foreign Policy of
Palmerston *(2 vols., London: G. Bell and Sons, Ltd., 1951).*

The impetus to emancipation was not derived from Britain, but from
the two revolutionary movements which transformed North America
and Europe at the end of the eighteenth century. That which resulted
in the United States provided an example to Latin America no less
than to Europe. The successful challenge to the old order affected the
minds of men all over the world, and not least in the rest of the
Americas. That was by far the greatest, and in a sense the only important contribution of the United States to the independence of Latin
America. But it was all-important. "The operation of that example,
sooner or later, was inevitable," was Canning's[1] own judgment. It
was indeed always present in the minds of British ministers throughout
these events to as great an extent as it was in those of the Latin
Americans themselves. Castlereagh appealed to it as a warning to
Spain, and as an inducement to her to seek some new system before

---

From Sir Charles Kingsley Webster (ed.), *Britain and the Independence of
Latin America, 1812–1830. Select Documents from the Foreign Office Archives*,
2 vols. (London: Oxford University Press, 1938), vol. 1, pp. 6–12. Reprinted
by permission of The British Council. This article appears as reprinted in
R. A. Humphreys and John Lynch (eds.), *The Origins of the Latin American
Revolutions, 1808–1826* (New York: Knopf, 1965), pp. 75–83. Deletion in text
is by R. A. Humphreys and John Lynch.

[1] George Canning was English foreign secretary from 1822 to 1827. His
predecessor was Robert Stewart, Viscount Castlereagh, who served from 1812 to
1822. [H. D.]

it was too late. Canning tried to use it to secure from Spain a recognition which Britain had refused to give until overwhelming odds had been brought against her. All states but one indeed recognized the force of that example. Spain herself was the only exception, and her refusal cost her dear.

For the rest the influence of the United States was not great. Some men and ships came from her to South America, but not in such numbers as came from Britain, for her own frontiers and future fully occupied the energies of her people. Her republicanism did something to ensure that republics should arise in Spanish America, but her influence in this respect was not so great as that which came from the French Revolution. The magnificent conception of federalism was imitated to a certain extent by the Latin Americans in the problem of organizing their own vast areas, but local conditions led them to develop the idea along very different lines. The recognition of the Spanish colonies by the United States in 1822 undoubtedly hastened the steps of Britain in the same direction, but the main principle had already been conceded. In preventing Europe from intervening on behalf of Spain it is now recognized that the United States played a minor role of no great importance. The Monroe Doctrine was for the future and for the interests of the United States more than for South America. . . . It was only as the pioneers of independence in the New World that the North Americans made their great contribution to the emancipation of Latin America from a control similar to that from which they had themselves escaped.

In the eighteenth century there was considerable ferment in Latin America which showed that some change was necessary. Revolts occurred, some, of the Indians against Spanish rule—a cause that was now hopeless—others, of the Creoles against the exactions and misgovernment of Spain. There was some relaxation of control and reorganization of the system. Towards the end of the century direct trade was at last allowed between the River Plate and Europe. The British right to send one ship a year to the Spanish colonies had enabled more European supplies to be introduced into South America, and there as elsewhere smuggling mitigated the barriers which governments and vested interests raised against international trade. The old monopoly of the Spanish merchants, however, still persisted, and they still regarded the trade with Spanish America as their own. In smuggling, and in the enjoyment of the right to the slave trade, the British traders played a greater part than those of all other nations, and their navy maintained and extended British interests in the Caribbean sea.

The expulsion of the Jesuits in 1767, a result of European rather than American forces, resulted in the destruction of the missions they had established with so much devotion and skill. Henceforth their

Order was a source of attack on the privileges of Spain in the New World, and affected the minds of many in Europe and Latin America. The ideas that were fermenting in Europe penetrated to some extent into Latin America, through Jesuit as well as through many other channels, but only a small portion of the upper classes were aware of them. The great mass of the people were still completely faithful to their king and church, which were closely identified, since the former had all ecclesiastical patronage in his hands.

The French Revolution acted on this seemingly almost impenetrable body in two ways: in the first place, by its ideas, and secondly, by the effect which it had on the mother countries. Anglo-Saxon ideas as distinct from Anglo-Saxon action have never had much influence on the minds of Latin Americans. The reasoning of the *Federalist* or the speeches of Burke were incomprehensible to them. But the French philosophers and orators spoke a language they could understand. As Senhor Oliveira Lima has testified, it had far greater effect upon their outlook than any republican theories produced in the United States. It gave the intellectual and emotional impetus which produced the energy of the men who led the people to resistance and eventual success. Rousseau was a far greater force in the struggle than Franklin or Hamilton.

But the French Revolution in its Napoleonic expression was the greatest of all the forces which made a revolution in Latin America inevitable. There were indeed revolutionary movements there before 1808, partly assisted by Britain, then at war with Spain. But little effect was produced until Spain's king was captive, her country invaded, and a revolutionary *junta,* and subsequently a democratic *cortes* in control of her government. These events shook the whole foundation of the Spanish empire, and, in their effort to preserve their balance, men found they were revolutionaries almost before they were aware of it. An authority assumed in the name of the king and a determination to resist French control developed into a resistance to the authority of Spain itself. Men inspired by the new ideas and the example of the United States were there to use the situation for their own ends. Thus before the struggle with Napoleon was over, the movement for independence had begun in practically every Spanish province. Meanwhile the same force had driven the Portuguese royal family overseas, and Brazil, become the metropole of the Portuguese empire, could never descend again to the position of a Portuguese colony.

In bringing about these events Britain had played a lesser part than either the United States or France. She had indeed for a long period coquetted with the idea of obtaining a part at least of the vast dominion for herself. Miranda, the great precursor, had long had connections with her statesmen, had lived on her pay and sought to divert her energies to the liberation of Spanish America, particularly of his native Venezuela. After fighting in the American revolutionary war, he had rightly seen that British sea power was the most powerful weapon he could use against Spain; and while Spain was in alliance with Napoleon his efforts met with some response. Trinidad was a convenient base whence expeditions against the mainland could be organized. But these were of small importance until Miranda interested some British commanders themselves in South America. Sir Home Popham's attack on Buenos Aires, partly a result of his propaganda, was in a sense as much a filibustering expedition as those of Drake and Hawkins, since it was not planned nor even authorized by the home government. Its immediate success in the capture of Buenos Aires in 1806, and its rapid defeat as soon as the Argentines had recovered from the first shock, are events of importance in the history of emancipation. They gave merited confidence and prestige to the victors, while at the same time they opened up to them the possibilities of a future under their own control. The soldiers and sailors were soon replaced by traders, and the River Plate was opened to what was in effect an unrestricted trade with such portions of the world as were left free to commerce by the British blockade. The British government had no serious designs of conquest in South America, and they showed little wisdom in endeavoring to recover their prestige by another expedition, which also experienced defeat, partly owing to the incapacity of its commander, General Whitelocke. What the British government and people were really seeking was not territory, but trade and bullion. They also wished to protect Brazil, and of course to prevent the extension of French power and influence in South America. Castlereagh in particular from the first wished to avoid "the hopeless task of conquering this extensive country against the temper of its population." "In looking to any scheme for liberating South America," he advised the cabinet, "it seems indispensable that we should not present ourselves in any other light than as auxiliaries and protectors." The object was admittedly a delicate one for a Power which still considered itself as fighting a revolutionary foe. But the advantages to be gained were considerable. A further expedition was thus planned, its first objective being not Argentina, but Mexico, whose mineral riches might supply the bullion necessary to finance the struggle against Napoleon. But Miranda still had hopes that he would at last secure the assistance so long solicited from Britain, and that the army assembled in Ireland which Sir Arthur Wellesley was to command would be sent to secure the liberation of his own country, Venezuela, from Spanish rule.

The situation was, however, suddenly transformed. Napoleon's invasion of the Spanish Peninsula diverted the expedition to another destination, and from its base at Lisbon it began the reconquest of Portugal and Spain from the French armies which had overrun them. The situation which thus arose naturally made Britain of supreme importance in the Latin American struggle. In any case, as the greatest sea power and trading nation she would have been a determining factor. Events now forced her into a position of peculiar delicacy which exercised great influence on the course of events.

Britain had long been the protector of Portugal. It was by her advice and with the escort of her ships that the Portuguese royal family and many of the court and upper classes emigrated to Brazil. Henceforward until the end of the war Britain practically governed as well as defended Portugal. The price that she asked and obtained was the treaties of 1810, which gave her goods entrance at low duties into all the territories governed by the House of Braganza.

But she was now forced also to become the defender of Spain. For five years her armies fought side by side with the Spaniards until Spain had recovered her freedom and her king. The alliance was an uneasy one, but it never faltered on either side in its main objective. Naturally in such circumstances Britain could not contemplate the conquest of Spain's colonies. She had indeed already renounced it. But she could not now give aid to any attempt to overthrow Spanish dominion. What she wanted was the right to trade. This her merchants, shut out from European markets, were already taking without permission. The Spaniards were as conscious as the South Americans that Britain was the most important factor in the situation. They were reluctant to give up their position of monopoly. But Britain was defending them against Napoleon, and the deputies of Venezuela, Bolívar amongst them, were in London. Thus a sort of permission to trade was granted by the Cádiz government, though how definite and how far to extend into the future was later a matter of dispute. Canning claimed in the famous Polignac Memorandum that the right to trade had been established at this time. This was an exaggeration, since permission was local and limited to the duration of the war. But at any rate by 1810 a definite stage had been reached in the relations of Britain to the Latin American world. She had secured an opportunity to trade directly with both Brazil and the Spanish colonies. It is a major element in all the negotiations which follow that under no circumstances would she abandon that privilege.

There was thus no special reason why British policy should desire the emancipation of the Spanish colonies or the establishment of Brazil as an independent state. But she could not view with indifference any threat of interference by any other Power in the relations between Spain and her colonies or between Portugal and Brazil. She was ready, and indeed for a period anxious, that the authority of the mother countries should be recognized by their colonies, to whom freedom of trade should be guaranteed. But the trade must remain. And remain it did through all the vicissitudes of the next fifteen years. Indeed it multiplied tenfold. British manufacturers and shipping interests therefore became more and more interested in Latin America, and their outlook exercised more and more influence over the activities of the British government.

In addition to her trading influence, the naval power of Britain gave her a commanding position which no other country could hope to challenge. The Napoleonic wars had established her command of the seas—every sea, including American waters. In spite of the victories of the United States in many combats in the War of 1812, Britain established naval control over the American coasts at the height of her war against Napoleon. In European waters French privateers persisted, but enemy fleets had ceased to sail the seas. This supremacy was retained after the peace, and in 1823, when French armies occupied Spain, the British fleet was four times as strong as that of France. No fleet could therefore move against Latin America unless Britain allowed it to do so. This strategical situation was always present in the minds of all the statesmen who were concerned with the question of recognition. John Quincy Adams no less than Villèle or Chateaubriand recognized that this fact dominated the situation. Only by means of the British fleet could Spain have re-established her power; only by permission of Britain could any other Power have assisted her to do so. The Latin Americans were equally conscious of the same fact. "Only England, mistress of the seas, can protect us against the united force of European reaction," wrote Bolívar as late as 1823. Though they might desire recognition from other Powers, and at times enter into negotiation with them, it was always to Britain that they naturally turned. From Miranda onwards the thoughts of their leaders were preoccupied with the idea of how they could turn this mighty instrument to their own purpose.

Thus from the beginning of the revolutionary movement, British influence was established by two main agencies—her trade and her fleet. As the former grew, the latter was called upon to defend it from the piratical warfare into which the struggle sometimes developed. The adventurers, who used the letters of marque granted by the Latin American States, and the Spanish *guarda costas* that were supposed to maintain the Spanish monopoly of commerce, were both liable to take a prize without enquiring too closely into its origin. Some vessels were little more than unabashed pirates. British shipping as the most numerous was the most hard-hit, and the archives are full of protests and protracted negotiations over these captures of British vessels. The necessity of regularizing the trade and giving to the South American states a legal and responsible position in the world was one of the major reasons that led Britain towards a policy of recognition.

In all this British statesmen were directed by the powerful motive of self-interest which is the determining factor in the policy of all nations. There were, however, other forces in Britain on the side of the emancipators. The growing liberal movement was from the first deeply interested in their success. In debates in the House and in the pages of the *Morning Chronicle,* their cause was sustained by followers of the same men who had defended the right of the North Americans to revolt. As early as 1809 the *Edinburgh Review* published a long article, inspired by Miranda himself, entitled "South American Emancipation." When the Napoleonic wars were over and Ferdinand had re-established absolutism and the Inquisition in Spain, the Spanish government became exceedingly unpopular in England. There was a real desire to see freedom triumph in South America, altogether apart from the commercial interests which dictated policy. Without the commercial interest the loans could not have been raised to buy the arms with which the Americans defended themselves against Spain. But the fact that the cause was also one which appealed to the liberal and Protestant feelings of the middle class undoubtedly helped to make it a success. Moreover, the emancipation of Spanish America resulted in the abolition there, not only of the Inquisition, but also of the slave trade. This fact made an immense appeal to the same classes, while the reluctance of Spain and Portugal to do the same thing made their governments unpopular. ... . Brazil's interest in the slave trade was one of the great obstacles to British recognition of her independence.

~§ 22 §~

Bolívar's Jamaica Letter

Simón Bolívar

The most celebrated figure of the revolutionary era, Simón Bolívar (1783–1830), was one of those Creoles who was steeped in the ideas of the Enlightenment. A forceful writer and penetrating thinker as well as a successful general, Bolívar expounded his political views in a number of documents. One of the best known is the letter from Jamaica, written in 1815 while Bolívar was in exile after suffering a series of reverses in Venezuela and New Granada. In the letter Bolívar bitterly condemns Spain for keeping the inhabitants of America in a state of political tutelage for three centuries. He also predicts the future that awaits the various parts of Spanish America and declares his own preference for strong, centralized, but republican, government.

. . . We are a young people. We inhabit a world apart, separated by broad seas. We are young in the ways of almost all the arts and sciences, although, in a certain manner, we are old in the ways of civilized society. I look upon the present state of America as similar to that of Rome after its fall. Each part of Rome adopted a political system conforming to its interest and situation or was led by the individual ambitions of certain chiefs, dynasties, or associations. But this important difference exists: those dispersed parts later reestablished their ancient nations, subject to the changes imposed by circumstances or events. But we scarcely retain a vestige of what once was; we are, moreover, neither Indian nor European, but a species midway between the legitimate proprietors of this country and the Spanish usurpers. In short, though Americans by birth we derive our rights from Europe, and we have to assert these rights against the rights of the natives, and at the same time we must defend ourselves against the invaders. This places us in a most extraordinary and involved situation. Not-

From Vicente Lecuna (comp.) and Harold A. Bierck, Jr. (ed.), *Selected Writings of Bolívar*, 2 vols. (Caracas: Banco de Venezuela, 1951), I, 110–122 *passim*. Reprinted by permission of the Banco de Venezuela, S. A. This article appears as reprinted in David Bushnell (ed.), *The Liberator, Simón Bolívar* (New York: Knopf, 1970), pp. 11–21. Deletions in the text are by David Bushnell.

withstanding that it is a type of divination to predict the result of the political course which America is pursuing, I shall venture some conjectures which, of course, are colored by my enthusiasm and dictated by rational desires rather than by reasoned calculations.

The role of the inhabitants of the American hemisphere has for centuries been purely passive. Politically they were nonexistent. We are still in a position lower than slavery, and therefore it is more difficult for us to rise to the enjoyment of freedom. Permit me these transgressions in order to establish the issue. States are slaves because of either the nature or the misuse of their constitutions; a people is therefore enslaved when the government, by its nature or its vices, infringes on and usurps the rights of the citizen or subject. Applying these principles, we find that America was denied not only its freedom but even an active and effective tyranny. Let me explain. Under absolutism there are no recognized limits to the exercise of governmental powers. The will of the great sultan, khan, bey, and other despotic rulers is the supreme law, carried out more or less arbitrarily by the lesser pashas, khans, and satraps of Turkey and Persia, who have an organized system of oppression in which inferiors participate according to the authority vested in them. To them is entrusted the administration of civil, military, political, religious, and tax matters. But, after all is said and done, the rulers of Ispahan are Persians; the viziers of the Grand Turk are Turks; and the sultans of Tartary are Tartars. China does not bring its military leaders and scholars from the land of Genghis Khan, her conqueror, notwithstanding that the Chinese of today are the lineal descendants of those who were reduced to subjection by the ancestors of the present-day Tartars.

How different is our situation! We have been harassed by a conduct which has not only deprived us of our rights but has kept us in a sort of permanent infancy with regard to public affairs. If we could at least have managed our domestic affairs and our internal administration, we could have acquainted ourselves with the processes and mechanics of public affairs. We should also have enjoyed a personal consideration, thereby commanding a certain unconscious respect from the people, which is so necessary to preserve amidst revolutions. That is why I say we have even been deprived of an active tyranny, since we have not been permitted to exercise its functions.

Americans today, and perhaps to a greater extent than ever before, who live within the Spanish system occupy a position in society no better than that of serfs destined for labor, or at best they have no more status than that of mere consumers. Yet even this status is surrounded with galling restrictions, such as being forbidden to grow European crops, or to store products which are royal monopolies, or to establish factories of a type the Peninsula itself does not possess. To this add the exclusive trading privileges, even in articles of prime necessity, and the barriers between American provinces, designed to prevent all exchange of trade, traffic, and understanding. In short, do you wish to know what our future held?—simply the cultivation of the fields of indigo, grain, coffee, sugar cane, cacao, and cotton; cattle raising on the broad plains; hunting wild game in the jungles; digging in the earth to mine its gold—but even these limitations could never satisfy the greed of Spain. So negative was our existence that I can find nothing comparable in any other civilized society. . . .

As I have just explained, we were cut off and, as it were, removed from the world in relation to the science of government and administration of the state. We were never viceroys or governors, save in the rarest of instances; seldom archbishops and bishops; diplomats never; as military men, only subordinates; as nobles, without royal privileges. In brief, we were neither magistrates nor financiers and seldom merchants—all in flagrant contradiction to our institutions.

Emperor Charles V made a pact with the discoverers, conquerors, and settlers of America; and this, as Guerra puts it, is our social contract. The monarchs of Spain made a solemn agreement with them, to be carried out on their own account and at their own risk, expressly prohibiting them from drawing on the royal treasury. In return, they were made the lords of the land, entitled to organize the public administration and act as the court of last appeal, together with many other exemptions and privileges that are too numerous to mention. . . . Thus, for themselves and their descendants, the *conquistadores* possessed what were tantamount to feudal holdings. Yet there are explicit laws respecting employment in civil, ecclesiastical, and tax-raising establishments. These laws favor, almost exclusively, the natives of the country who are of Spanish extraction. Thus, by an outright violation of the laws and the existing agreements, those born in America have been despoiled of their constitutional rights as embodied in the code.

From what I have said it is easy to deduce that America was not prepared to secede from the mother country; this secession was suddenly brought about by the effect of the illegal concessions of Bayonne and the unrighteous war which the regency unjustly and illegally declared on us.[1] . . .

The first steps of all the new governments are marked by the

---

[1] The "concessions of Bayonne" represent the forced abdication of the Spanish royal family, imposed by Napoleon in 1808. When the Spanish Americans formed juntas of their own to govern in the absence of their legitimate monarch, the anti-Napoleonic rump government in Spain normally refused to recognize their authority to do so—hence the "unrighteous war" unleashed by the Spanish Council of Regency. [D. B.]

establishment of juntas of the people. These juntas speedily draft rules for the calling of congresses, which produce great changes. Venezuela erected a democratic and federal government, after declaring for the rights of man. A system of checks and balances was established; and general laws were passed granting civil liberties, such as freedom of the press and others. In short, an independent government was created. New Granada uniformly followed the political institutions and reforms introduced by Venezuela, taking as the fundamental basis of her constitution the most elaborate federal system ever to be brought into existence. . . .

Events in Costa Firme[2] have proved that institutions which are wholly representative are not suited to our character, custom, and present knowledge. In Caracas party spirit arose in the societies, assemblies, and popular elections; these parties led us back into slavery. Thus, while Venezuela has been the American republic with the most advanced political institutions, she has also been the clearest example of the inefficacy of the democratic and federal system for our newborn states. In New Granada, the large number of excess powers held by the provincial governments and the lack of centralization in the general government have reduced that fair country to her present state. For this reason her foes, though weak, have been able to hold out against all odds. As long as our countrymen do not acquire the abilities and political virtues that distinguish our brothers of the north, wholly popular systems, far from working to our advantage, will, I greatly fear, bring about our downfall. Unfortunately, these traits, to the degree in which they are required, do not appear to be within our reach. On the contrary, we are dominated by the vices that one learns under the rule of a nation like Spain, which has only distinguished itself in ferocity, ambition, vindictiveness, and greed.

It is harder, Montesquieu has written, to release a nation from servitude than to enslave a free nation. This truth is proven by the annals of all times, which reveal that most free nations have been put under the yoke, but very few enslaved nations have recovered their liberty. Despite the convictions of history, South Americans have made efforts to obtain liberal, even perfect, institutions, doubtless out of that instinct to aspire to the greatest possible happiness, which, common to all men, is bound to follow in civil societies founded on the principles of justice, liberty, and equality. But are we capable of maintaining in proper balance the difficult charge of a republic? Is it conceivable that a newly emancipated people can soar to the heights of liberty, and, unlike Icarus, neither have its wings melt nor fall into an abyss? Such

[2] The "mainland" or Spanish Main; the northern coast of South America. [D. B.]

a marvel is inconceivable and without precedent. There is no reasonable probability to bolster our hopes.

. . .

M. de Pradt[3] has wisely divided America into fifteen or seventeen mutually independent states, governed by as many monarchs. I am in agreement on the first suggestion, as America can well tolerate seventeen nations; as to the second, though it could easily be achieved, it would serve no purpose. Consequently, I do not favor American monarchies. My reasons are these: The well-understood interest of a republic is limited to the matter of its preservation, prosperity, and glory. Republicans, because they do not desire powers which represent a directly contrary viewpoint, have no reason for expanding the boundaries of their nation to the detriment of their own resources solely for the purpose of having their neighbors share a liberal constitution. They would not acquire rights or secure any advantage by conquering their neighbors unless they were to make them colonies, conquered territory, or allies, after the example of Rome. But such thought and action are directly contrary to the principles of justice which characterize republican systems; and, what is more, they are in direct opposition to the interests of their citizens, because a state, too large of itself or together with its dependencies, ultimately falls into decay. Its free government becomes a tyranny. The principles that should preserve the government are disregarded, and finally it degenerates into despotism. The distinctive feature of small republics is permanence: that of large republics varies, but always with a tendency toward empire. Almost all small republics have had long lives. Among the larger republics, only Rome lasted for several centuries, for its capital was a republic. The rest of her dominions were governed by divers laws and institutions.

The policy of a king is very different. His constant desire is to increase his possessions, wealth, and authority; and with justification, for his power grows with every acquisition, both with respect to his neighbors and his own vassals, who fear him because his power is as formidable as his empire, which he maintains by war and conquest. For these reasons I think that the Americans, being anxious for peace, science, art, commerce, and agriculture, would prefer republics to kingdoms. And, further, it seems to me that these desires conform with the aims of Europe.

We know little about the opinions prevailing in Buenos Aires, Chile, and Peru. Judging by what seeps through and by conjecture, Buenos Aires will have a central government in which the military,

---

[3] The Abbé de Pradt, one of the leading European propagandists for Latin American independence. [D. B.]

as a result of its internal dissensions and external wars, will have the upper hand. Such a constitutional system will necessarily degenerate into an oligarchy or a monocracy, with a variety of restrictions the exact nature of which no one can now foresee. It would be unfortunate if this situation were to follow because the people there deserve a more glorious destiny.

The Kingdom of Chile is destined, by the nature of its location, by the simple and virtuous character of its people, and by the example of its neighbors, the proud republicans of Arauco,[4] to enjoy the blessings that flow from the just and gentle laws of a republic. If any American republic is to have a long life, I am inclined to believe it will be Chile. There the spirit of liberty has never been extinguished; the vices of Europe and Asia arrived too late or not at all to corrupt the customs of that distant corner of the world. Its area is limited; and, as it is remote from other peoples, it will always remain free from contamination. Chile will not alter her laws, ways, and practices. She will preserve her uniform political and religious views. In a word, it is possible for Chile to be free.

Peru, on the contrary, contains two factors that clash with every just and liberal principle: gold and slaves. The former corrupts everything; the latter are themselves corrupt. The soul of a serf can seldom really appreciate true freedom. Either he loses his head in uprisings or his self-respect in chains. Although these remarks would be applicable to all America, I believe that they apply with greater justice to Lima, for the reasons I have given and because of the cooperation she has rendered her masters against her own brothers, those illustrious sons of Quito, Chile, and Buenos Aires. It is plain that he who aspires to obtain liberty will at least attempt to secure it. I imagine that in Lima the rich will not tolerate democracy, nor will the freed slaves and *pardos* accept aristocracy. The former will prefer the tyranny of a single man, to avoid the tumult of rebellion and to provide, at least, a peaceful system. If Peru intends to recover her independence, she has much to do.

From the foregoing, we can draw these conclusions: The American provinces are fighting for their freedom, and they will ultimately succeed. Some provinces as a matter of course will form federal and some central republics; the larger areas will inevitably establish monarchies, some of which will fare so badly that they will disintegrate in either present or future revolutions. To consolidate a great monarchy will be no easy task, but it will be utterly impossible to consolidate a great republic.

It is a grandiose idea to think of consolidating the New World into

---

[4] The Araucanian Indians of southern Chile, whose resistance to Spanish rule had never been fully overcome. [D. B.]

a single nation, united by pacts into a single bond. It is reasoned that, as these parts have a common origin, language, customs, and religion, they ought to have a single government to permit the newly formed states to unite in a confederation. But this is not possible. Actually, America is separated by climatic differences, geographic diversity, conflicting interests, and dissimilar characteristics. How beautiful it would be if the Isthmus of Panama could be for us what the Isthmus of Corinth was for the Greeks! Would to God that some day we may have the good fortune to convene there an august assembly of representatives of republics, kingdoms, and empires to deliberate upon the high interests of peace and war with the nations of the other three-quarters of the globe. This type of organization may come to pass in some happier period of our regeneration. But any other plan, such as that of Abbé St. Pierre, who in laudable delirium conceived the idea of assembling a European congress to decide the fate and interests of those nations, would be meaningless.

Among the popular and representative systems, I do not favor the federal system. It is overperfect, and it demands political virtues and talents far superior to our own. For the same reason I reject a monarchy that is part aristocracy and part democracy, although with such a government England has achieved much fortune and splendor. Since it is not possible for us to select the most perfect and complete form of government, let us avoid falling into demagogic anarchy or monocratic tyranny. These opposite extremes would only wreck us on similar reefs of misfortune and dishonor; hence, we must seek a mean between them. I say: Do not adopt the best system of government but the one that is most likely to succeed.

By the nature of their geographic location, wealth, population, and character, I expect that the Mexicans, at the outset, intend to establish a representative republic in which the executive will have great powers. These will be concentrated in one person, who, if he discharges his duties with wisdom and justice, should almost certainly maintain his authority for life. If through incompetence or violence he should excite a popular revolt and it should be successful, this same executive power would then, perhaps, be distributed among the members of an assembly. If the dominant party is military or aristocratic, it will probably demand a monarchy that would be limited and constitutional at the outset, and would later inevitably degenerate into an absolute monarchy; . . . only a people as patriotic as the English are capable of controlling the authority of a king and of sustaining the spirit of liberty under the rule of scepter and crown.

The states of the Isthmus of Panama, as far as Guatemala, will perhaps form a confederation. Because of their magnificent position between two mighty oceans, they may in time become the emporium of the world. Their canals will shorten distances throughout the world, strengthen commercial ties between Europe, America, and Asia, and bring to that happy area tribute from the four quarters of the globe. There some day, perhaps, the capital of the world may be located—reminiscent of the Emperor Constantine's claim that Byzantium was the capital of the ancient world.

New Granada will unite with Venezuela, if they can agree to the establishment of a central republic. Their capital may be Maracaibo or a new city to be named Las Casas (in honor of that humane hero) to be built on the borders of the two countries, in the excellent port area of Bahía-Honda. This location, though little known, is the most advantageous in all respects. It is readily accessible, and its situation is so strategic that it can be made impregnable. It has a fine, healthful climate, a soil as suitable for agriculture as for cattle raising, and a superabundance of good timber. The Indians living there can be civilized, and our territorial possessions could be increased with the acquisition of the Goajira Peninsula. This nation should be called Colombia as a just and grateful tribute to the discoverer of our hemisphere. Its government might follow the English pattern, except that in place of a king there will be an executive who will be elected, at most, for life, but his office will never be hereditary, if a republic is desired. There will be a hereditary legislative chamber or senate. This body can interpose itself between the violent demands of the people and the great powers of the government during periods of political unrest. The second representative body will be a legislature with restrictions no greater than those of the lower house in England. The Constitution will draw on all systems of government, but I do not want it to partake of all their vices. As Colombia is my country, I have an indisputable right to desire for her that form of government which, in my opinion, is best. It is very possible that New Granada may not care to recognize a central government, because she is greatly addicted to federalism; in such event, she will form a separate state which, if it endures, may prosper, because of its great and varied resources.

.   .   .

Surely unity is what we need to complete our work of regeneration. The division among us, nevertheless, is nothing extraordinary, for it is characteristic of civil wars to form two parties, *conservatives* and *reformers*. The former are commonly the more numerous, because the weight of habit induces obedience to established powers; the latter are always fewer in number although more vocal and learned. Thus, the physical mass of the one is counterbalanced by the moral force of the other; the contest is prolonged, and the results are uncertain. Fortunately, in our case, the mass has followed the learned.

I shall tell you with what we must provide ourselves in order to expel the Spaniards and to found a free government. It is *union*, obviously; but such union will come about through sensible planning and well-directed actions rather than by divine magic. America stands together because it is abandoned by all other nations. It is isolated in the center of the world. It has no diplomatic relations, nor does it receive any military assistance; instead, America is attacked by Spain, which has more military supplies than any we can possibly acquire through furtive means.

When success is not assured, when the state is weak, and when results are distantly seen, all men hesitate; opinion is divided, passions rage, and the enemy fans these passions in order to win an easy victory because of them. As soon as we are strong and under the guidance of a liberal nation which will lend us her protection, we will achieve accord in cultivating the virtues and talents that lead to glory. Then will we march majestically toward that great prosperity for which South America is destined. Then will those sciences and arts which, born in the East, have enlightened Europe, wing their way to a free Colombia, which will cordially bid them welcome. . . .

23

Bolívar in His Camp

Hiram Paulding

The liberation of portions of Venezuela and New Granada was accompanied by the creation of the republic of Colombia, of which Ecuador later became a part. Although Bolívar was elected president of the new republic, he preferred to prosecute the war against Spain in person and launched campaigns against royalist forces in Ecuador and Peru. While in Peru in 1824, Bolívar received a visit from Hiram Paulding (1797–1878), an American naval officer who bore dispatches from the commander of the United States Pacific Squadron. Paulding's account of his meetings with Bolívar reveals his own favorable impression of the Liberator and sheds light on Bolívar's ideas on politics, religion, and other matters.

. . . I was ushered into a long hall where General Bolívar was seated at dinner with about fifty of his officers in splendid uniforms. His Excellency rose from the table, I was introduced as an officer of the United States, he asked my rank, shook me cordially by the hand, and bade me be seated alongside of him. He invited me to dine, but readily excused me when I declined doing so. "I presume you have had little wine on the road you have traveled," said he, "and therefore you will not refuse to take a glass of champagne with me."

He asked me a variety of questions about my journey, talked freely upon various subjects, bade the officers to fill round with wine, and introduced me by drinking my health in a bumper. His cordiality, his frankness, and his unceremonious courtesy relieved me entirely from the awkward feeling I had experienced at my first introduction. He continued to talk incessantly and with great animation while he remained at the table, which was but for a short time after my arrival. When he desired no longer to continue the pleasures of the table, he became silent, and rising from his seat the officers immediately took their leave. After the company had retired I asked whether His Ex-

From Rebecca Paulding Meade, *Life of Hiram Paulding, Rear-Admiral, U.S.N.* (New York, 1910), pp. 62–64, 68–72, 74–76. This article appears as reprinted in David Bushnell (ed.), *The Liberator, Simón Bolívar* (New York: Knopf, 1970), pp. 93–98. Deletions in the text are by David Bushnell.

cellency would then receive the despatches I had the honor of bearing to him or whether they should be delivered on the following day,
to which he replied, "I will receive them now and examine them
immediately. You shall return to your Commander with my reply
as soon as it is possible to have it prepared for you." He apologized
for not entertaining me in his own house, saying there was not a room
in it unoccupied, and, calling to him Captain Wilson, one of his aides,
bade him obtain comfortable lodgings for me in the house of some
citizen. . . .

At half-past four [on the following day] dinner was announced. A
large number of officers were assembled in the hall. They saluted as
he made his appearance; and, placing me at his right hand and my
companion at his left, the company was seated round the table furnished in the plainest possible manner. During the whole morning
his countenance had been grave and thoughtful, even to deep and
settled melancholy; but from the moment he took the head of his table,
surrounded by the officers of his army, the whole man appeared to
undergo an entire change. The settled gloom passed from his care-
worn features, his eyes sparkled with animation, and with a flow of
eloquent raillery or good-natured sarcasm, addressing himself from
one to another of his guests, he threw such a charm around the social
board that all eyes were fixed upon him with gratification and delight.

To the veteran Colonel Sands, an Irishman whose long career of
useful service in Colombia gave him a high place in the Liberator's
esteem and who arrived on the preceding day at the head of a regiment called the "Rifles," he spoke of their former campaigns, asking
whether on the plains of Houca [i.e., Jauja] (where in a few days the
Spaniards were expected to have been met) his gallant regiment could
maintain the glory they had acquired in so many hard-fought battles.
The Colonel, as remarkable for his diffidence as he was for his in-
trepidity, blushed deeply as he replied in the affirmative. The Liberator, then addressing the company, related a number of brilliant
achievements performed by the regiment and of individuals belonging
to it. From Colonel Sands and the "Rifles," with a grace peculiar to himself, he turned the eulogium upon other regiments and divisions of
the Colombian Army, in all of which some of the officers present had
acquired a reputation. He said that history, whether ancient or modern, could not furnish brighter examples of patriotic devotion or individual heroism than were recorded in the history of the revolution
of Colombia. In confirmation he went on to recount with minuteness
and perspicuity the brilliant achievements of some of the martyrs to
liberty with whom he had been personally acquainted or whose efforts
were in unison with his own in the great struggle for emancipation.

It surprised me not a little to hear the comparisons he made in passing from Colombia to Peru. He condemned the people of Peru in

general terms, said they were cowards and as a people did not possess a single manly virtue. I thought, though his remarks were just, they were both impolitic and ill timed, and calculated to injure him seriously in the estimation of the people of that country, while it could not possibly answer any useful purpose. I was informed that he was accustomed to speak in the same terms of the Peruvians on all occasions; and to this I believe it may be reasonably ascribed that the inhabitants of Peru did not evince more gratitude toward the Colombians for their fraternal assistance in driving the Spaniards from their country.

The dinner was served after the Spanish custom of placing it on the table in different courses, as many as seven or eight of which came in succession. The Liberator ate very heartily and I think must have had his plate changed a dozen times in making his dinner. He drank freely of wine and encouraged his guests to do so. He gave out a number of toasts, several of which were drunk with acclamation. Among those in compliment to my country was the memory of Washington, drunk standing.

Calling on me for a toast, I gave "Success to the liberating army of Peru and the Washington of the south, may glory attend them." In the course of the repast he turned to me, saying, "My enemies abuse me very much and among other falsehoods they have told of me they say I use gold knives." Holding toward me the knife he was using at the time, which was of a very ordinary kind, much worn, he said, smiling, "Does that look like gold? They say I wish to establish an empire in Peru, or, uniting Peru to Colombia, establish an absolute government and place myself at the head of it. It is all false," said he; "they do me great injustice. If I know my own heart," putting his right hand upon his left breast, "I would rather walk in the footsteps of Washington and die the death of Washington than to be the monarch of the whole earth; and this is known to all who know me well."

.   .   .

In the course of the repast some allusion was made to the Spanish Army in upper Peru, when the Liberator, embracing every opportunity of inspiring confidence in his officers, spoke of the Spaniards in the severest terms of scorn and contempt, intimating in the course of his remarks that one Colombian was equal to two or three Spaniards on the field of battle. . . .

On the following morning, June 13,[1] I went again to breakfast with the Liberator. He rose from his seat when he saw me enter the court and advanced to receive me. He took my hands, said he was better,

[1] Really two days later; on the 12th, Bolívar was not feeling well, and Paulding's account for that day has been omitted. [D. B.]

and invited me to be seated in his audience room. At one end of the room there was a small chapel with tapers burning, such as is often seen in Catholic gentlemen's houses. Pointing to it he said, "You do not go to mass I suppose." I replied that although no Catholic, I sometimes went to mass when in a Catholic country. "What is your religion?" said he. I replied, "The Protestant." "Now," he observed, "religion depends a good deal on fashion." I asked if the Protestant religions were tolerated in Colombia. "When the constitution of Colombia was framed," said he, "knowing that toleration of other than the Catholic religion would not be received, I took care that nothing should be said about religion, so that as there was no clause prescribing the manner of worship, strangers worship as they please."

Three priests came in richly dressed and were politely received by the Liberator, with whom they sat and conversed for some time. When they retired he saw them to the door; and, turning from them toward his seat, he remarked, "Esos moncas son ton feo como diablos." [2] I asked whether the priests were generally favorable to the revolution. He replied that those were friendly to it who were born in the country but that all the Spanish priests were opposed to it. Although their power was much lessened and was daily decreasing, they had still, he said, a great deal of influence. "No old Spaniard," said he, "is friendly to the revolution. They will pretend to favor the cause of the patriots while we have them in our power, but the moment they can aid the royalists they will do so. Their customs, their manners, their sentiments, their principles, and even their color are all bad. They come here bringing with them a combination of all the vices of our nature. They have corrupted the people of the country. They have mixed with negroes and Indians and devils and have formed the most accursed race that ever lived. This country," said he, "can never prosper for a hundred years to come. Two generations must pass away first. The people of Europe and North America must be encouraged to settle here, bringing with them their commerce, their arts and sciences. These advantages, an independent government, free schools, and inter-marriages with Europeans and North Americans would change," he said, "the whole character of the people and make them intelligent and prosperous."

I was unacquainted with the constitution of Colombia and in the course of this morning's conversation asked him if it were similar to that of the United States. He replied that it differed materially from that of the United States. "Your Government," said he, "cannot last. The executive has not power enough. The States have too much. Dissension and disunion will be the ultimate consequence. It is much

---

[2] The correct Spanish would be: "Esos monjes son tan feos como diablos." In English: "Those monks are as ugly as devils." [D. B.]

to be regretted. With a stronger Government your country would be the most powerful in the world in fifty years. Your commerce must be extensive, your countrymen are brave and enterprising, you have fine harbors and an abundance of timber and iron, and the time must come when you will drive England from the ocean. All Europe, imbibing the principles of America, will become free, and the civilized world in less than a hundred years will be governed by philosophy. There will no longer be kings. The people will find out their power and the advantages of liberty."

24

San Martín in Peru

──◄─◆─►──

Basil Hall

The outstanding figure of the revolutionary wars in the southern half of South America was José de San Martín (1778–1850). San Martín, the son of a Spanish army officer, was a professional soldier, unlike Bolívar, and remained primarily a military man. He shared Bolívar's dislike of federalism but differed from the northern liberator in his preference for monarchical government. Bolívar and San Martín met only once, on the occasion of the controversial Guayaquil interview (July 27, 1822), which was followed by San Martín's permanent retirement from the struggle against Spain. Earlier (1820–1821) San Martín had landed in Peru and had occupied Lima; now the task of liberating Peru fell to Bolívar.

In this selection, Basil Hall (1788–1844), a captain in the British navy, describes San Martín on the eve of his entry into Lima in July 1821 and records some of San Martín's remarks on contemporary politics. Captain Hall later wrote an account of his Travels in North America in the Years 1827 and 1828 *(Edinburgh: Cadell and Co., 1829), which provoked angry criticism in the United States because of its depiction of American society.*

25th of June

I had an interview this day with General San Martín, on board a little schooner, a yacht of his own, anchored in Callao Roads for the convenience of communicating with the deputies, who, during the armistice, had held their sittings on board a ship in the anchorage.

There was little, at first sight, in his appearance to engage the attention; but when he rose up and began to speak, his superiority was apparent. He received us in very homely style, on the deck of his vessel, dressed in a large surtout coat, and a large fur cap, and seated at a table made of a few loose planks laid along the top of some empty

---

From Captain Basil Hall, *Extracts from a Journal Written on the Coasts of Chili, Peru, and Mexico in the Years 1820, 1821, 1822,* 2 vols., 4th ed. (Edinburgh: Archibald Constable and Co., 1825), vol. 1, pp. 213–247. Italicized bracketed notes in the text are by Helen Delpar.

casks. He is a tall, erect, well-proportioned, handsome man, with a large aquiline nose, thick black hair, and immense bushy dark whiskers, extending from ear to ear under the chin; his complexion is deep olive, and his eye, which is large, prominent, and piercing, is jet black; his whole appearance being highly military. He is thoroughly well-bred, and unaffectedly simple in his manners; exceedingly cordial and engaging, and possessed evidently of great kindliness of disposition: in short, I have never seen any person, the enchantment of whose address was more irresistible. In conversation he went at once to the strong points of the topic, disdaining, as it were, to trifle with its minor parts; he listened earnestly, and replied with distinctness and fairness, showing wonderful resources in argument, and a most happy fertility of illustration; the effect of which was, to make his audience feel they were understood in the sense they wished. Yet there was nothing showy or ingenious in his discourse; and he certainly seemed, at all times, perfectly in earnest, and deeply possessed with his subject. At times his animation rose to a high pitch; when the flash of his eye, and the whole turn of his expression, became so exceedingly energetic as to rivet the attention of his audience beyond the possibility of evading his arguments. This was most remarkable when the topic was politics; on which subject, I consider myself fortunate in having heard him express himself frequently. But his quiet manner was not less striking, and indicative of a mind of no ordinary stamp: he could even be playful and familiar, when such was the tone of the moment; and whatever effect the subsequent possession of great political power may have had on his mind, I feel confident that his natural disposition is kind and benevolent.

During the first visit I paid to San Martín, several persons came privately from Lima to discuss the state of affairs, upon which occasion his views and feelings were distinctly stated; and I saw nothing in his conduct afterwards to cast a doubt upon the sincerity with which he then spoke. The contest in Peru, he said, was not of an ordinary description—not a war of conquest and glory, but entirely of opinion; it was a war of new and liberal principles against prejudice, bigotry, and tyranny.—"People ask," said San Martín, "why I don't march to Lima at once; so I might, and instantly would, were it suitable to my views—which it is not. I do not want military renown—I have no ambition to be the conqueror of Peru—I want solely to liberate the country from oppression. Of what use would Lima be to me, if the inhabitants were hostile in political sentiment? How could the cause of independence be advanced by my holding Lima, or even the whole country, in military possession?—Far different are my views. I wish to have all men thinking with me, and do not choose to advance a step beyond the gradual march of public opinion; the capital being now ripe for declaring its sentiments, I shall give them the opportunity

of doing so in safety. It was in sure expectation of this moment that
I have hitherto deferred advancing; and to those who know the full
extent of the means which have been put in action, a sufficient explanation is afforded of all the delays that have taken place. I have
been gaining, indeed, day by day, fresh allies in the hearts of the
people. In the secondary point of military strength, I have been, from
the same causes, equally successful in augmenting and improving the
liberating army; while that of the Spaniards has been wasted by want
and desertion. The country has now become sensible of its own interest, and it is right the inhabitants should have the means of expressing what they think. Public opinion is an engine newly introduced
into this country; the Spaniards, incapable of directing it, have prohibited its use; but they shall now experience its strength and importance."

On another occasion I heard San Martín explain the peculiar necessity there was for acting in this cautious, and, as it were, tardy manner,
in revolutionizing Peru. Its geographical situation had, in his opinion,
great influence in continuing that state of ignorance so favourable to
the mistaken policy of the Spaniards; long after the other countries
of South America had awakened from their apathy. Buenos Ayres,
from its vicinity to the Cape of Good Hope, and the facility of intercourse between it and Europe, had many years before acquired the
means of gaining information, which had not yet reached Peru. Chili
originally derived her knowledge through Buenos Ayres, but more
recently by direct communication from England and North America.
Columbia, although the scene of terrible wars, had the advantage of
being near the West Indies and North America; and Mexico was also
in constant communication with those places, as well as Europe. Thus
they had all more or less enjoyed opportunities of obtaining much
useful knowledge, during times little favourable, it is true, to its culture, but which did not, indeed could not, prevent its influence from
being salutary. In Peru, however, cut off unfortunately by nature from
direct communication with the more enlightened countries of the
earth, it was only very recently that the first rays of knowledge had
pierced through the clouds of error and superstition; and the people
were still not only very ignorant of their own rights, but required
time and encouragement to learn how to think justly on the subject.
To have taken the capital, by a *coup de main*, therefore, would have
answered no purpose, and would probably have irritated the people,
and induced them to resist the arms of the Patriots, from a misconcep-
tion of their real intentions.

The gradual progress of intelligence in the other states of South
America, said San Martín, had insensibly prepared the people's minds
for the revolution. In Chili and elsewhere, the mine had been silently
charged, and the train required only to be touched;—in Peru, where

the materials were yet to be prepared, any premature attempt at explosion must have been unsuccessful.

· · ·

12th of July 1821

This day is memorable in the annals of Peru, from the entry of General San Martín into the capital [*following the abandonment of Lima by the Spanish viceroy*]. Whatever intermediate changes may take place in the fortunes of that country, its freedom must eventually be established: and it can never be forgotten, that the first impulse was due entirely to the genius of San Martín, who planned and executed the enterprise, which first stimulated the Peruvians to think and act for themselves. Instead of coming in state, as he was well entitled to have done, he waited till the evening, and then rode in without guards, and accompanied by a single aid-de-camp. Indeed, it was contrary to his original intention that he came into the city on this day; for he was tired, and wished to go quietly to rest in a cottage about half a league off, and to enter the town before daybreak next morning. He had dismounted accordingly, and had just nestled himself into a corner, blessing his stars that he was out of the reach of business; when in came two friars, who, by some means or other, had discovered his retreat. Each of them made him a speech, to which his habitual good nature induced him to listen. One compared him to Cæsar, the other to Lucullus. "Good Heavens!" exclaimed the General, when the fathers left the apartment, "what are we to do? this will never answer."—"Oh! Sir," answered the aid-de-camp, "there are two more of the same stamp close at hand."—"Indeed! then saddle the horses again, and let us be off."

Instead of going straight to the palace, San Martín called at the Marquis of Montemira's[1] on his way, and the circumstance of his arrival becoming known in a moment, the house, the court, and the street, were soon filled. I happened to be at a house in the neighbourhood, and reached the audience-room before the crowd became impassable. I was desirous of seeing how the General would behave through a scene of no ordinary difficulty; and he certainly acquitted himself very well. There was, it may be supposed, a large allowance of enthusiasm, and high-wrought expression, upon the occasion; and to a man innately modest, and naturally averse to show, or ostentation of any kind, it was not an easy matter to receive such praises without betraying impatience.

---

[1] The Marquis of Montemira had been named governor of Lima by the viceroy prior to his departure. [H. D.]

At the time I entered the room, a middle-aged fine-looking woman was presenting herself to the General: as he leaned forward to embrace her, she fell at his feet, clasped his knees, and looking up, exclaimed, that she had three sons at his service, who, she hoped, would now become useful members of society, instead of being slaves as heretofore. San Martín, with much discretion, did not attempt to raise the lady from the ground, but allowed her to make her appeal in the situation she had chosen, and which, of course, she considered the best suited to give force to her eloquence: he stooped low to hear all she said, and when her first burst was over, gently raised her; upon which she threw her arms round his neck, and concluded her speech while hanging on his breast. His reply was made with suitable earnestness, and the poor woman's heart seemed ready to burst with gratitude for his attention and affability.

He was next assailed by five ladies, all of whom wished to clasp his knees at once; but as this could not be managed, two of them fastened themselves round his neck, and all five clamoured so loudly to gain his attention, and weighed so heavily upon him, that he had some difficulty in supporting himself. He soon satisfied each of them with a kind word or two, and then seeing a little girl of ten or twelve years of age belonging to this party, but who had been afraid to come forward before, he lifted up the astonished child, and kissing her cheek, set her down again in such ecstasy, that the poor thing scarcely knew where she was.

His manner was quite different to the next person who came forward: a tall, raw-boned, pale-faced friar: a young man, with deep-set dark-blue eyes, and a cloud of care and disappointment wandering across his features. San Martín assumed a look of serious earnestness while he listened to the speech of the monk; who applauded him for the peaceful and Christian-like manner of his entrance into this great city —conduct which, he trusted, was only a forerunner of the gentle character of his future government. The General's answer was in a similar strain, only pitched a few notes higher; and it was curious to observe how the formal cold manner of the priest became animated, under the influence of San Martín's eloquence: at last, losing all recollection of his sedate character, the young man clapped his hands and shouted, "Viva! viva! nuestro General!"—"Nay, nay," said the other, "do not say so; but join with me in calling, Viva la Independencia del Peru!"

The *Cabildo,* or town-council, hastily drawn together, next entered, and as many of them were natives of the place, and liberal men, they had enough to do to conceal their emotion, and to maintain the proper degree of stateliness belonging to so grave a body, when they came, for the first time, into the presence of their liberator.

Old men, and old women, and young women, crowded fast upon him: to every one he had something kind and appropriate to say;

always going beyond the expectation of each person he addressed. During this scene I was near enough to watch him closely; but I could not detect, either in his manner or in his expressions, the least affectation; there was nothing assumed, or got up; nothing which seemed to refer to self; I could not even discover the least trace of a self-approving smile. But his manner, at the same time, was the reverse of cold; for he was sufficiently animated, although his satisfaction seemed to be caused solely by the pleasure reflected from others. While I was thus watching him, he happened to recognize me, and drawing me to him, embraced me in the Spanish fashion. I made way for a beautiful young woman, who, by great efforts, had got through the crowd. She threw herself into the General's arms, and lay there full half a minute, without being able to utter more than "Oh mi General! mi General!" She then tried to disengage herself, but San Martín, who had been struck with her enthusiasm and beauty, drew her gently and respectfully back, and holding his head a little on one side, said with a smile, that he must be permitted to show his grateful sense of such good will, by one affectionate salute. This completely bewildered the blushing beauty, who, turning round, sought support in the arms of an officer standing near the General, who asked her if she were now content: "Contenta!" she cried, "O Señor!"

It is perhaps worthy of remark, that, during all this time, there were no tears shed, and that, even in the most theatrical parts, there was nothing carried so far as to look ridiculous.

It is clear that the General would gladly have missed such a scene altogether; and, had his own plan succeeded, he would have avoided it; for he intended to have entered the city at four or five in the morning. His dislike of pomp and show was evinced in a similar manner when he returned to Buenos Ayres, after having conquered Chili from the Spaniards, in 1817. He there managed matters with more success than at Lima; for, although the inhabitants were prepared to give him a public reception, he contrived to enter that capital without being discovered.

BIBLIOGRAPHY

Recent scholarship on the revolutions for independence in Latin America is reviewed in R. A. Humphreys, "The Historiography of the Spanish American Revolutions," *Hispanic American Historical Review*, 31 (1956), 81–93 and in the Pan American Institute of Geography and History, *La emancipación latinoamericana: Estudios bibliográficos* (Mexico: Instituto Panamericano de Geografía e Historia, 1966). Charles W. Arnade, Arthur P. Whitaker, and Bailey W. Diffie, "Causes of Spanish American Wars of Independence," *Journal of Inter-American Studies*, 2 (1960), 125–144 is a general survey.

In addition to the works on eighteenth-century Spanish America listed in the bibliographical suggestions to Part I, students interested in the causes of the independence movements should consult R. A. Humphreys, "The Fall of the Spanish American Empire," *History*, 37 (1952), 218–227; R. A. Humphreys and John Lynch (eds.), *The Origins of the Latin American Revolutions, 1808–1826* (New York: Knopf, 1965); and Hernán Ramírez Necochea, *Antecedentes económicos de la independencia de Chile*, 2nd ed. (Santiago: Universidad de Chile, 1967). The essays in Arthur P. Whitaker (ed.), *Latin America and the Enlightenment*, 2nd ed. (Ithaca, N.Y.: Cornell University Press, 1961), illustrate the various ways in which Enlightenment thought manifested itself in the Spanish colonies and in Brazil. Also relevant are Bernard Moses, *The Intellectual Background of the Revolutions in South America, 1810–1824* (New York: Reprint House International, 1926; reissued, New York: Russell, 1966); Arthur P. Whitaker, "The Elhuyar Mining Missions and the Enlightenment," *Hispanic American Historical Review*, 31 (1951), 557–585; J. T. Lanning, *The Eighteenth-Century Enlightenment in the University of San Carlos de Guatemala* (Ithaca, N.Y.: Cornell University Press, 1956); and Arthur Robert Steele, *Flowers for the King: The Expedition of Ruiz and Pavón and the Flora of Peru* (Durham, N.C.: Duke University Press, 1964). Foreign influences may be further traced in William Spence Robertson, *France and Latin American Independence* (Baltimore: Johns Hopkins Press, 1939); Charles C. Griffin, *The United States and the Disruption of the Spanish Empire, 1810–1822* (New York: Columbia University Press, 1937); Arthur P. Whitaker, *The United States and the Independence of Latin America, 1800–1830* (Baltimore: Johns Hopkins Press, 1941); and in the introduction to Sir Charles Kingsley Webster (ed.), *Britain and the Independence of Latin America, 1812–1830. Select Documents from the Foreign Office Archives*, 2 vols. (London: Oxford University Press, 1938).

The best biography of Bolívar is Gerhard Masur, *Simón Bolívar* (Albuquerque: University of New Mexico Press, 1948). Victor Andrés Belaúnde, *Bolívar and the Political Thought of the Spanish American Revolution* (Baltimore: Johns Hopkins Press, 1938) discusses the evolution of Bolívar's political philosophy; José Luis Salcedo-Bastardo, *Visión y revisión de Bolívar*, 3rd. ed. (Caracas: privately printed, 1957) examines his social and economic views as well. David Bushnell (ed.), *The Liberator, Simón Bolívar: Man and Image* (New York: Knopf, 1970) illustrates both the adulation and the denigration that have been heaped upon Bolívar. Ricardo Rojas, *San Martín, Knight of the Andes* (Garden City, N.Y.: Doubleday, 1945; reissued, New York: Cooper Square Publishers, 1967) is an uncritical biography. William Spence Robertson, *The Rise of the Spanish-American Republics as Told in the Lives of Their Liberators* (New York: Appleton-Century, 1918; reissued, New York: Free Press, 1965) includes a biographical sketch of Mariano Moreno, who is also the subject of Eugene M. Wait, "Mariano Moreno: Promoter of Enlightenment," *Hispanic American Historical Review*, 45 (1965), 359–383. English-language works dealing with the revolutions for independence in Mexico, Chile, and other parts of Spanish America include Hugh M. Hamill, Jr., *The Hidalgo Revolt* (Gainesville: University of Florida Press, 1966); William H. Timmons, *Morelos: Priest, Soldier, Statesman* (El Paso: Texas Western College Press, 1963); Charles W. Arnade, *The Emer-*

gence of the Republic of Bolivia (Gainesville: University of Florida Press, 1957); Simon Collier, *Ideas and Politics of Chilean Independence 1808–1833* (Cambridge, Eng.: Cambridge University Press, 1967); Jay Kinsbruner, *Bernardo O'Higgins* (New York: Twayne, 1968); and Stephen Clissold, *Bernardo O'Higgins and the Independence of Chile* (New York: Praeger, 1969).

Charles C. Griffin, "Economic and Social Aspects of the Era of Spanish-American Independence," *Hispanic American Historical Review*, 29 (1949), 170–187 is an early effort to determine the extent to which independence was accompanied by or has resulted in social and economic change in Spanish America; for Griffin's subsequent reflections on the same subject, see his *Temas sociales y económicos en la epoca de la independencia* (Caracas: Fundación John Boulton and Fundación Eugenio Mendoza, 1962). Specific aspects of this topic are examined in Harold A. Bierck, Jr., "The Movement for Abolition in Gran Colombia," *Hispanic American Historical Review*, 33 (1953), 365–386; David Bushnell, *The Santander Regime in Gran Colombia* (Newark: University of Delaware Press, 1954); and William Lofstrom, "Attempted Economic Reform and Innovation in Bolivia Under Antonio José de Sucre," *Hispanic American Historical Review*, 50 (1970), 279–299.

Alexander Marchant, "Tiradentes in the Conspiracy of Minas," *Hispanic American Historical Review*, 21 (1941), 239–257, analyzes an abortive revolutionary effort in eighteenth-century Brazil. Two articles by E. Bradford Burns cast additional light on the Enlightenment in Brazil: "The Enlightenment in Two Colonial Brazilian Libraries," *Journal of the History of Ideas,* 25 (1964), 430–438 and "The Role of Azeredo Coutinho in the Enlightenment of Brazil," *Hispanic American Historical Review,* 44 (1964), 145–160. A nearly contemporary account of the events that led to Brazilian independence is John Armitage, *The History of Brazil,* 2 vols. (London, 1836). John Armitage was a young British merchant who spent several years in Brazil. On Dom Pedro I, see Alan K. Manchester, "The Paradoxical Pedro, First Emperor of Brazil," *Hispanic American Historical Review,* 12 (1932), 176–197 and a popular biography by Sérgio Corrêa da Costa, *Every Inch a King* (New York: Macmillan, 1950). See also three essays in Henry H. Keith and S. F. Edwards (eds.), *Conflict and Continuity in Brazilian Society* (Columbia: University of South Carolina Press, 1969): Manoel Cardozo, "Azeredo Coutinho and the Intellectual Ferment of His Times"; Alan K. Manchester, "The Transfer of the Portuguese Court to Rio de Janeiro"; and Harry Bernstein, "The Lisbon *Juiz do Póvo* and the Independence of Brazil, 1750–1822."

Glossary

adelantado [Sp.]   A title held by many early conquerors of Spanish America. It conferred many powers and privileges upon them, including the right to govern any territory they conquered.

alcalde mayor [Sp.]   An official responsible for the administration of a territory within the jurisdiction of an *audiencia*.

alcalde ordinario [Sp.]   A member of a municipal council, who was also a magistrate, in colonial Spanish America.

audiencia [Sp.]   A tribunal in colonial Spanish America that exercised administrative as well as judicial powers.

cabildo [Sp.]   A municipal council in colonial Spanish America.

cacique [Sp.]   A word of Arawak origin meaning Indian chieftain. It was used throughout Spanish America, but after the colonial period it was applied to any local boss regardless of race.

campesino [Sp.]   Countryman, peasant.

capitão-mor [Port.]   A district official in colonial Brazil with extensive military and administrative powers.

casta [Sp.]   or caste   A designation for persons of mixed racial ancestry in colonial Spanish America.

caudillo [Sp.]   A leader, usually a dictator. Government by *caudillos* is known as *caudillismo*.

chapetón [Sp.]   In colonial South America, a disparaging name for a Spaniard.

científicos [Sp.]   A name applied to a group of influential Mexican intellectuals and government officials during the latter part of the dictatorship (1876–1911) of Porfirio Díaz. They were so called because of their emphasis on "scientific" methods of encouraging economic development.

colegio [Sp.] or colégio [Port.]   A secondary or preparatory school.

compadrazgo [Sp.] or compadrio [Port.]   Ritual kinship contracted between the parents and godparents of a child.

comuneros [Sp.]   In colonial Spanish America, participants in a popular uprising against royal officials in Paraguay from 1721 to 1735 or in an insurrection to protest high taxes in New Granada from 1779 to 1781.

continuismo [Sp.]   The continuation in office of a chief executive beyond his constitutionally prescribed term, usually by the expedient of amending the constitution to permit consecutive reelection.

corregimiento [Sp.]   In colonial Spanish America, a territorial subdivision governed by an official called a *corregidor*.

Creole or *Criollo* [Sp.]   In colonial Spanish America, a person born in America of Spanish parents.

descamisados [Sp.]   Literally "shirtless ones." A name applied to the working-class followers of Juan D. Perón in Argentina.

ejido [Sp.]   In Mexico, land belonging to a rural community. A member of a community who receives a plot of such land to cultivate during his lifetime is called an *ejidatario*.

encomienda [Sp.]   The granted tribute of a group of Indians to a Spaniard in colonial Spanish America. The recipient of an *encomienda,* who was known as an *encomendero,* was obligated to safeguard the spiritual and physical welfare of his charges and to render certain services to the crown if the need arose.

fazenda [Port.]   A plantation.

Flota [Sp.]   See *Galeones y Flotas.*

fuero [Sp.]   A body of privileges granted to an organization or institution.

gachupín [Sp.]   In Mexico, a disparaging name for a Spaniard.

Galeones y Flotas [Sp.]   The collective name given to the two fleets of merchantmen and warships that sailed from Spain to the colonies each year. The fleet dispatched to Panama and northern South America was known as the *Galeones;* the Mexican fleet was called the *Flota.*

gamonal [Sp.]   In South America, a local political boss or strongman.

hacendado [Sp.]   Owner of an *hacienda,* a large landowner.

hidalgo [Sp.]   A member of the petty nobility of Spain.

jefe político [Sp.]   The chief administrative official of a district.

latifundium [Lat.; plural latifundia]   A large landed estate, especially one that is inefficiently or inadequately exploited. The prevalence of *latifundia* in a region is known as *latifundismo.*

mestizo [Sp.]   A person of mixed European and Indian ancestry.

mita [Sp.]   A word of Quechua origin used in colonial Peru for the periodic conscription of Indians to perform forced, paid labor.

oidor [Sp.]   A judge of an *audiencia.*

pardo [Sp.]   A free person of African ancestry.

patrón [Sp.]   A patron, master, or landlord.

peninsulares [Sp.]   Natives of the Iberian peninsula, that is, Spaniards.

pensador [Sp.]   Thinker, a term often applied to intellectuals in Spanish America.

pronunciamiento [Sp.]   An uprising or insurrection.

real patronato [Sp.]   The power of the Spanish crown to exercise patronage over the Catholic Church in America, particularly the right to make nominations to ecclesiastical office.

reduction   A mission village in colonial Latin America inhabited by Indian converts to Christianity and directed by members of the clergy.

regimento [Port.]   A set of instructions or rules.

repartimiento [Sp.]   Distribution or allotment. In colonial Spanish America, the word might refer to (a) the distribution of Indians to Spaniards, as in an *encomienda;* (b) the periodic conscription of Indians to perform forced, paid labor; (c) the forceable sale of merchandise to Indians by Spanish officials.

senzala [Port.]   A slave hut on a plantation.

sertão [Port.; plural sertões]   Backland or hinterland, especially the semi-arid interior of Northeast Brazil.

sesmaria [Port.]   A grant of land.

visita [Sp.]   An official investigation into the conduct of an officeholder or the administration of a province.

zambo [Sp.]   A person of mixed Indian and African ancestry.